New Elites in Old States

New Elites in Old States
Ideologies in the Anglo-American Democracies

Neil Nevitte & Roger Gibbins

Toronto New York London
OXFORD UNIVERSITY PRESS
1990

Oxford University Press, 70 Wynford Drive, Don Mills, Ontario M3C 1J9

Toronto   Oxford   New York
Delhi   Bombay   Calcutta   Madras   Karachi   Petaling Jaya
Singapore   Hong Kong   Tokyo   Nairobi   Dar es Salaam
Cape Town   Melbourne   Auckland

and associated companies in
Berlin   Ibadan

Canadian Cataloguing in Publication Data

Nevitte, Neil
  New elites in old states

Includes bibliographical references and index.
ISBN 0-19-540803-9

1. Ideology. 2. Political science. 3. Youth –
Attitudes. 4. Elite (Social sciences).
I. Gibbins, Roger, 1947–   . II. Title.

JA71.N48 1990   320.5'0835   C91-093129-1

Copyright © Neil Nevitte and Roger Gibbins 1990
OXFORD is a trademark of Oxford University Press

www.oupcanada.com

Table of Contents

	Preface	ix
CHAPTER ONE:	Ideological Change in the Anglo-American Democracies	1
CHAPTER TWO:	Mapping the Ideological Terrain	27
CHAPTER THREE:	Gender and Feminism	64
CHAPTER FOUR:	Minorities on the Ideological Landscape	85
CHAPTER FIVE:	Equality: Of Opportunity or Result?	108
CHAPTER SIX:	Ideology and Political Influence	130
CHAPTER SEVEN:	Common Themes and National Variations	163
APPENDIX A:	Sample Questionnaire	174
APPENDIX B:	List of Universities Sampled	186
APPENDIX C:	Factor Analytic Procedures	187
APPENDIX D:	Scale Construction	193
	Bibliography	195
	Index	207

TABLES

Table 1.1	System Characteristics of the Anglo-American Democracies
Table 1.2	Income and the Workforce
Table 1.3	Percentage Change in the Proportion of the Workforce Employed in Primary, Secondary and Tertiary Economic Sectors, 1965-1985
Table 1.4	Anglo-American Populations: Size, Distribution, and Fertility Rates
Table 2.1	The Data Set
Table 2.2	Factor Pattern Matrix
Table 2.3	Questions Included in the Government Scale
Table 3.1	The Gender Environment
Table 3.2	Economic Position of Women in the Anglo-American Democracy
Table 3.3	Pearson Correlations between Feminism and Left-Right by Nationality and Gender
Table 4.1	National Differences in Response to Minority Poverty Question
Table 4.2	National Differences in Partisan Mean Scores on Minority Scale
Table 4.3	Correlation between Feminism and Minority Scales
Table 4.4	Left-Right Differences in Perceptions of Media Coverage
Table 5.1	Equality of Opportunity or Result?
Table 5.2	Left-Right Differences in Orientations Towards Equality
Table 6.1	The Influence Gap: Perceptions and Preferences
Table C-1	Factor Pattern Matrix
Table D-1	Standardized Alpha Coefficients for Scales

FIGURES

Figure 1.1	Percentage of Women in the Workforce, 1966 and 1988
Figure 2.1	National Left-Right Self-Placement Locations
Figure 2.2	Left-Right Ideological Space Occupied by Partisans
Figure 2.3	Comparison of Means of National Party Identifiers on the Left-Right Scale
Figure 2.4	National Locations on the Government Scale
Figure 2.5	Comparison of Means of Left, Centre and Right Identifiers on Government Scale
Figure 2.6	Comparison of Means of National Party Identifiers on Government Scale
Figure 2.7	Parties in Government—Left/Right Space

List of Figures | vii

Figure 2.8	Government Scale Mean Inter-Item Correlations (Xr) and Left-Right Pearson Correlation (r)
Figure 3.1	National Locations on Feminist Scale
Figure 3.2	Feminist Scale Mean Inter-Item Correlations (Xr) and Left-Right Pearson Correlation (r)
Figure 3.3	Comparison of Means of Left, Centre and Right Identifiers on Feminism Scale
Figure 3.4	Comparison of Means of National Party Identifiers on Feminism Scale
Figure 3.5	Parties in Feminism—Left/Right Space
Figure 3.6	Combined Government and Feminism Scale Mean Inter-Item Correlations (Xr) and Left-Right Pearson Correlation (r)
Figure 4.1	National Locations on the Minority Scale
Figure 4.2	Minority Scale Mean Inter-Item Correlations (Xr) and Left-Right Pearson Correlation (r)
Figure 4.3	Comparison of Means of Left, Centre and Right Identifiers on Minority Scale
Figure 4.4	Comparison of Means of National Party Identifiers on Minority Scale
Figure 4.5	Parties in Minority—Left/Right Space
Figure 4.6	Combined Minority, Feminism and Government Scale Mean Inter-Item Correlations (Xr) and Left-Right Pearson Correlations (r)
Figure 5.1	National Locations on Equality Scale
Figure 5.2	Equality Scale Mean Inter-Item Correlations (Xr) and Left-Right Pearson Correlation (r)
Figure 5.3	Comparison of Means of Left, Centre and Right Identifiers on Equality Scale
Figure 5.4	Comparison of Means of National Party Identifiers on Equality Scale
Figure 5.5	Parties in Equality–Left/Right Space
Figure 5.6	Combined Equality, Minority, Feminism and Government Scale Mean Inter-Item Correlations (Xr) and Left-Right Pearson Correlations (r) [A: Britain; B: United States; C: Australia; D: New Zealand; E: Canada]
Figure 5.7	Combined Equality, Minority, Feminism and Government Scale Mean Inter-Item Correlations (Xr) and Left-Right Pearson Correlations (r) [English Canada and French Canada]
Figure 6.1	Measuring Influence
Figure 6.2	Perceived Influence in Society
Figure 6.3	Preferred Influence in Society
Figure 6.4	Gender Differences in the Perceived and Preferred Influence Ratings of Feminists

Figure 6.5   Gender Differences in the Perceived and Preferred Influence Ratings of Minorities
Figure 6.6   Perceived and Preferred Influence—Left
Figure 6.7   Perceived and Preferred Influence—Right
Figure 6.8   The Influence Hierarchy of National Lefts and Rights—Unions and Business
Figure 6.9   The Influence Hierarchy of National Lefts and Rights—Feminists and Minorities
Figure 6.10   Preferred Influence in Society by National Left Parties
Figure 6.11   Preferred Influence in Society by National Right Parties
Figure 6.12   Preferred Influence Ratings of Business and Unions by National Partisan Lefts and Rights
Figure 7.1   National Locations on Factor Scales
Figure 7.2   Locations of National Lefts and Rights on Factor Scales

Preface

This book is about the political belief systems of new elites, the youth elites of the 1980s, in the Anglo-American democracies—the old states. The similarities and differences among and between the political cultures of Australia, Britain, Canada, New Zealand, and the United States have been probed, debated, re-examined, and debated again for more than half a century. In the 1960s, newly developed cross-national survey techniques produced evidence that added fuel to those speculations. Remarkably, however, no cross-national attitudinal research comparing all five countries followed the path-breaking studies of the 1960s. This study aims to go some distance towards filling that gap, and the argument it proposes is a simple one. Enormous changes swept across all advanced industrial states during the last two decades. The Anglo-American democracies, like other countries, experienced the globalization of their economies, the information revolution, profound structural transformations, and dramatic shifts in population replacement. Long-standing patterns of political behaviour eroded, traditional alliances unravelled, and new issues forced their way onto political agendas. The ideological climate of the 1980s, we suggest, bore little resemblance to the ideological climate of the 1960s and, for a variety of reasons, those shifts in ideology were disproportionately concentrated in the ranks of the new generations. In what respects, then, are the political belief systems of new elites in the Anglo-American democracies similar? In what respects are they different? These are the questions we ask, and we answer them with comparative cross-national survey evidence from all five countries.

This book is written with a broad audience in mind. Our aim is to make the results of the study accessible to those without formal training in quantitative methods and to those who are being introduced to, or who have a general interest in, the contemporary politics of the Anglo-American democracies. Where possible, we present our findings by way of graphic illustrations. Where we resort to summary statistical presentation of evidence, we rely on relatively few simple measures, which are explained in the text. Our hope is that this study will contribute to a revitalized debate about politics both in and between each of the five countries as well as about the transformation of advanced industrial states in general.

This project was truly a collaborative effort. We drew heavily upon the goodwill of many colleagues and institutions in all of the five countries represented in the study. We are happy to be able to acknowledge publicly our gratitude for their help.

The study was ten years in the making. In the late 1970s, while orchestrating the Cross National Survey Project, Sidney Verba co-ordinated a number of brainstorming sessions at the Center for International Affairs, Harvard University, dealing with the opportunities, difficulties, and practicalities of cross-national survey research. It was during those stimulating meetings that the prospect of undertaking a comparative Anglo-American study was first discussed. This project would never have been started, undertaken, or completed without the intellectual leadership and moral support of Sidney Verba. We thank him for allowing us to use the American data for this project. More importantly, we are very grateful for his continual encouragement.

Several other institutions and individuals were also crucial to the project. The Australian field work was conducted from the Australian National University at both Canberra and Darwin. The University of Essex gave us work space from which we co-ordinated the British segment of the study. Tony King, Ian Budge, and Ivor Crewe were very gracious hosts. Nigel Roberts and Rod Alley made the New Zealand component of the study possible. And in Canada we were willingly aided in a variety of ways by colleagues across the country. We particularly appreciate the contributions of Herman Bakvis, André Blais, Marsha Chandler, Jean Crête, Barry Kay, Richard Johnston, and Richard Simeon. Some of the analysis was undertaken at the Center for Political Studies, University of Michigan. Sam Barnes and Ronald Inglehart made that workspace a home.

The project placed a unique burden on our own institution, the University of Calgary. For steering us through a maze of computing related matters we are grateful to Thomas Huang and Ted Ziajka. We were very lucky to have extremely able research assistants: Robert Burge got the project underway and Lori Galbraith held it together, carrying the bulk of the computational and graphics work through to its conclusion. We are very appreciative of their efforts and abilities. We also thank our colleagues in the department of political science for their congenial support.

The Social Sciences and Humanities Research Council of Canada provided the financial wherewithal for the project (SSHRC grant #410-88-0221). We thank them not only for underwriting the hard costs but also for providing sabbatical leave fellowships that enabled us to conduct the field work and to start attacking the analysis. Several individuals provided us with constructive criticism of the early drafts of various parts of the book. Seymour Martin Lipset, Paul Sniderman, and Sylvia Bashevkin were particularly helpful. Robert Boardman, Jon Pammett, and Campbell Sharman read the entire manuscript and provided both thoughtful commentary and a number of helpful suggestions. We are very grateful to them, and to Richard Teleky, managing editor of Oxford University Press, who coaxed us along with the manuscript.

Both of us borrowed time from our families. We extend a special thanks to Susan Bloch-Nevitte and Isabel Gibbins, who were understanding when we fell short on what we imagine to be the normal responsibilities of spouses in normal families.

Neil Nevitte
Roger Gibbins
Calgary, June 1990

*To some special members of the next generation—
Lee Bishop Nevitte, Christopher Gibbins, and Daniel Gibbins*

CHAPTER ONE

Ideological Change in the Anglo-American Democracies

Introduction

This study examines the nature of political belief systems[1] in the five Anglo-American democracies—Australia, Britain, Canada, New Zealand, and the United States. Perhaps no other five countries in the industrialized world are more alike; they share not only roughly comparable economies, social structures, and cultural environments, but also the same political tradition. Compared with other industrially advanced states, each of the Anglo-American democracies has a long history of open, stable, and liberal democratic style of government. For the most part, citizens of the Anglo-American democracies view their systems of government as legitimate, and the transfer of power has rarely taken place in an atmosphere of crisis; it has been routine. Throughout this century political contests have not been battles about the rules of the game; instead, the battles have been about ideas, policies, leaders, and parties.

It is not surprising, then, that comparative social scientists often regard the Anglo-American democracies as a special subset of advanced industrial states, a distinct analytic category. This practice gained considerable momentum in the 1950s and early 1960s with the publication of such landmark works as Louis Hartz's *Founding of New Societies*, Alexander Brady's *Democracy in the Dominions*, Gabriel Almond and Sidney Verba's *Civic Culture*, and Robert Alford's *Party and Society*. These studies, along with a number of influential articles by Seymour Martin Lipset, Gabriel Almond, and others, all underscored the same point: Australia, Britain, Canada, New Zealand, and the United States were all 'different examples of the same type'. Some scholars emphasized the remarkably similar 'climate' or 'spirit' of politics in the five states. Others identified secularism and homogeneity as the unifying themes, while yet others pointed up similarities in styles of political combat and political values—pluralism, pragmatism, individualism, and the non-ideological sense of compromise. The language differed but the message was the same—all five countries shared a common political culture beyond what one might expect from their similar status as Western industrialized states.

By the middle of the 1960s, however, the conceptual tide turned. Armies of scholars drawing upon a variety of analytical traditions, and working from national rather than cross-national perspectives, challenged the notion that the Anglo-American democracies were 'essentially the same'. The historical vineyards were re-worked to show that 'significant differences' existed, and could be traced to variations in founding traditions. Variations in political institutions, social structures, and literary traditions were probed to bolster the case for the essential differences between national political cultures. Canadian scholars, for example, reacting perhaps to concerns about the 'Americanization' of Canadian culture, entered the fray contending that the differences between Canadian and American values were not 'mere nuances', but fundamental. American analysts, meanwhile, busily mounted a powerful and incidentally complementary case for American exceptionalism. Throughout the Anglo-American democracies, the effort and conclusions focused on contrasts, not similarities.

Today the friction between these two visions persists, and in the final analysis it hinges on one central empirical question: Are there significant differences between and among the contemporary political cultures of the five Anglo-American democracies? Certainly there are countless national arguments to support, for example, the expectation that the political culture of Australia will differ significantly from that of Britain, and that of Britain from the political culture of the United States. For readers and scholars in those countries whose main concern is to explain national political cultures to domestic populations, idiosyncratic features are often to be treasured and vigorously defended. At the same time, however, we have compelling reasons to expect cultural similarity. The Anglo-American democracies not only share the structural characteristics common to all industrial states; they also share a common political tradition. Thus the expectation of similarity is driven not only by more general patterns of structural and ideological convergence within the Western world, but also by history. At root, however, remains the basic empirical question: Are there significant national differences in political culture? Until and unless such differences can be demonstrated, it is premature to speculate on the reasons why national differences might persist in an era of global ideological convergence.

Methodological Overview

Our entry into this debate about cross-national similarities and differences in political values is shaped by three themes that regularly emerge in these disputes. First, we accept, of course, that competing interpretations of the same phenomena are a normal part of academic debate in all disciplines, as are attempts to resolve discrepancies of interpretation. In this instance, for example, it might be argued that the differences between the two visions of the Anglo-American democracies can be squared away simply by acknowledging that each operates at a different level of generalization. After all, what appears close up to be an 'important difference' easily fades into insignificance when global comparisons are entertained. Australians and Canadians might be expected to be alert and sensitive to differences between the two countries, whereas an observer from Africa could be excused for emphasizing their similarities (climatic differences notwithstanding!). But that line of reasoning is not entirely convincing either, because it obscures the fact that much of the debate centres around the same unit of observation—national values—and that the empirical question still remains as to whether or not significant differences exist.

Second, most comparative judgements about values in the five Anglo-American democracies rely almost entirely upon indirect evidence. National differences in crime rates, for example, might be used to speculate on the importance of citizen deference to political elites in the civic cultures of the countries under examination. However, forming conclusions about contemporary public attitudes on the basis of inherited political institutions and social patterns is risky and contentious. It is equally hazardous to rely on a theory about founding traditions to make inferences about the national values of populations several generations removed from founding circumstances. The problem is that to get from institutional, social structural, literary, and historical evidence to conclusions about national values in the 1980s and beyond requires a logical leap of faith. Many of the existing studies that rely on these impressionistic sources are both imaginative and persuasive, but they do not escape the limitations of having to rely on inference. This debate about comparative similarities and differences has raged now for more than twenty-five years, during which time comparative social scientists have continued to use the Anglo-American democracies as a major analytic category. From that standpoint, it is remarkable that no single study has ever provided direct comparative evidence of national values in all five countries.

Third, and relatedly, if claims to the effect that the Anglo-American democracies share 'essentially the same political values' ring hollow in the absence of direct evidence of those similarities, then so do counterclaims about national uniqueness. In practical terms, it is much easier to make the case for the uniqueness of any single country than it is to establish the common properties of five countries. The burden of proof is lighter; dig deep enough, press hard enough, and any country will yield to the conclusion that it is unique. But from the cross-national perspective, what is gained in our understanding of political cultures from the assumption that no two countries are 'the same'? The more important question is not whether differences exist, but whether such differences are significant when viewed against the backdrop of broader cultural patterns and trends.

In a related sense, two-country comparisons also fall short. For example, and only by way of illustration, we could undertake a comparison of British and Australian values. We could identify areas of value difference, proclaim the differences 'significant', denounce the Anglo-American democracies as a flawed category, and expect a round of applause. That performance, however, cuts little ice with those who take the category 'Anglo-American democracies' seriously, much less with those who are interested in broader patterns of ideological organization and change in the Western world. It is unconvincing because critical questions remain unanswered. Which set of national values is unique? Which country is the outlier? (In a two-nation comparison, each is unique and each is an outlier.) In the final analysis, the burden of proof is not lighter; it is precisely the same.

In the present analysis, we report direct evidence of values in each of the five Anglo-American democracies. Our strategy is deliberately cross-national, and the goal is to make some progress towards filling a gaping hole in the comparative literature. Thus our examination of political beliefs in these similar systems is explicitly comparative. More particularly, our comparison is focused. The political belief systems are explored from the common vantage point of a single segment of each of the five societies—from the perspective of more than 3,000 senior undergraduate students located on fifty campuses across the five countries. Thus the ideological landscapes that we map are seen through a distinct but very useful analytical optic.

Our focus is a useful one for a combination of three reasons. The first has to do with the social location of these students. We refer to them as 'new elites' or 'youth elites' because while they do not yet stand at the command posts of society, they are strategically located in the sense that they form the pool from which the future elites of each society will be drawn. Second, our new elites are the educated strata of a particular generation occupying a significant and interesting historical location. The generation coming to maturity in the 1980s was raised in an economic and social environment shaped by conditions dramatically different from those of a quarter-century ago. Unlike the populations analysed in the pioneering studies of Alford (1963) and Almond and Verba (1965), studies that still serve as the major reference points for generalizations about the ideological contours of Anglo-American democracies, none of our youth elites experienced first-hand the traumas of economic depression or world war. Relatedly, the ideological climate of the 1980s in all of the Anglo-American democracies was also markedly different from that which prevailed during earlier studies. Simply put, the 1980s was a decade of ideological flux. After generations of stability, and for a variety of reasons, the ideological configurations of these societies suddenly became more fluid as new ideological polarities emerged (Inglehart, 1977; Flanagan, 1982; Offe, 1984). Of perhaps even greater significance, available evidence indicates that new ideological polarities are disproportionately concentrated in the generations born since 1945 (Inglehart, 1977, 1990; Dalton, 1988).

The third reason for focusing upon our new elites is more technical. Because these people are highly educated, they are politically more sophisticated and ideologically more articulate than the general populations of which they are a part (Bishop, 1976; Luskin, 1987). As a consequence, their political belief systems are more sharply defined (Converse, 1964), and it is thus easier to identify the *underlying structure* of those systems. It is also easier to identify the similarities and differences in the belief systems across the five national settings we explore. In addition, we know that the political belief systems of these youth elites not only are well formed already, but are also relatively resilient and will remain resistant to change throughout the life cycle. This in turn gives us some confidence that the belief systems identified in the following analysis will have some staying power, that they are not simply an ephemeral artifact of the 1980s, but will continue to find reflection in the Anglo-American democracies as we move into the twenty-first century. In sum, then, by focusing on a particular generation in five similar countries, we can shed light on how, in an age of ideological turmoil, the new elites of the 1980s organize their ideological worlds. Insofar as the belief systems of the new elites remain stable, and to the extent that these elites will be recruited to the command posts of society, our analysis may also provide us with a glimpse of the future shape of political discourse in each of the old democracies.

In bringing this methodological overview to a close, we must emphasize that the project is exploratory and limited in important respects. Our analysis relies on survey evidence gathered in the 1980s from senior university students; we are not reporting on the political values of entire national populations. Instead, we present a one-time snapshot of the attitudes of a single well-educated segment of the same generation of citizens in the five countries. Furthermore, our focus is restricted to political belief systems.

Finally, we must address the issue of change over time. Contemporary generalizations about values in the Anglo-American democracies still rely to a remarkable extent on the classic studies undertaken in the 1950s and 1960s. The political winds of the 1980s were undoubtedly quite different from those of the 1960s, and not least of all where ideological orientations were concerned. Thus any study of values and value change necessarily confronts a moving target. (Of course, opinions differ about how quickly values change and in what direction; some observers speculate, for instance, that the value differences between the Anglo-American democracies have diminished with the passage, and under the pressures, of time.) No study that relies on data collected at a single time, as ours does, can definitively lay to rest hypotheses about value change. Nonetheless, two aspects of this project are relevant to that line of speculation. First, a mountain of evidence indicates that value changes are led by new, well-educated generations within the middle class. Second, the structure of attitudes within that group is relatively enduring. Our focus, then, is upon that group within which value changes are most likely to have taken place. The emphasis here is not upon the likely sources of value differences or similarities, but upon the outcomes.

The Anglo-American Political Tradition

In his landmark study of the founding of Australia, Robert Hughes (1988: 41) notes that the rebellion of the American colonies in 1775 touched off a crisis for British jails. No longer could British convicts be sent to the New World:

> The American air filled with nobly turned resolutions against accepting criminals from England, for a new republic must not be polluted with the Crown's offal. This was cant, since the American economy was already heavily dependent on slavery. The real point was that the trade in black slaves had turned white convict labor into an economic irrelevance. On the eve of the American Revolution, 47,000 African slaves were arriving in America every year—more than English jails had sent across the Atlantic in the preceding half-century. Beside this labor force, the work of white indentured convicts was inconsequential; the Republic did not need it.

As Hughes goes on to explain, the stopping-up of the American outlet for convicts caused the English prisons to overflow. Faced with the choice of building expensive new prisons or finding an alternative destination to which convicts could be transported, Britain looked to Australia as the site for a new convict settlement. Thus the Revolution was not only a dramatic turning point in the histories of Britain and the United States; it also touched off the British settlement of Australia and, eventually, New Zealand.

The American Revolution also helped to lay the foundations for the Canadian society. Of the approximately 100,000 United Empire Loyalists who fled the Revolution, over 40,000 went north. More than 30,000 settled in Nova Scotia, tripling that colony's population and spilling into New Brunswick, which was consequentially established as a separate colony in 1784. Others formed the bedrock of what is now Ontario, while, as historian A.R.M. Lower explains (1953: 109), 'the influx of Anglophone loyalists, pushed by expropriation or drawn by good farmland, changed Quebec once and for all from a homogeneous French-Canadian society to one with a prosperous and vocal English minority'. It is in this sense, then, that Lower described Canada as a 'by-product' of the American Revolution.

Thus Australia, Britain, Canada, New Zealand, and the United States were all touched by the American Revolution, though not, of course, in the same way. As Robert Alford (1963: 31) aptly put it, 'America was born of revolution, Australia was born of revolutionaries without a revolution, Canada was born out of forces opposed to revolution, and modern Britain was not born at all, but has evolved under the guidance of the aristocracy to its present state.' Extending that characterization, we might add that New Zealand was born of revolutionaries once, if not twice, removed.

Admittedly, and from a narrow viewpoint, it is easy to argue that every country, from its inception and throughout the course of its evolution, is essentially unique. Thus in the case of the Anglo-American democracies, the novelty of each country's response to the American Revolution could be emphasized. Attention could be called to differences in the social strata that settled each country, and the importance of timing could be highlighted by focusing, as does Hartz (1964) in his discussion of social fragments, on the precise moment at which each founding culture was spun out of Britain's orbit. Certainly, some differences in founding circumstances are reflected in the variety of charter myths. The powerful resonance of America's revolutionary charter myth and its 'rugged individualism', for example, might be compared with Australia's 'radical' tradition, or 'mateship', and in turn, both could be contrasted with New Zealand's more muted, middle-class founding ethos.

What the narrow viewpoint misses are the powerful lessons that might be learned from a broader comparative perspective, one in which the similarities among the five countries are striking. All five find a common point of departure in the Great Britain of the eighteenth and nineteenth centuries, as British immigrants created the cultural core of the settler societies in Australia, English-speaking Canada, New Zealand, and the United States. The full significance of that common British heritage was best underscored by Tocqueville more than a century ago. 'In the Middle Ages,' he observed, 'the tie of religion was sufficiently powerful to unite all the different populations of Europe in the same civilization. The British of the New World have a thousand other reciprocal ties; and they live at a time when the tendency toward equality is general among mankind' ([1835], 1966: 451). It is doubtful that even Tocqueville could have predicted how resilient those cultural links would turn out to be, for the five countries continue to share a great deal in common despite the physical distance that separates most of them and despite the fact that each has experienced more than a century of independent development. Britain and the United States, countries divided by a common language, continue to serve as major cultural reference points for each other; both also provide benchmarks, and sometimes foils, for interpreting the collective experiences of Australia, Canada, and New Zealand.

If for the moment we can paint with a very broad brush, it is possible to highlight some of the more obvious similarities among the five countries. All are democratic, industrialized, relatively wealthy, highly literate, predominantly urban and middle class, mostly white, and mainly English-speaking.[2] Each society can be characterized as stable, open, and pluralist. Although the configurations of political arrangements within the countries are far from identical, there are strong parallels and substantial overlaps. Australia, Canada, and the United States are all transcontinental federal states. Australia, Britain, Canada, and New Zealand are all parliamentary democracies with similar parliamentary institutions and legal systems (see Table 1.1). These political systems might be contrasted with the American presidential system; however, as historians have pointed out, the American system of government, despite its revolutionary origins, shares many of the political practices associated with the English tradition (Lower, 1958: 5-6). The similarities also extend beyond formal institutional structures to include party systems. All five countries are often regarded as classic examples of the competitive two-party model (Sartori, 1976: 185-9), and while this model is fraying at the edges in Canada and Australia, and is under growing strain in Britain, the five countries nonetheless continue to share a relatively distinctive pattern of partisan combat.

Table 1.1 System Characteristics of the Anglo-American Democracies

	AUSTRALIA	BRITAIN	CANADA	NEW ZEALAND	UNITED STATES
Institutional features	parliamentary federal bicameral	parliamentary unitary bicameral	parliamentary federal bicameral	parliamentary unitary unicameral	presidential federal bicameral
Electoral system	mixed	single-member district	single-member district	single-member district + minority seats	single-member district
Voting age	18	18	18	18	18
% Vote for two major parties	77.6 (Dec. '84)	78.2 (June '87)	75.6 (Nov. '88)	90.2 (Aug. '87)	99.1 (Nov. '88)
Electoral participation rate (%)	94.5	74.6	75.9	89.1	50.3

In addition to the parallels that can be found in the domestic political arrangements, there are also countless examples of 'reciprocal ties' between and among the Anglo-American democracies, ties that have been continually strengthened. Cultural ties have been reinforced by successive waves of immigrants from Britain.[3] All the countries are enmeshed in overlapping economic, political, and security arrangements: Britain, Canada, and the United States are all member states of the North Atlantic Treaty Organization, while Australia, Britain, Canada, and New Zealand are senior partners in the Commonwealth of Nations. 'Special' relationships abound within the group, including such examples as the Canada-US and Australia-New Zealand free-trade agreements. All five countries fought as allies in the First and Second World Wars; Australian and American troops fought together in Vietnam; Britain, Canada, and the United States are members of the Group of Seven; and so the list could continue.

The rich texture of similarities among the Anglo-American democracies, however, cannot be fully captured just by listing common institutional traits or noting a long record of international co-operation. No list can adequately express, for example, how founding circumstances have interacted with institutional arrangements in their economic and social settings. Almond and Verba (1965) were closer to the mark in suggesting that Britain, the United States, and the Old Commonwealth countries were broadly alike in that they shared the same political culture; that they drew from a common store of ideas and beliefs about politics. As we will show, that common store extends to include *comprehensive ideological structures* and *systems of political belief*.

Here there is little question that the historical forces shaping the Anglo-American democracies also structured their ideological landscapes in similar ways. Political discourse in each of the five countries takes on a similar ideological hue precisely because it is filtered through the lens of a similar ideological tradition. The core of that tradition, as Louis Hartz (1964) has pointed out, is a liberal one, although if we limit our focus to the five Anglo-American democracies and employ a powerful microscope, national differences in the ideological centre of gravity become more prominent. Thus the Lockean individualism of American liberalism might be contrasted with the Australian variant, which more closely resembles the liberalism of J.S. Mill. Similarly, when the microscope is turned to one side of the ideological spectrum, differences in the Anglo-American lefts appear. The American left, for instance, is tinged by populism, while the others are shaded more in the Fabian colours of Owen, Morris, and the Webbs. When the microscope is turned to the other side of the spectrum, the rights can be differentiated according to the extent to which collectivism and Toryism are embraced or rejected, and the extent to which Burkean conservatism works to give those rights coherence.

In making cross-national generalizations about similarities or differences, perspective is everything. Thus when we discard the microscope, those differences fade. If we step back and observe the ideological contours of the Anglo-American democracies against the backdrop of, say, the old continental European democracies, it is the similarities among the Anglo-American democracies that are striking. Unlike the old continental European societies, the Anglo-American democracies lack an absolutist tradition, and their liberal core is flanked by quite different ideological alternatives. The Anglo-American left, for example, is social reformist and gradualist; it has not been shaped by sustained encounters with organized Marxism. Moreover, none of the Anglo-American rights have lapsed into totalitarianism, nor have they been haunted by fascism in ways comparable to the continental European experience. From this broader perspective, it is the sheer expanse of the liberal core that sets the ideological terrain of the Anglo-American democracies apart from that of other old states in the industrialized world.

With respect to the focus on political beliefs that shapes the analysis to come, it is important to note at the outset that all five countries have experienced all or most of the same collective events, even though such events were played out in a somewhat idiosyncratic fashion within each country. Thus, for example, Australia, Canada, New Zealand, and the United States were all settler societies, and in all four cases early settlers encountered significant aboriginal populations. As noted above, the five countries all fought on the same side and in most of the same theatres in the First and Second World Wars. All five were rocked by the Great Depression, and all five enjoyed rapidly expanding material prosperity following the end of the Second World War. The point to stress is not only that each country was settled early on by migrants from the same culture, but also that citizens of the five countries shared many of the same collective experiences; they have lived through common traumas of war, depression, and prosperity. Moreover, those collective experiences have been interpreted through the language of a common ideology. Thus when we turn to examine the contemporary political belief systems in the five countries, we should expect to find common echoes of very similar, if not identical, collective memories.

Twenty-Five Years of Economic and Social Change

Until recently, scholars could have confidently described the ideological trajectories of the Anglo-American democracies in terms of two broad themes: continuity and similarity. But in the last twenty-five years, accumulating evidence suggests that the ideological mainstream has been buffeted by significant cross currents; it has changed course. The political discourse of the 1980s bears little resemblance to the discourse of the 1960s; there is a new political agenda, and accompanying the rise of that new agenda have been substantial shifts in styles of political participation. For example, all five countries now have articulate, organized, and powerful feminist movements that are reshaping the contours of social, political, and economic life in significant ways. In all five countries, concerns about the 'quality of life' are challenging traditional patterns of economic development and exploitation. All five also face increasingly vocal visible minorities demanding changes in the distribution of both political and public goods. Hence citizens of the five Anglo-American democracies not only inherit many of the same collective memories, albeit viewed through distinctive national optics; they also confront many of the same new realities that have profoundly transformed the ideological terrain of other advanced industrial states (Barnes and Kaase, 1979; Inglehart, 1990).

The more than 3000 youth elites incorporated in this study thus stand at an intriguing ideological nexus. Their world views must embrace the classical ideological debates that have shaped their national societies in the past, which echo through similar collective memories, and which continue to shape political discourse in the five countries. In ideological terms, they must come to grips with questions concerning the distribution or redistribution of income, the role of the state in the management of the economy and society, and the appropriate scale and reach of government programs. At the same time, they confront a host of relatively new issues about the role of women in society and the economy, about the status of minorities, and about the quality of life. Therefore the question to ask, the question pursued in this study, is: *How and to what extent do new elites in the five countries weave together new and old concerns into reasonably coherent ideological garments?* How do they make sense out of an increasingly complex and turbulent ideological environment? In trying to construct ideological maps for this new environment, do they employ similar values and beliefs as landmarks? Do they employ the same ideological signposts in the same way? In summary: *Are the ideological maps employed by the five sets of youth elites similar to one another despite national differences in the political terrain, or are the maps idiosyncratic to the distinctive national environments?*

In addressing these questions, our attention is focused on the ideological make-up of a particular political generation. To paraphrase Marx, members of this generation do not live under conditions they choose, they live under conditions inherited from the past. Yet the socio-economic conditions confronting this generation are profoundly different from the conditions that prevailed only twenty-five years ago. In other words, the environment in which these new elites live is quite different from the environment that prevailed when Alford explored the relationship between class and party in the Anglo-American democracies, and when Almond and Verba outlined the features of the Anglo-American civic culture. Most scholars suggest that dramatic structural changes have transformed advanced industrial societies in the last twenty-five years, and that as a consequence of this transformation a new ideological agenda has emerged.

First and foremost have been substantial changes in economic structure and performance. Along with other advanced industrial societies, all five Anglo-American democracies have experienced substantial economic growth. Admittedly, that expansion has not always been even; it stalled and even temporarily reversed during the OPEC oil crisis and the recession of the early 1980s. But the overall pattern has been one of accumulating wealth. In real terms, the Gross Domestic Product of each of the five countries at least doubled over the last twenty-five years (IMF, 1986).

Increased levels of aggregate economic productivity have been reflected, in turn, in increased levels of individual income. The Anglo-American democracies, by any measure, have consistently been among the wealthiest countries of the world, and contemporary living standards have reached unprecedented levels of affluence (see Table 1.2).

Table 1.2 Income and the Workforce

	AUSTRALIA	BRITAIN	CANADA	NEW ZEALAND	UNITED STATES
GNP per capita (US dollars)	11,588	11,718	15,571	10,360	18,413
Labour-force participation (aged 15-64 years)	72.5	74.5	77.0	65.8	76.0
% Primary	6	2	5	11	3
% Secondary	26	30	25	28	27
% Tertiary	68	68	70	60	70

SOURCE: Labour force statistics: 1966-86 (Paris: OECD, 1988).

Economic expansion has been accompanied by a variety of other trends, including the globalization of markets. Significantly, in the last twenty-five years each of the Anglo-American democracies has sought and entered into trading agreements that enable each country to exploit more fully its comparative economic advantages and to protect and maximize the economic benefits that accrue from stable access to expanded markets.[4] With the internationalization of economic markets, shifts have occurred in the structure of domestic economies. Most notable here has been a sustained expansion of the tertiary and service sectors of each economy. These changes, of course, are reflected in the character of the workforce and in the occupational structures of society. As Table 1.3 shows, in all instances, the proportion of the workforce devoted to primary, extractive, and agricultural activities has slipped, and the proportion of the workforce engaged in the secondary manufacturing sector has dropped off even more dramatically. The significant point is that all of the Anglo-American democracies have crossed an important threshold. According to Daniel Bell's criteria (1973), all now qualify as 'post-industrial' societies, for in each more than half of the workforce is now employed in the tertiary sector.

A driving force behind economic change has been technological innovation. In the last quarter-century it has revolutionized information processing and dissemination (Dizard, 1989). The surge in technologically driven segments of the economy, along with the expansion of the service sector, has generated new demands on the workforce; the premium is upon 'knowledge-based' skills. Consequently, the rapid transformation of the economies of the Anglo-American democracies has been complemented by a dramatic expansion in educational opportunities. The growth of university education throughout the Western world has been characterized as 'a virtual explosion' (Dalton, Flanagan, and Beck, 1984: 6), and over the last twenty-five years the proportion of the population attending colleges and universities has at least doubled in all of the Anglo-American democracies (Taylor and Jodice, 1983). The citizens of the Anglo-American democracies, then, are not only more affluent than ever before; they are also better educated.

Table 1.3 Percentage Change in the Proportion of the Workforce Employed in Primary, Secondary, and Tertiary Economic Sectors, 1965-1985

COUNTRY	PRIMARY	ECONOMIC SECTOR SECONDARY	TERTIARY
Australia	−3.2%	−9.7%	+13.1%
Britain	−1.3	−14.8	+16.1
Canada	−4.8	−7.7	+12.2
New Zealand	−1.6	−7.1	+ 8.7
United States	−3.2	−7.5	+10.6
Average Change	−2.8%	−9.4%	+12.1%

SOURCE: Labour force statistics, 1966-86 (Paris: OECD, 1988).

These transformations have reached far beyond the economic domain to have a profound impact on the nature of each society. In all five countries the expansion of educational opportunities, pulled along by the requirements of a changing economy, has helped to shake loose traditional barriers to occupational, geographic, and social mobility. One measure of increased social mobility is the growth of the middle class. That middle class, however, has not just increased in size; its composition has changed. A new, socially diverse, better educated and technologically more sophisticated middle class has emerged alongside the old. Mobility has also affected family life as traditional ideas about the family unit and gender roles have been challenged by a dramatic shift in the gender composition of the workforce. By 1988, in all the Anglo-American democracies, more than half of the female population of working age were part of the paid workforce. Indeed, as Figure 1.1 shows, the female workforce participation rates in all five countries have far exceeded the 50 per cent benchmark.

Figure 1.1: Percentage of Women in the Workforce, 1966 and 1988

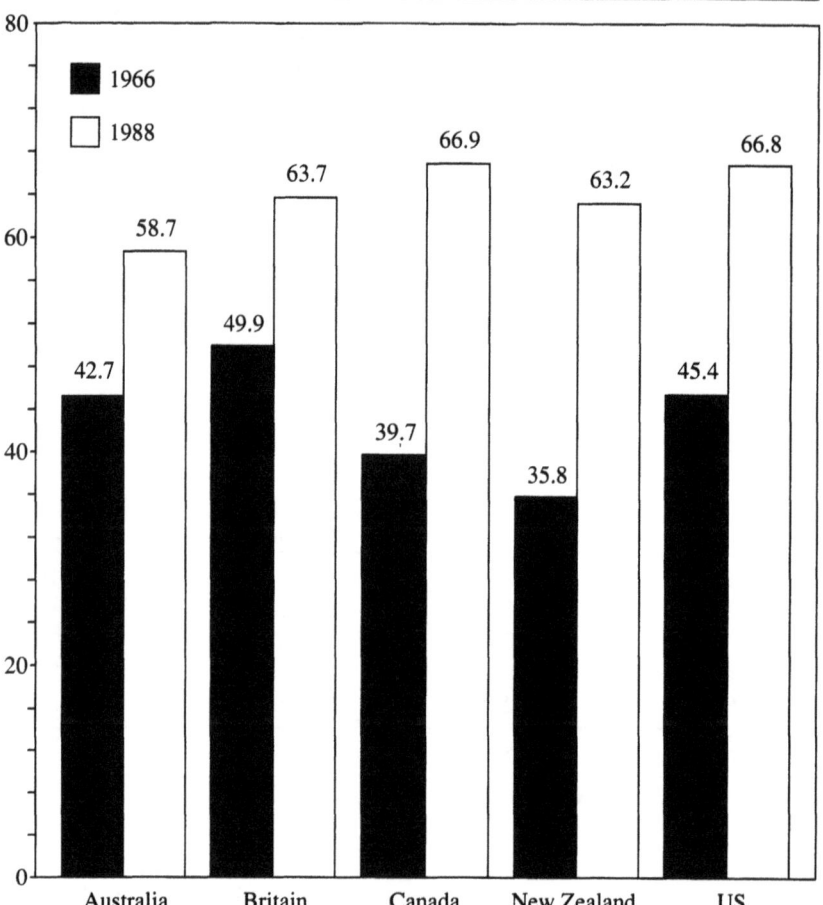

Source: Employment Outlook (Paris: OECD, 1989): 214.

The context of social life has changed in other respects as well. With the decline of rural economies and the concentration of service sectors in metropolitan areas, urban centres have become more powerful population magnets than ever before. In 1960 the Anglo-American democracies already ranked among the ten most urbanized countries of the world in relative terms; since then, the absolute rate of urban growth has continued apace. On average, seven out of every ten citizens of the old democracies now live in urban settings (Taylor and Jodice, 1983). Such social indicators as higher divorce rates, lower fertility rates, and increased levels of delinquency, crime, and suicide probably reflect the stresses of mobility and urban life.

The high levels of occupational, geographic, and social mobility that have characterized social change in the Anglo-American democracies over the last twenty-five years have been linked to other significant changes, most notably increased levels of cognitive mobility (Inglehart, 1977; Dalton, 1988). The expansion of the middle class has meant greater affluence and more leisure time. Foreign travel, once the privilege of a few, is now within the reach of many. The ease of travel, domestic and foreign, along with increased levels of education and the explosion of information from popular sources such as television, has dramatically expanded the cognitive horizons of citizens in all advanced industrial societies (Inglehart, 1977). The effect has been to erode pockets of parochialism and to produce a citizenry that is better informed than ever before about all aspects of social and political life. While economies have become global, the world has also shrunk in other ways. Physical distance was once a significant barrier that insulated most Anglo-American democracies from each other, but the mobility of populations and the information revolution have dramatically reduced the significance of such geographic obstacles (Dizard, 1989). Thus the cross-fertilization of ideas among the Anglo-American democracies—ideas about politics as well as popular culture—has never been easier. Not only are those ideas transmitted through the shared medium of a common language, and often through the same magazines, books, movies, and television programs, but they are also received by societies with shared cultural reference points.

Social change, of course, is not driven solely by technological innovation and economic impulse. Population replacement is one form of change that no country can escape; it is imposed by the passage of time. The dynamics of population replacement, however, differ substantially from country to country. Some reproduce themselves entirely, and thus minimize the likelihood of social change, while others draw heavily upon immigration to supplement natural increase, and thus increase the likelihood of demographically induced change. For example, Australia, Canada, New Zealand, and the United States all started as settler societies, and the first three have continued to rely heavily upon immigration as a means for achieving population growth. In fact, relative to population size, Australia's immigration intake is larger than that of any other country in the world. In 1981, for example, 20 per cent of Australians were foreign-born. The figures for Canada (16 per cent) and New Zealand (15 per cent) are somewhat lower, but they are still substantial (Statistics Canada, 1981).

Since the early 1960s two trends have developed in all five societies, both representing significant departures from the traditional patterns of population replacement. First, as shown in Table 1.4, fertility rates have fallen to the point that none of the Anglo-American democracies can sustain present population levels through natural increase; thus the burden of achieving population growth has shifted entirely to immigration.

Second, immigrants to the Anglo-American democracies are increasingly being drawn from non-traditional, non-European, sources. In Australia, for instance, immigrants from Britain account for less than 20 per cent of all newcomers, while one in three Australian immigrants comes from Asia (Dept. of Immigration, Local Government and Ethnic Affairs, 1987).[5] Between 1956 and 1960, Canadian immigrants from traditional sources outnumbered those from non-traditional sources by a ratio of 15 to 1. By 1980 that trend had completely reversed; immigrants from non-traditional sources outnumbered those from traditional sources by 2 to 1 (Beaujot and Rappak, 1988). Canada may be the most extreme case, but available aggregate data indicate that the more recent trends in all four settler societies are essentially the same (United Nations, 1984). The important point to emphasize is that the joint effect of both trends has been to change the ethnic, racial, and religious contours of all Anglo-American societies, including Britain. Thus the societies occupied by the new elites, both the European fragment societies and Britain, are culturally far more diverse than ever before—they are less 'European'.

Table 1.4 Anglo-American Populations: Size, Distribution and Fertility Rates

	AUSTRALIA	BRITAIN	CANADA	NEW ZEALAND	UNITED STATES
Population ('000)	16,090	56,648	25,334	3,397	247,498
% Urban	85.0	92.5	75.9	84.0	79.2
% English-speaking	99	99	61	99	79
Fertility rate	1.8	1.8	1.6	2.0	1.8

SOURCE: UN Statistical Yearbook (New York: 1986).

Twenty-Five Years of Political Change

There is little question that the socio-economic changes sweeping across the Anglo-American democracies have had a profound impact on the political life of each country, not least by re-shaping the environments within which politics is conducted. In the last quarter-century, each of the Anglo-American democracies has experienced marked departures from long-standing patterns of political behaviour, including changes in the traditional bases of party support, in the way people vote, in the policies pursued by governments, in the activities of interest groups, and in other forms of political participation. Overall, the political climate has become more fluid and less predictable.

Evidence of these changes can be found in the decline of old patterns of conflict and the emergence of new ones. For example, prior to the 1960s, class stood out as a critical axis of political conflict dividing communities within all of the old democracies; it structured party loyalty, voting, and many other aspects of associational life (Alford, 1963). In the last twenty-five years, however, the capacity of class to structure political behaviour seems to have weakened in each of the five countries (Abramson, 1975; Kemp, 1978; Bean, 1980; Sarlvik and Crewe, 1983; Pammett, 1987).[6] Some explain the decay of class in terms of population turnover, and note that the populations reared in the class cauldron of the 1920s and 1930s have now been completely replaced (Dalton, Flanagan and Beck, 1984). Others emphasize the importance of the dynamics of advanced industrialism, increased social mobility, education, affluence, and the growth of the middle class (Huntington, 1974). Regardless of which explanation applies, the consequences of class dealignment have been similar across all of the Anglo-American democracies. Loyalties to political parties have become more frail, party support less stable, and electorates more volatile, while traditional coalitions between social groups and political parties have weakened or unravelled (Wattenburg, 1982; LeDuc, 1985; Vowles, 1988). Significantly, party loyalties are weakest among the young and well-educated (Nie, Verba and Petrocik, 1976; Aitken, 1983; Alt, 1984).

Social and demographic changes can be linked to other new patterns of domestic political conflict. Until the 1960s, most observers would have associated racial tension in the Anglo-American democracies with the politics of black-white relations in the United States; although racial politics has been a part of the subterranean historical record of all of the old Commonwealth democracies, most lacked a racial minority of any significant size until recently. New patterns of immigration have changed that, and since the 1960s racial divisions have become increasingly politicized throughout all five countries. By the 1980s both Britain and Canada could be added to the list of Anglo-American countries experiencing the contemporary politicization of race. Until the 1960s, similarly, conflict between linguistic communities in the Anglo-American democracies was largely limited to English-French relations in Canada. But the politics of language conflict has spread as well. For example, the Hispanic community in the United States now stands at some 20 million—six times the entire population of New Zealand—and in such states as Florida and California efforts have been made to legislate English as the official language.

Examples of the rise of communal tensions based on language, religion, race, and ethnicity can therefore be supplied for all the old democracies. While the new trends in immigration are not the sole cause for the rise of communal politics, they have revitalized and added new dimensions to historic conflicts between majorities and Aborigines in Australia, Maoris in New Zealand, and Native peoples in Canada and the United States.

The point is that in the course of the last twenty-five years, communal politics has moved from the margins of debate to the centre of political controversy in each of the five countries. As new communal divisions have sprouted and become entangled with old ones, the patterns of communal politics have become more complex.

Fierce competition between groups can be seen as 'normal politics', especially in open democratic systems of government. In some instances, as in the case of communal politics, the emergence of new political conflicts might be directly related to specific social changes such as population turnover. But in most cases the links between socio-economic change and political change are much more subtle. The outcomes of battles between groups pursuing interests hinge on the relative distribution of political resources (Goodin and Dryzek, 1980). Socio-economic change disturbs the political status quo when it redistributes resources that can be used to achieve political goals. Thus socio-economic change can revitalize some groups at the expense of others, pump new life into some issues while consigning others to the sidelines, and, in the process, reshape political agendas and place new demands on governments.

The politicization of women's issues is an example of how socio-economic change has empowered historically marginalized groups in similar ways in all of the Anglo-American democracies. The old democracies were among the first countries of the industrialized world to grant women the franchise; they won the right to vote in New Zealand in 1893, and by 1928 women in all five countries had the franchise on an equal footing with men. Until the 1960s, however, few women sought public office, and women's interests received little serious consideration except in the context of traditional notions about family life. In the last twenty-five years, gender issues have emerged full force onto the agenda of all Anglo-American democracies, and in all five cases the politicization of women can be attributed to greater access to such resources as higher education, information, and the income and skills that accrue from greater participation in the workplace (Anderson, 1975; Welch, 1977; Norris, 1987). In the last twenty-five years the women's movement has emerged as a powerful, well-organized, and politically sophisticated lobby in each country. Such groups as the National Organization for Women in the United States and the Women's Electoral Lobby in Australia have their counterparts in Britain, Canada, and New Zealand, and all pursue greater gender equality by promoting such issues as the extension of women's legal rights, the greater political representation of women, equal pay for work of equal value, greater access to credit, and the availability of day care. As might be expected, not all women agree about either the priorities or the strategies for promoting the causes of women. The important point, however, is that women are no longer political bystanders. In many senses, women are still not full participants across all levels of the political field of play, but they now have the capacity to force issues onto the public agenda. Significantly, the gladiators within the women's movement in the 1980s were the young and the articulate, those who benefited most from the expansion of post-secondary education in the 1960s.

The apparent decline of class politics, demographic change, and the rise of newly empowered groups, such as women, go some distance towards indicating how the political environment has become more fluid. But a more complete explanation for why new political agendas have emerged in the old democracies would also have to consider evidence of the spread of new values across advanced industrialized societies (Inglehart, 1977, 1981, 1990; Flanagan, 1982; Dalton, 1988). Traditional conflicts typical of early industrialized societies revolved around battles between classes, between the haves and the have-nots, and the gap between the rich and the poor is still present in even the wealthiest societies. Underclasses, the destitute, remain trapped in the cycle of poverty, homelessness, mental and physical illness; for them, the primary concern—subsistence—has not changed. But for substantial segments of the Anglo-American populations—the middle classes—the issues *have* changed. The vigorous expression of new concerns about the environment and the quality of life (Lowe and Goyder, 1983; Milbrath, 1984; Hay and Haward, 1988) reflects the fact that growing proportions of these societies are no longer driven by the single-minded pursuit of wealth.

The precise scope and depth of the value change implied by the emergence of concerns about the quality of life is a matter of dispute, and scholars emphasize different aspects of the value change. Daniel Bell (1973), for instance, argues that it entails a declining concern for economic security while Scott Flanagan (1982) suggests that the value change encompasses a decline in respect for authority, traditional religious values, conformity, and the work ethic. Ronald Inglehart casts a wider net by linking value change to the structural transformations of advanced industrial societies. He claims (1977, 1981) that such subsistence needs as physical security, food, and shelter have been superseded by higher-order needs like self-esteem, the need to belong, self-actualization, and the search for aesthetic and intellectual satisfaction. Regardless of differences in emphasis and scope, there is broad agreement, first, that these values represent a basic shift away from traditional economic, social, and political concerns; second, that they are lodged predominantly in the younger generations that have been raised in an environment of physical security and economic affluence; and third, that the rise of new values may have important implications for the future political order of advanced industrial societies.

Twenty-Five Years of Ideological Change?

In focusing on political belief systems, our main concern is with the ideological contours of the Anglo-American democracies. But ideology is not 'disembodied', and we cannot ignore how social and economic change, or the ebb and flow of political cleavages, may have refashioned ideological landscapes in the old democracies in the last twenty-five years. Indeed, ideology is so thoroughly entangled with all aspects of political life that the shifting patterns of political behaviour might themselves be taken as evidence of ideological instability (Cooper et al., 1988). Such indicators as electoral change and the emergence of new issues, however, represent just the tip of the ideological iceberg. From a broader historical standpoint it is clear that the roots of ideological turmoil precede the 1980s; they can be traced back to the disintegration of the ideological consensus that underpinned policy-making in the old democracies throughout most of the postwar period. That consensus was erected upon the structures of Keynesian economic theory and wrapped in the ideological garments of social democracy.

Keynes provided the theoretical bridge justifying greater government intervention in the economy for the purposes of moderating inequalities and other social costs—most notably, cycles in unemployment—associated with the dramatic fluctuations of free market economies. All of the Anglo-American democracies crossed that bridge with more or less enthusiasm. The political acceptability of Keynesianism was undoubtedly helped by fresh memories of the economic collapse of the 1930s, and it gained momentum as a result of wartime experiences (Deane, 1978). The sustained pursuit of Keynesian politics, however, had two large consequences. First, notions of citizens' social rights broadened. Second, as governments expanded the scope of welfare provisions, the size of the state in the old democracies grew apace.

The energy driving the post-Depression expansion of the state was given coherent ideological focus by political parties of the left. In Britain and New Zealand, the Labour Party 'welfare leaders' found the redistributive consequences of Keynesianism to be particularly congenial to their social democratic goals. In Canada, the New Democratic Party, the 'party of conscience', led the way, as did the Labor Party in Australia. In the United States, the 'welfare laggard,' the Democrats—the party of the New Deal and Great Society programs—served similar purposes (Flora and Heidenheimer, 1981). Significantly, however, the welfare effort in all of the Anglo-American democracies continued to expand even when parties of the right were in power, indicating a significant measure of ideological consensus.

It is difficult to pinpoint the exact moment when this Keynesian consensus ran out of steam or when one set of 'ruling ideas' replaced another, but significant ruptures were clearly evident by the 1970s (King, 1987). Keynesianism was attacked on two fronts. First, economists argued that the advent of 'stagflation', the coexistence of high unemployment and high inflation, contradicted a central tenet of Keynes's theory. They noted too that the worst-performing economies—Britain and Italy, those with the highest unemployment and the lowest growth—were precisely the ones that had most fully embraced Keynesianism. On a second front, others argued that governments bent on pursuing Keynesian policies were inviting serious crises of overload, ungovernability (King, 1975; Huntington, 1975), and even political bankruptcy (Rose and Peters, 1978); while public expectations about government services remained high, the costs of providing those services had outstripped the rate of economic growth.

There is little question that these arguments have struck a responsive chord in publics disenchanted with the welfare state policies that had formed the cornerstone of left-wing programs since the Second World War. Parties of the right were victorious in 1979 in Britain and in Canada, and in the following year in the United States. Whether these 1979 and 1980 victories were ideologically motivated is difficult to tell; they could be explained in terms of the alternating electoral rhythms typical of two-party systems, or as a reaction to the poor economic records of preceding governments (Lipset, 1981; Hibbs, 1987). In retrospect, though, two factors suggest that a shift in ideological mood played some role. First, each of the parties came to power voicing similar priorities. In the United States, the Republicans, in the wake of tax revolts, aimed 'to get the governments off the backs of the people'. In Britain, the Conservatives stressed the virtues of 'self-reliance', and in 1984 the Canadian Progressive Conservatives declared that the country was 'open for business'. Second, parties of the right in Britain and the United States were consistently returned to power throughout the 1980s, and their counterparts in Canada held office for most of the decade. It is the repeated electoral success of parties promoting similar kinds of policies that suggests a collective 'shift to the right'.

There is another sense in which the victories of right-wing parties, particularly in Britain and the United States, represented ideological discontinuity; they reflected an ideological discontinuity within the right. The electoral success of Margaret Thatcher's Conservatives did not signify a return to power for the Tories of old; 'Thatcherism' had little in common with the traditional 'One Nation' conservatism of the Macmillan, or even Heath, eras. Indeed, the label 'Thatcherism' itself came to symbolize a new brand of conservatism. Similarly, the 'Reagan Revolution' in the United States implied a decisive ideological break with traditional Republicanism. Furthermore, the new ideological trajectories of the right in Britain and the United States seemed to converge. In many respects Thatcher and Reagan were ideological bedfellows; both rode to power on the shoulders of ideas and interests clustered under the label of 'the New Right'; and when in power both pursued objectives reflecting the influence of the New Right. In the economic domain those objectives included halting and then reversing the advance of the welfare state, limiting the role of government in the economy, and giving market forces freer play in the allocation of resources and rewards—all goals reminiscent of nineteenth-century liberalism (Lipset, 1988). At the same time, the rationale provided for pursuing these objectives was not exclusively economic; also at play was a more or less explicit set of conservative social and moral values, values that linked the expansion of the welfare state, the permissiveness of the 1960s, and the rise of feminism to a sort of moral flabbiness, or decay, that had eroded the spirit of individualism, sapped national pride, and undermined the traditional family (King, 1987).[7] The project of the New Right, then, was to reverse both economic and moral decay.

The ideological 'shifts to the right' were most vividly displayed in Britain and the United States, perhaps because they were so energetically pursued by such striking personalities. Yet evidence suggests that the same kind of ideological discontinuity also took place, albeit with considerably less fanfare, within the Canadian right. The conservatism of Brian Mulroney is not the conservatism of John Diefenbaker, and the Progressive Conservatives became significantly more 'conservative' and much less 'progressive' in the course of the decade (Gibbins, 1988).

The ideological discontinuities emerging in Australia and New Zealand by the mid-1980s were equally remarkable, though for quite different reasons. The state occupies a central place in the political traditions of both Australia and New Zealand; it was a crucial catalyst and instrument of early political development and figured as a prominent ally in popular conceptions of 'progressive democracy'. Both countries developed full-blown welfare states relatively early and easily, and historically the scope of the welfare state deepened and broadened when Labor governments were in power. That pattern changed dramatically in the mid-1980s. In both Australia and New Zealand, Labor governments initiated a series of economic policies that amounted to a radical departure from the historic course set by previous left-wing parties. In Australia, for example, the Hawke government lowered tax rates for the wealthy, deregulated financial markets, persuaded labour unions to agree to cuts in real wages, and planned to privatize such state-owned enterprises as banks, airlines, and telecommunications. In New Zealand, the Lange government's 'Rogernomics' policies cut an even deeper swath. They included lowering taxes for the wealthy and corporations, rolling back welfare payments, reducing subsidies to industry, and turning government enterprises into profit-seeking corporations. Thus by the mid-1980s 'left-wing' governments in Australia and New Zealand were pursuing policy objectives that closely resembled the programs of 'right-wing' governments in Britain, Canada, and the United States (Boston, 1987).

Three aspects of these ideological shifts are significant. First, they suggest the ideological convergence and ascendance of the right in all the old democracies. The policies vigorously initiated by the Thatcher and Reagan governments in the the early part of the decade spread throughout the old democracies in the space of a few short years. By the mid-

1980s four broad economic priorities were central to government policy in each of the Anglo-American democracies: (1) controlling inflation; (2) increasing the efficiency and cost-effectiveness of welfare programs; (3) reforming tax structures to reduce average and marginal income tax rates in order to sharpen work incentives and increase productivity; and (4) deregulating financial, product, and labour markets. The scope and scale of these measures differed from one national setting to the next, but the policy direction was the same. Together they suggest that the ideological initiative had been seized by the right.

Second, the ideological transformations illustrate the fluidity of the ideological environment. If the ideological transitions in Britain, Canada, and the United States could be characterized as a 'shift to the right' led by parties of the right, then the disjunctures in Australia and New Zealand could be described as a 'shift to the right' led by parties of the left. The change of course *within* the right in Britain, Canada, and the United States involved turning the ideological rudder perhaps 45 degrees; but in Australia and New Zealand it seemed to be more a case of 'reverse engines'. Neither the Australian Labor Party nor the New Zealand Labor party, however, was penalized by electorates for such a reversal. In fact, both were re-elected. Paradoxically, the re-election of both parties provides further evidence of just how much the traditional Keynesian policy cornerstone of left-wing parties had crumbled. The Australian and New Zealand Labor parties abandoned important elements of Keynesianism and were returned to power while the fragmented British Labour Party clung to Keynesianism and in 1987 suffered its worst electoral defeat since 1918.

Third, and relatedly, the shifts in electoral support and the policy changes of the 1980s illustrate the hazards of forming conclusions about the ideological locations of political parties on the basis of inherited historical wisdom. Parties born under one set of circumstances may adapt quickly to new conditions. Some parties, like New Zealand Labor, are more nimble at moving across the ideological spectrum than others. For example, after comparing Anglo-American political parties about twenty-five years ago, Leslie Lipson (1959) formed the conclusion that in New Zealand 'the centre of political gravity has moved so far over on the left that the conservatism of the National party would be damned as outright communism by many a conservative in other lands'. In 1988 another analyst observed that the Labor government had moved 'considerably to the right of the National Opposition', and noted that 'National under Robert Muldoon largely rejected the international movement towards "New Right" economic and social doctrines while Labor under Roger Douglas embraced them with a fervour unmatched by Margaret Thatcher or Ronald Reagan' (Gustafson, 1988).

In focusing upon the decline of Keynesianism, the rise of the New Right, and the frailty of traditional electoral alignments, we have drawn attention to obvious markers of ideological flux. The growing rifts between traditional and neo-liberal elements within parties of the right, the decline and fragmentation of some left-wing parties, and the policy reversals of others all suggest a shift to the right. That interpretation gains more momentum when changes in political leadership, Thatcherism, and the Reagan revolution are added to the picture. Nonetheless, shifting partisan allegiances and changes in the character of political leadership provide still only a partial view of the depth and scope of the tremors that reverberated throughout the Anglo-American democracies during the 1970s and 1980s.

That picture is filled out somewhat when we take into account how political agendas changed. By the 1980s citizens in each of the Anglo-American democracies confronted a bewildering array of issues. New life was pumped into such old questions as what to do about poverty, social assistance for the needy, equal opportunity, and affirmative action (Glazer, 1988). But new issues were also added to those revitalized old ones, contributing further to complex policy dilemmas. As we have indicated, some of those issues have been traced to profound social, cultural, and economic changes that have taken place since the 1960s. Yet others, such as concern about work, stress, leisure, and the quality of life, have been linked to structural transformations associated with post-industrialism. To characterize the totality of these changes as 'ideological flux' implies that they were merely part of the normal ideological rhythms of post-war politics. But when the simultaneous shifts in partisan allegiance, political leadership, and political agendas are placed against the backdrop of other profound and irreversible changes—changes in demography, the workforce, technology, and domestic, economic, and social structures, as well as globalization—they might be interpreted as indicating more than ideological flux; they suggest deeper turbulence, perhaps even re-polarization.

The Path Ahead

Our focus in the following chapters is not upon the fate of parties or even political leaders; it is upon how informed observers, new elites, make ideological sense out of an often bewildering world. As we suggested at the outset, the new elites who are the focus of this study stand at an interesting ideological nexus; they are at the vortex of ideological turmoil. They are the inheritors of five national ideological traditions, and yet the objective social, economic, and cultural realities of their lives are profoundly different from those that structured the lives of previous generations. The changes we have described amount to substantial cross-currents that challenge the continuity of the ideological traditions of each country, so much so that the ideological maps of the Anglo-American democracies sketched only twenty-five years ago may provide unreliable guides for traversing the ideological landscapes of the 1980s and beyond.

Our youth elites thus provide a useful perspective from which to explore the ideological turmoil of the old democracies precisely because their cognitive horizons are more expansive than those of previous generations, because they are less wedded to traditional avenues of political participation, and because their life spans do not encompass the great traumas that shaped the perspectives of preceding generations. Rather, their life experiences were framed on the one hand by early memories of a vigorous left, an expanding state, and the paroxysms of the 1960s, and on the other hand by recent experience with a triumphant right, a retreating state, and a political agenda that embraces a complex mixture of both old and new issues. Precisely how these new elites in five similar countries sharing a similar political tradition organize that new and complex world, and whether the national ideological signatures retain the distinctive imprint of their founding traditions, are the questions to which we now turn.

In so doing, we should explain the nature of our own approach. We have suggested that the five Anglo-American democracies emerged from distinctive national settings, albeit ones rooted in a common political tradition. We have also argued that the Anglo-American democracies have experienced substantial and wide-ranging social change since the end of the Second World War; that the structural dynamics of that change have been similar across the five national communities; and that the change has had a similar impact on the underlying political cultures. In short, Western industrialized states, within which the five Anglo-American democracies constitute a distinct but not aberrant community, have been exposed to common patterns of social change manifested in such things as feminism, environmentalism, the information revolution, and the globalization of the economy.

Overall, the character of social change raises the expectation of ideological convergence and homogenization, an expectation that received some initial support in the above discussion of the 'new right'. However, this expectation must be placed against the contrary expectation that significant national differences do exist, that it 'matters' whether an individual lives in Sydney, Calgary, or New York when we come to explain how he or she makes sense out of the political world. While national political cultures have been exposed to common patterns of social change, we cannot quickly or cavalierly dismiss the resiliency of distinctive national political cultures.

Hence our central question: *Are there significant differences between and among the contemporary political cultures of the five Anglo-American democracies?* To answer this question, we turn in Chapter 2 to a discussion of the left-right scale, and to a broader discussion of respondent orientations towards the role of government in contemporary society. In Chapters 3, 4, and 5 the examination of national differences, or the lack thereof, takes on a sharper focus as we address in turn respondent orientations towards feminism, minority rights, and equality. In Chapter 6 the discussion turns to an examination of respondent perspectives on political power, its distribution within the contemporary society, and its ideal distribution. And in the final chapter of this study we return to consider the saliency of national differences in the face of well-grounded expectations about cultural homogeneity.

NOTES

[1] 'Ideology' is a contentious term that raises a variety of epistemological and normative issues, issues that have been discussed extensively elsewhere (Mannheim, 1954; Bell, 1960; Lane, 1962; Larrain, 1979). Nonetheless, throughout this volume we use the terms 'ideology', 'political ideology', 'political belief systems', and their derivatives interchangeably. Following Converse (1964), we consider an ideology to entail a coherent world view, a comprehensive system of political beliefs in which ideas are central.

[2] Canada, where approximately 26 per cent of the national population is francophone, has proportionately the largest non-English-speaking population.

[3] The degree of population migration between the five countries is impressive. For example, 69 per cent of those who emigrate from Australia relocate to the other Anglo-American democracies (Department of Immigration, Local Government and Ethnic Affairs, 1987). Similarly, in 1980, the Canadian-born population living in the United States amounted to 843,000, or 3.5 per cent of the 1981 population of Canada. The American-born population living in Canada consistently hovers around the 300,000 mark (Beaujot and Rappak, 1988).

[4] Britain's entry into the European Economic Community (1973) represented a departure from historic trading patterns with Empire and Commonwealth, whereas the Australia-New Zealand Closer Economic Relations Trade Agreement (1983) and the Canada-United States Free Trade Agreement (1989) solidified emerging trade patterns.

[5] The Asian component of Australia's immigrant intake increased from 9.5 per cent in 1969 to 40.2 per cent in 1989 (*Australia Report*, 12 May 1990).

[6] One calculation, based on voting data from five Western democracies between 1947 and 1988, indicates that class-based voting is less than half as strong as it was a generation ago. See Inglehart (1990: 260-1).

[7] King argues that while Britain has no real counterpart to Jerry Falwell's 'moral majority' in the United States, Mrs Thatcher's approving references to the strength of Victorian values nonetheless operated as a secular equivalent. He also notes that Norman Tebbit, the Conservative Party Chairman, attributed increased levels of social violence in Britain to 'the era and attitudes of post-war funk which gave birth to the Permissive Society' (King, 1987: 20).

CHAPTER TWO

Mapping the Ideological Terrain

Debates about national differences in political culture, and thus about national differences in underlying ideological structures, are notoriously difficult to resolve because there is no consensus on the appropriate research strategy. We have seen how very different kinds of evidence—ranging from voting behaviour through the performance of political parties and constitutional conventions—can be used to identify the ideological mainstreams of the Anglo-American democracies. Although each approach can provide useful insights about the ideological mood of the times, each also operates on its own particular assumptions about which aspects of ideology are most significant. Such methodological diversity is not spurious; it reflects genuine disagreement about the meaning and dimensions of the term *ideology*. To avoid further confusion, then, it is useful to be clear at the outset about how we aim to explore the ideologies of youth elites, about which assumptions guide our approach and, consequently, about which questions are central to the analysis.

Following the well-established tradition informed by the work of Converse (1964) and others (for example, Inglehart and Klingemann, 1979), we identify ideological thinking with a coherent world view, a *comprehensive system of beliefs*. More particularly, our approach explores the degree of *constraint*, or the extent of *linkage*, among political beliefs. In this sense, a political ideology is a relatively wide-ranging system of political beliefs and values, a system that displays a reasonable measure of constraint and coherence. Put somewhat differently, an ideology exists when knowledge about one set of component beliefs allows an observer to predict, with a reasonable degree of confidence, what other beliefs and values might be. Thus an ideology is distinguished by the linkage or relationship among its parts, and not by the character of the parts *per se*.

Ideologies are economical ways of interpreting and evaluating a complex political reality. Therefore to understand ideological patterns of political thought, we must seek out the common principles, the core beliefs (Feldman, 1988) that underpin more specific attitudes and attitude structures. The goal is to isolate those core beliefs and to see how efficiently they organize the politically relevant worlds of respondents. Thus we are not concerned with such epistemological issues as which ideology is true, or with such normative questions as which ideology is best. Instead, our goal is to address such exploratory empirical questions as: Which principles underpin political belief systems? Are similar principles at work across the five Anglo-American democracies? Do they work in the same direction, with the same force, and with the same effect? Do they embrace similar sets of attitudes and concerns? Do ideological structures display similar degrees of coherence and constraint? More bluntly, are there any significant national differences?

A number of assumptions are embedded in this approach. One is the idea that ideologies are *cultural products* transmitted from generation to generation by institutions and individuals. Individuals do not create idiosyncratic ideological structures—or if they do, such structures are not accessible to survey research; they lie in the domain of psychiatry, not social science. Rather, individuals buy into ideological 'packages' that exist and compete within the political culture. This does not mean, however, that political belief systems are completely determined, rigid or fixed. Although the prevailing ideology of any country may well be shaped significantly, even decisively, by founding circumstances and may retain the imprint for generations, ideologies are not disembodied, severed from objective socio-economic reality. They will yield to, and become transformed by, structural and environmental change.

Another assumption of our approach is that direct evidence is stronger than indirect evidence. The implications that flow from this distinction are far-reaching and touch most research about political ideologies, but the central point can be illustrated briefly enough. Suppose that we want to compare the political ideologies of two voting citizens—say, an American and a Briton. On the basis of indirect evidence—for instance, knowing only that the American votes Republican and the Briton votes Conservative—we might conclude that the two voters are ideologically similar. Yet that conclusion is risky because several inferences are required for it to hold water. We have to assume that vote *is* a good indicator of ideology, *and* that both individuals voted the way they did because of ideology, *and* that US Republicans and British Conservatives *are* ideologically similar, and so on. As the chain of reasoning gets longer, the links holding it together become more tenuous and the number of plausible explanations multiplies. An alternative strategy, and the approach followed here, is simply to ask both voters directly about how they see the political world. Direct evidence is stronger not just because it yields more information but because it requires fewer inferences; it reduces the logical distance between evidence and conclusions and allows us to place greater confidence in those conclusions.

Finally, because we are concerned with identifying national similarities and differences in political belief systems, we confront a range of obstacles and call upon a variety of assumptions generic to comparative research (e.g., Verba, 1967; Przeworski and Teune, 1970; Lijphart, 1971). More specifically, to map the ideological terrain of youth elites in five countries implies not only that direct evidence of individual attitudes provides the empirical key unlocking the doors to those ideological worlds, but also that, once those doors have been opened, we have a conceptually reliable compass to guide us across that terrain. Comparative research more or less explicitly entails the use of some yardstick, or baseline, against which the object of comparison, in this instance political belief systems, can be meaningfully measured. Throughout our analysis, the *left-right polarity* provides us with the conceptual compass for exploring and comparing the ideologies of youth elites in the five Anglo-American democracies.

The Language of Ideological Discourse: Left and Right

The terms 'left' and 'right' have been used to describe the ideological landscapes of societies for more than two hundred years. In the beginning, they referred to the seating arrangements of the clergy (on the right) and the nobility (on the left) at the first post-revolutionary meeting of the French Estates General in 1789 (Laponce, 1981). As usage of the terms spread beyond the walls of the French Parliament, the meanings attached to the left-right polarity broadened. With the industrialization of Western Europe, for example, left and right came to signify different ideological orientations towards the emergent conflicts associated with the processes of industrialization, and particularly class conflict. Later, following the diffusion of Keynesianism, left and right reflected competing perspectives about such large issues as the redistribution of wealth and power, and the role of government in the economy. Today, and as we illustrated in Chapter 1, the labels are still central to ideological discourse in the Anglo-American democracies, and across the world. Indeed, they are so central that it is difficult to imagine how political debates could be conducted without them. As one observer (Inglehart, 1990: 292-3) has noted:

> The Left-Right dimension, as a political concept, is a higher-level abstraction used to summarize one's stand on the important political issues of the day. It serves the function of organizing and simplifying a complex political reality, providing an overall orientation toward a potentially limitless number of issues, political parties, and social groups. The pervasive use of the Left-Right concept through the years in Western political discourse testifies to its usefulness. Insofar as political reality can be reduced to one underlying dimension, then one can distinguish readily between friend and foe, and between the good and bad positions on given issues, in terms of relative distances from one's own position on this dimension.

The left-right concept provides a useful starting point for analysing political ideologies for three basic reasons. First, even though the left-right dimension is a higher level abstraction, the use of these terms should not imply that every individual has a carefully thought-out, complex theory about political life; this is clearly not the case. Nevertheless, a substantial body of evidence indicates that very large proportions of the general public in advanced industrial societies, the Anglo-American democracies included, do meaningfully employ and respond to the left-right labels (Klingemann, 1979; Sankiaho, 1984; Dalton, 1988). Left-right usage, then, is not restricted to a few sophisticated political analysts; the polarity enjoys almost universal recognition. In industrialized societies at least (Arian and Shamir, 1983), left and right are useful conceptual categories precisely because they are both the formal tools of political analysis *and* the informal currency of casual political debates within and between all strata of society.

Second, the left-right polarity applies to a wide range of political objects. Not only can most individuals easily locate *themselves* on the left-right ideological scale (Klingemann, 1979), but they can also use that scale to organize and evaluate *other* phenomena in the larger political world. In Britain, for example, the public readily associates Prime Minister Thatcher with 'the right'. Similarly, Australians routinely see the Labor Party as being 'to the left of' the Liberal Party, just as New Zealanders interpret privatizing state-owned enterprises in terms of 'right-wing' policies. The left-right polarity, then, operates as an ideological grid within which the ideological self is located and against which political parties, leaders, policies, and even countries are routinely measured; the polarity is a conceptual bridge linking the ideological self to the rest of the politically relevant world. For most people, and for our analysis, left and right anchor the rough conceptual baseline used to organize the political world.

The third reason has to do with the cross-national range of left and right. Exactly why the left-right dichotomy is so pervasively used is not very clear; one speculation is that it has visual and spatial qualities that are immediately and easily understood (Laponce, 1981). But from the comparative perspective, the significant point is that left and right are not just robust indicators of ideological orientations towards political parties, leaders, and issues *within* societies; they are also powerful and stable indicators for making comparative judgements about the ideological worlds of *different* societies (Finlay, Simon and Wilson, 1974; Laponce, 1981). Insofar as ideologies are cultural products, and to the extent that the Anglo-American democracies were spun out of the same cultural orbit, we might expect a direct comparison of the left-right worlds of our respondents in these societies to be particularly revealing.

Research Design and Data

Our knowledge about the contemporary political belief systems of the Anglo-American democracies is distinctly lumpy. That unevenness can be attributed to a number of factors including national differences in prevailing analytical styles and discrepancies in the availability of research resources. At one end of the scale, the ideological pulse of various segments of the American public is regularly taken and a substantial body of high-quality research has been generated at an impressive clip (Hochschild, 1981; Abramson, 1983; McCloskey and Zaller, 1984; Verba and Orren, 1985; Neuman, 1986). Australia, Canada, and New Zealand fall to the other end of the scale. Unlike Britain, which along with the United States is often taken as a benchmark and test site for the ideological orientations of the English-speaking industrialized world (Almond and Verba, 1965; Dahl, 1966; Barnes and Kaase, 1979; Dalton, 1988), Australia, Canada, and New Zealand rarely feature as cases even in the most comprehensive comparisons of advanced industrial states. As a consequence, attempts to draw reliable conclusions about the political belief systems of the Anglo-American democracies have been crippled by the absence of direct and explicitly comparative cross-national research evidence encompassing all five countries. Most evidence is country-specific, and making cross-national generalizations on the basis of multiple sets of single-country studies typically runs into a number of difficulties. Even if evidence generated for the purposes of exploring political belief systems in one country could be reliably compared with roughly equivalent data generated in other countries, single-country studies are usually tuned to explore the uniqueness of the national experience, just as analyses comparing two countries end up focusing on contrasts. It is only through the comparison of a larger set of countries that similarities and common themes emerge, and that deviations or exceptions can be readily recognized.

In this instance, our analysis relies upon direct, self-reported attitudinal evidence drawn from mailed questionnaires (Appendix A) returned by 3,127 final-year students at 50 universities throughout Australia, Britain, Canada, New Zealand, and the United States (Appendix B). The resultant data set has important advantages for comparative exploration of political belief systems in the five countries. First, precisely the same principles were followed in constructing the survey instrument for each country. All questionnaires contained a common core of 118 items probing attitudes towards a host of issues ranging across the political, social, and economic debates present in most advanced industrial states. Moreover, in every instance questionnaires were introduced in the same way, the same scales were used, and questions were presented in the same order.

Second, identical stratified random sampling procedures were employed, with all national samples stratified according to three criteria. To a greater or lesser extent, all of the Anglo-American democracies are regionally divided societies, and thus to take into account such significant regional cleavages as the North-South divide in Britain and East-West differences in Canada, the universities included in the sample were selected from different regions of each country. Then, because student populations are themselves ideologically diverse, social science students being more 'left-wing' than others (Klineberg and Zavalloni, 1979), the university samples were stratified equally between four general areas of study: Arts and Humanities; Business and Commerce; Natural Sciences and Engineering; and Social Sciences. Finally, and in response to research (Gibbins and Nevitte, 1989) showing gender differences across a range of issue areas, each sample was stratified by gender.

In addition to these explicit controls, the data set also incorporates a number of implied controls that are particularly relevant to the focus of this study. It has been conclusively shown that level of formal education is a crucial variable in the analysis of attitude structures (Bishop, 1976; Converse, 1964), and by limiting our samples to include just final-year students we tighten our control on this important variable. We know that all respondents have undergone several years of university education and that most presumably anticipate entering the work world in the near future. But we can also assume that because the surveys were conducted within a similar time frame, plus or minus three and a half years, and because all respondents were of approximately the same age, they belong to the same cohort lodged in the same segment of life cycle. Therefore we can discount cohort differences and life-cycle effects (Abramson, 1989; Braungart and Braungart, 1989; Jennings, 1984; Jennings and Niemi, 1981) as plausible explanations for any significant cross-national variations that may emerge from the analysis.

Apart from issues relating to the survey instrument and sampling techniques, precautions were taken to maximize equivalence in other phases of the research process. In each case, samples were drawn 'blind' from lists prepared by the registrar's offices in the 50 universities, and the same mail-back procedures were followed to retrieve the questionnaires. As Table 2.1 shows, the 3127 completed and returned questionnaires represent a 56 per cent response rate, a level as high as that usually achieved through in-person survey interviews. In all five countries response rates exceeded 50 per cent, and standard checks provide no indication of systematic biases in any of the national respondent pools.

Table 2.1 The Data Set

COUNTRY	NUMBER OF UNIVERSITIES SAMPLED	SAMPLE SIZE	RESPONSE RATE	YEAR OF SURVEY
Australia	11	670	58%	1987
Britain	14	715	52%	1986
Canada	9	779	53%	1983
New Zealand	6	599	56%	1987
United States	10	364	63%	1980
Total	50	3127	53%	

Although the research design employed identical sampling procedures, and a common core of questions across the five countries, some national differences could not and should not have been avoided. For instance, no study of Canadian political belief systems can fail to consider the presence of a significant francophone linguistic minority. Thus a francophone subsample was included in the Canadian survey, and those respondents were provided with a French version of the questionnaire. Even among anglophone communities slight differences in language usage obtain, and on the few occasions when these differences could be anticipated they were accommodated by making minor modifications in the wording of items in the survey instrument; for example, in Australia the survey asked questions about *trade unions* while in Canada the phrase *labour unions* was used. Here it should also be noted that elements of national uniqueness, or social conditions shared by some but not all of the Anglo-American democracies, need not be viewed only as obstacles to comparative research; they also present unique research opportunities. In this survey one such opportunity was exploited when Australian, Canadian, and New Zealand respondents were asked additional questions probing attitudes towards Aborigines, Native People, and Maoris. Overall, providing francophones with French questionnaires, substituting terms to achieve functional equivalence, and adding questions to some national surveys all modify the survey instrument. However, such modifications are inherent to any cross-national survey research; the comparative logic of the study remains intact.

In essence, the study constitutes a straightforward quasi-experimental design (Campbell and Stanley, 1966) that circumvents some of the more flagrant difficulties plaguing cross-national research on political ideologies. Because of the efforts made to ensure cross-national comparability in the research design, our data are 'even', not 'lumpy', and we have the full complement of five matching data sets. Taken together, the test group was sampled from that proportion of the population most likely to exhibit clear patterns of ideological coherence. The sample design imposed, at the point of data collection, a variety of controls on those respondent characteristics that often obscure a clear reading of political belief systems. By administering the same 'test'—asking the same 118 questions—in the same way to respondents who are the same with respect to all significant characteristics except nationality, we have brought national differences into bold relief. In a more technical sense, within-group variance has been minimized so as to sharpen the focus on between-group variance.

Entering the Left-Right Ideological World

We begin our analysis by exploring the left-right ideological worlds of our youth elites. As indicated earlier, 'left' and 'right' are quintessentially ideological labels; they are familiar terminology in ideological debates throughout all Anglo-American democracies. The traditional left-right scale, which was included in the core battery of 118 items presented to all youth elites, asked: 'In general, how would you describe your views of political matters?' Respondents were then presented with a closed, seven-point scale anchored at the one end by 'far left' and at the other by 'far right'.

We note first that the vast majority of our respondents (90 per cent) had no difficulty placing themselves on the left-right scale (Australia, 87 per cent; Britain 93 per cent; Canada, 90 per cent; New Zealand, 84 per cent; United States, 93 per cent).[1] Few responded by indicating 'don't know' and fewer still chose not to respond at all. As we would expect of well-informed segments of these national populations, the 90 per cent response level is substantially higher than that typically found among general publics responding to the same question (for example, Dalton, 1988; Neuman, 1986), and closely matches the response levels of other student samples asked similar questions about left and right (Laponce, 1970, 1981; Klineberg and Zavalloni, 1979).

Figure 2.1 illustrates how the national samples of youth elites are distributed across the left-right scale. The figure is drawn to scale such that the *width* of the blocs representing each national respondent pool indicates the extent to which national samples are spread across the scale (measured in standard deviations). The *location* of each bloc is centred around the average score ($\bar{x}$) of each respondent pool on the seven-point left-right scale. (The *height* of each national bloc is varied for presentation purposes only; it has no substantive meaning.)

Two basic findings are brought into focus by Figure 2.1. First, all national samples share a similar ideological centre of gravity, one located slightly to the left of the scale's mid-point. The mean scores and percentage distributions show that Australian respondents outflank others to the right and American respondents, on average, outflank others to the left. However, the ideological distance between the right-most and left-most samples is small by any measure—a mere .8 on the seven-point scale; no national sample emerges as an obvious outlier, or a deviant case. Second, a comparison of the standard deviation scores indicates that the national samples are spread across the left-right scale to about the same extent. Although national differences are not entirely absent, the similarities are more striking than the differences; the latter are of degree, not of kind. The five sets of respondents, then, essentially share the same ideological space, at least so far as self-placement on the left-right scale is concerned.

Summary aggregate data such as those presented in Figure 2.1 are a useful place to start. They provide us with broad impressions about the relative ideological positions of our five national respondent pools, and the very modest national differences foreshadow the analysis to come. But by themselves these impressions do not take us very far, because they capture only one aspect of the ideological worlds of our respondents. As

Figure 2.1: National Left-Right Self-Placement Locations

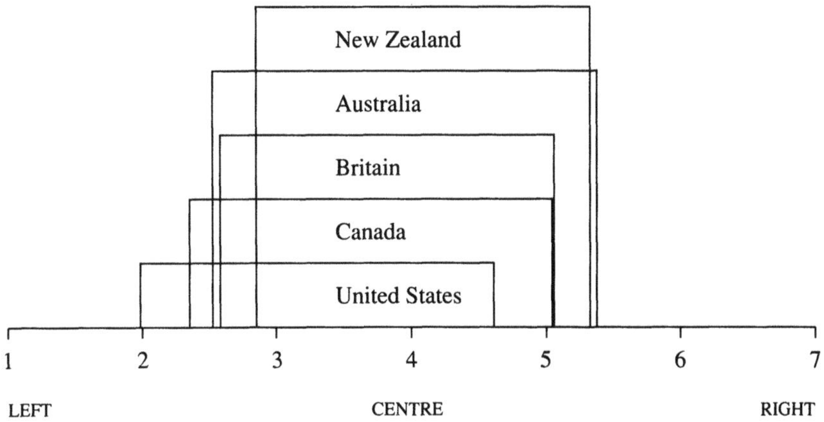

```
                    ┌──────────────────────┐
                    │      New Zealand     │
              ┌─────┼──────────────────────┼─────┐
              │     │       Australia      │     │
              │  ┌──┴──────────────────────┴──┐  │
              │  │          Britain           │  │
              │  │  ┌──────────────────────┐  │  │
              │  │  │        Canada        │  │  │
        ┌─────┼──┼──┼──────────────────────┼──┼──┼─────┐
        │     │  │  │    United States     │  │  │     │
├───────┴──┬──┴──┴──┴──┬──────────────┬────┴──┴──┴──┬──┤
1          2           3              4             5   6           7
LEFT                              CENTRE                        RIGHT
```

Distribution of Left-Right Scale (%)

COUNTRY	LEFT	CENTRE	RIGHT
Australia ($\bar{x} = 3.91$ s $= 1.40$)	45	17	38
Britain ($\bar{x} = 3.80$ s $= 1.25$)	46	22	32
Canada ($\bar{x} = 3.71$ s $= 1.33$)	47	24	29
New Zealand ($\bar{x} = 4.00$ s $= 1.25$)	39	23	38
United States ($\bar{x} = 3.20$ s $= 1.23$)	66	16	18

$\bar{x}$: mean s: standard deviation

we noted before, the left-right scale is not just a metric for ideological *self*-placement; it is an encompassing ideological grid in which *other* political objects are placed and against which a variety of political phenomena—policies, issues, even countries—are routinely measured. Therefore, although the five national samples project similar left-right profiles as far as self-placement is concerned, there is no guarantee that the left-right optic will work in the same way when it is used for viewing other political objects or issues. For example, left-right self-placement may be a powerful predictor of attitudes towards income redistribution in New Zealand but not in Canada. Or it may be a very discriminating indicator of opposition to nuclear power in Britain but not in the United States. How well, then, does the same left-right optic work when it is applied to the same political objects across five different countries?

The case of political parties is a particularly useful example to explore for a variety of reasons. Parties play a crucial role in liberal democratic political systems; they are the main vehicles linking individuals to governments, and as such they are essential instruments for maintaining the legitimacy of regimes. Parties are the chief combatants in the main political struggles of the day; as architects and critics of public policy, they compete for public affection, and publics, in turn, keep parties 'honest' by supplying or withdrawing their support. Not surprisingly, parties are commonly characterized, compared, and contrasted according to where they sit in left-right ideological space (Butler and Stokes, 1969; Barnes, 1971; Sani, 1974; Sartori, 1976). Indeed, parties actively encourage the use of left-right labels to help voters 'make sense' of the party system (Sani, 1974), with the result that the left-right ideological labels are often taken as proxies for party identification.[2] With respect to the Anglo-American democracies, one observer has noted that 'political parties in these countries more than those in most others, fall along the classic Left-Right continuum; they lack the complications introduced by strong totalitarian or religious parties that cut across the Left-Right dimension' (Alford, 1963: 11). At the same time, the shifting electoral fortunes of left and right parties in the Anglo-American democracies have been taken as one indication of changing ideological climate over the last twenty-five years (Nie, Verba and Petrocik, 1976; Crewe, 1980; LeDuc, 1985). Moreover, and of particular relevance here, the emergence of the new political generation has been linked to those ideological changes (Jennings, 1984).

How, then, does left-right ideological self-location work to structure the partisan identifications of our youth elites in the Anglo-American democracies? All respondents were asked the same standard question about party identification: 'Generally speaking, do you usually consider yourself as ... [the party labels listed here varied according to national setting]?' The ideological distributions of party identifiers are illustrated in Figure 2.2, in which each bloc, drawn to scale, captures a particular partisan camp. The location of each bloc is fixed, or anchored, by the mean left-right score of respondents identifying with each party, and the width of each bloc reflects the ideological spread, measured by standard deviations, of partisans' scores on the seven-point left-right scale.

These data reveal a number of significant national differences. First, self-placement on the left-right scale is clearly a very efficient predictor of partisan identification for the Australian respondents. In essence, identifiers with both the Australian Labor Party and the Liberals occupy unique left-right ideological space. The same is true, though to a lesser

Mapping the Ideological Terrain | 37

Figure 2.2: Left-Right Ideological Space Occupied by Partisans

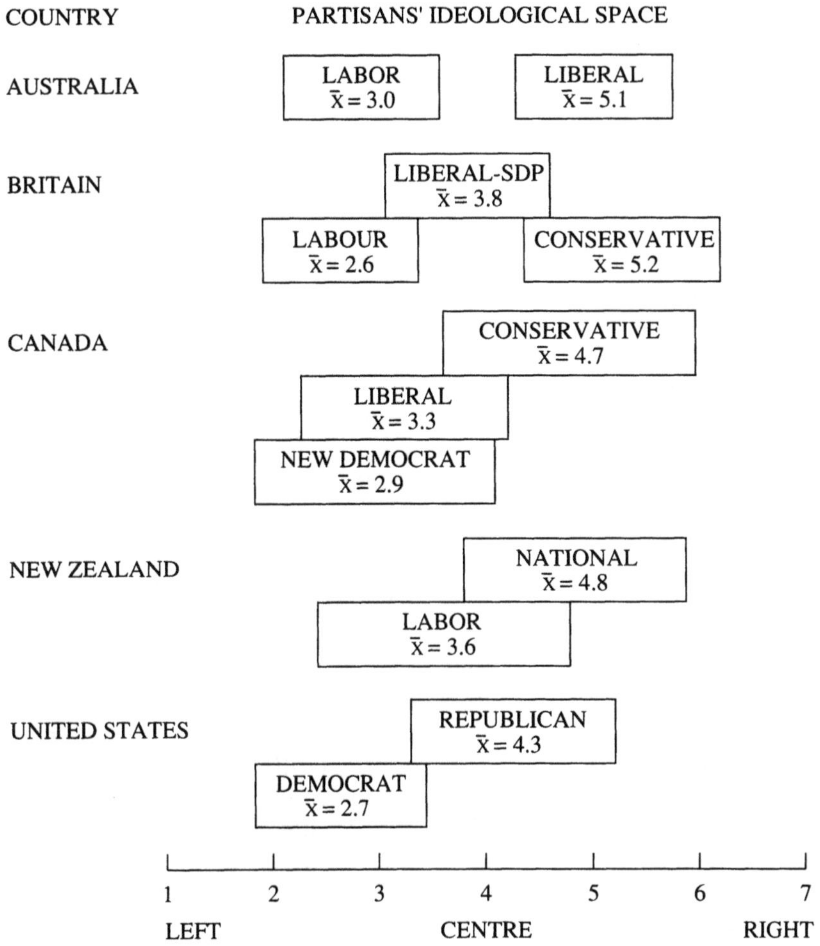

COUNTRY	PARTISANS' IDEOLOGICAL SPACE

AUSTRALIA: LABOR $\bar{x} = 3.0$ | LIBERAL $\bar{x} = 5.1$

BRITAIN: LIBERAL-SDP $\bar{x} = 3.8$ | LABOUR $\bar{x} = 2.6$ | CONSERVATIVE $\bar{x} = 5.2$

CANADA: CONSERVATIVE $\bar{x} = 4.7$ | LIBERAL $\bar{x} = 3.3$ | NEW DEMOCRAT $\bar{x} = 2.9$

NEW ZEALAND: NATIONAL $\bar{x} = 4.8$ | LABOR $\bar{x} = 3.6$

UNITED STATES: REPUBLICAN $\bar{x} = 4.3$ | DEMOCRAT $\bar{x} = 2.7$

```
  1      2      3      4      5      6      7
 LEFT                 CENTRE                RIGHT
```

extent, for partisans in British and American samples; in both cases, those identifying with the major parties of the left and right occupy relatively discrete ideological space. Indeed, in the British case the gap between the two exceeds the Australian gap, and even identifiers with the British Liberal-SDP occupy an almost discrete ideological space. The Canadian and New Zealand data, however, display a different pattern as left-right self-location turns out to be a poorer predictor of party identification. In the Canadian case, all three parties compete for centre-left identifiers, while in the New Zealand sample the National and Liberal parties battle for support from centre-right identifiers.

Not surprisingly, Figure 2.2 shows that left-identifiers support the traditional parties of the left (Labour, Labor, the NDP and the US Democrats) while right-identifiers support the traditional parties of the right (the Republicans, Conservatives, Nationals, and Australian Liberals). What is more surprising is the cross-national comparison. By reading the data vertically and comparing, first, the party identifications of left-identifiers in all five countries and then the party identifications of right-identifiers, we can see that parties of the left and right stack on top of each other fairly neatly; they occupy about the same ideological space. This 'stacking' of parties on the left may reflect the fact that the parties, at least in the four Commonwealth states, were cut from the same Fabian cloth and thus share common historical and ideological roots. Conversely, the stacking of parties on the right may reflect the international currents of neoconservatism that were so readily apparent in the 1980s. Before these speculations can be pursued further, however, we need a more precise measure of ideological similarity and distinctiveness. Only with such a measure in hand can we determine if the Anglo-American lefts are more similar to one another than are the Anglo-American rights.

Figure 2.3 presents the results of a Scheffe test, a difference-of-means test that identifies whether there are statistically significant differences between the mean scores of any pair of groups.[3] The groups, in this instance political parties, are ranked and numbered according to each subsample's mean score on the self-anchoring left-right scale. The column numbers (1 through 12) correspond to the group labels (British Conservative through British Labour) indicated in the rows at the left side of the matrix in Figure 2.3. We read the results of the Scheffe test by examining the location and distribution of the asterisks. The *presence* of an asterisk in the matrix indicates statistically significant differences in group mean scores on the left-right scale. For example, identifiers with the British and Canadian Conservative parties are significantly different in their self-placement on the left-right scale; British Conservatives are farther to the right than are their Canadian counterparts. The *absence* of an asterisk means that group differences are not significant. Thus, for example, although British Labourites and American Democrats have different mean scores on the left-right scale, the difference is not statistically significant.

To determine whether the Anglo-American partisan rights are more ideologically similar than are the Anglo-American partisan lefts, we have to compare *two* sets of five groups according to the relative ideological consensus or fragmentation within those sets. In more technical terms, we want to know whether the statistical differences within partisans of the left on the left-right scale are greater, or smaller, than the statistical differences within partisan rights. We draw attention to the groups we are comparing by enclosing the national partisan lefts in one box at the lower quadrant and enclosing the national rights in another box at the upper quadrant. The results of the comparison-of-means test are revealing on several accounts.

Figure 2.3: Comparison of Means of National Party Identifiers on the Left-Right Scale

NATIONAL PARTY IDENTIFIERS	1	2	3	4	5	6	7	8	9	10	11	12	LEFT-RIGHT SCALE MEAN SCORES
1. Britain Conservative													5.2
2. Australia Liberal													5.1
3. New Zealand National													4.8
4. Canada Conservative	★	★											4.7
5. United States Republican	★	★											4.3
6. Britain Liberal-SDP	★	★	★	★									3.8
7. New Zealand Labor	★	★	★	★	★								3.6
8. Canada Liberal	★	★	★	★	★	★							3.3
9. Australia Labor	★	★	★	★	★	★	★						3.0
10. Canada New Democrat	★	★	★	★	★	★	★						2.9
11. United States Democrat	★	★	★	★	★	★	★	★					2.7
12. Britain Labour	★	★	★	★	★	★	★	★					2.6

★ represents pairs of party identifiers with Left-Right mean scores significantly different at p < .05

First, supporters of the left-most parties from each national sample (lower quadrant) do *not* emerge as a solid ideological bloc. Although partisans from four out of the five parties of the left occupy contiguous ideological space, New Zealand Labor partisans are statistically significant outliers, separated from other left-wing partisans by Canadian Liberals. Therefore the difference-of-means test reveals some discontinuity, or fragmentation, among the partisan lefts, although Australian Labor, Canadian New Democrats, American Democrats, and British Labour form a very sizeable and statistically indistinguishable cluster. The ideological solidarity of the partisan lefts dissipates more noticeably as one moves towards the centre. Canadian Liberals share common ground with Australian Labor and with their co-nationals in the New Democratic party, but the outlying New Zealand Laborites share ideological territory only with Canadian Liberals.

When we turn to consider the partisans of the right (upper quadrant of Figure 2.3), and when we inspect the pairwise comparisons again, a quite different pattern emerges. As with the lefts, the data show that the rights do not form a single ideologically cohesive bloc. But there are two clearly identifiable ideological clusterings within the partisan rights. American Republicans and Canadian Progressive Conservatives are statistically indistinguishable, as are British Conservatives and Australian Liberals. Furthermore, both pairs differ significantly ($p<.05$) from one another. In effect, New Zealand Nationals provide a bridge, a common link that ideologically hitches both of these groups together; the Nationals' ideological location is statistically indistinguishable from that of any other partisan right.

For the moment, this discussion of partisan differences with respect to the left-right scale does little more than raise the curtain on an extended analytical comparison of the left and right, and of national differences within the left and right. The relative coherence of the left and right is an issue to which we will return. At this point, it is important to move on to a conceptual matter that lies at the very heart of our analysis. Simply put: *How much does left-right self-location tell us about the political belief systems of youth elites in the 1980s?* Although a student in Vancouver and a student in Melbourne, or Houston, may locate themselves on the same left-of-centre location on the scale, and may all support left-wing parties, does this mean that they view the world in the same way? Do they share the same political ideals, values, and beliefs?

Drawing conclusions about political belief systems on the basis of left-right self-location alone is a risky business, not least of all because location on the left-right scale by itself provides no specific clues about what *substantive meanings* the labels left and right might carry in each national setting. We noted before that left and right originally referred to ideological divisions between the nobility and the clergy in eighteenth-century France, and we also pointed out that the meanings attached to left and right have continually expanded and evolved to embrace novel positions on the most salient political issues and ideological conflicts of the day. As Sartori has indicated, left and right were ideologically loaded terms from the very start, and in the last 150 years the terms have been unloaded and reloaded several times (1976: 335). This 'semantic flexibility' may well explain why the terms themselves have survived for so long as cornerstones of our ideological vocabulary, but it also poses serious problems of interpretation. If left and right are *not* anchored in any particular set of meanings, if they are so fluid, then *how can we be certain that left and right mean the same things even in such similar countries as the Anglo-American democracies?* Of course, we might try to reconstruct the contemporary meanings assigned to left and right in each country by delving into the particular historical meanings of the terms, and by projecting those meanings onto contemporary national circumstances. But that strategy runs into trouble too; it fails to take into account substantial variations in the content of left and right even *within* the same national population. More to the point, it ignores a substantial body of evidence indicating that the meanings of left and right vary systematically across age cohorts (Jennings, 1984; Inglehart, 1984; Bucklin, 1985; Dalton, 1986).

To provide a comprehensive picture of the ideological worlds of our youth elites we must flesh out, or fill in, the specific meanings that respondents attach to left and right. We must also specify how the contents of those lefts and rights relate to the larger underlying structures that shape and give coherence to national political belief systems. To accomplish this we could proceed in two different ways. We could determine how the left-right scale correlates with a variety of dependent variables tapping orientations to a range of political issues and objects in each national setting. By looking at the strongest correlations we might be able to construct profiles of the lefts and rights for each national sample, and then compare those profiles. But this approach is cumbersome, and it involves a good deal of trial and error.[4] Moreover, the left-right profiles that would be produced by such a strategy depend entirely upon which variables are included in the analysis. More importantly, we would have no way of knowing, beyond intuition, which *underlying attitude structures* are responsible for shaping those left-right profiles. The second approach, and the one followed here, reduces the amount of guesswork involved by starting at the other end of the problem. First we identify the common primary dimensions shaping the political belief systems of youth elites. We then turn to see how those structures are reflected in, and shape, the left-right polarity in each of the five national samples. In this second approach the left-right scale provides the foundation upon which we can construct more complex ideological structures.

Common Attitude Structures: Four Dimensions

Our search for underlying attitude structures employs exploratory factor analysis—a statistical procedure that scans the interrelationships among responses to a large number of questions and reduces those relationships to a limited, and statistically most efficient, set of underlying dimensions, or 'factors'. The factor analysis was first applied to the pooled data set encompassing *all* respondents because our goal was to identify *common* attitude structures. In all, 44 items tapping orientations towards a variety of social, economic, and political issues, and common to all five national surveys, were subjected to an initial screening factor analysis (unrotated). Items that failed to load onto a significant factor—that is, a factor with an eigenvalue greater than one—were dropped from further consideration and a second, clarifying factor analysis (oblique rotation) was performed on the remaining 26 items. Four discrete factors emerge from the terminal solution. The full text of the item questions retained in the terminal factor solution are reported in Appendix C, and the full matrix in Table C-1. The results of the final four-factor solution are summarized in Table 2.2.

The first factor, 'Government', encompasses nine items linking concerns about government intervention in the economy with traditional welfare-state issues. The factor is driven primarily by questions addressing the appropriate size of government, whether the government should provide jobs, and how much government control should be exercised over business. It also contains classic questions concerning redistribution—about the gap between the rich and the poor, the role of taxation in reducing disparities in wealth, the fairness of the free-enterprise economy, and the preferred scope of government services to such groups as the old and the handicapped. More peripherally, it taps orientations towards the traditional gladiators in battles for economic rewards—business and unions. The government factor contains the largest number of items and it explains by far the highest proportion of variance (about 34 per cent). In more qualitative terms, the power of the government factor is surprising because it suggests that the ideological tensions associated with the advance of the post-war left are far from settled. Those tensions continue to resonate powerfully even in the generation that is the farthest removed from the conditions that gave rise to the welfare state, and the generation that would seem least likely to have need of the kinds of supports provided by the welfare state.[5]

The second most powerful dimension to emerge from the factor analysis, 'Feminism', relates to gender equality. This dimension is not analytically tidy. It contains questions on whether it is appropriate for women to pursue careers instead of staying home, and whether women with employed husbands should be laid off before other workers, concerns that reach back into the early history of the women's movement. But it also includes issues of more recent vintage, questions about a woman's right to abortion, whether lesbians and homosexuals should be allowed to teach in schools, and whether there should be laws eliminating distinctions in the treatment of men and women. Thus the gender concerns tapped by the factor are both broad and diversified, which is appropriate given that the feminist agenda itself grafts new issues onto long-standing

Table 2.2 Factor Pattern Matrix*

ITEM	GOVERNMENT	FEMINISM	MINORITIES	EQUALITY	COMMUNALITY
1. Size of Government	.79499				.59
2. Government and jobs	.70204				.51
3. Government regulation	.68226				.51
4. Rich/poor income gap	.54463				.53
5. Welfare benefits	.52040				.38
6. Private enterprise	.51184				.61
7. Progressive tax system	.49701				.54
8. Power of business	.49255				.51
9. Power of unions	.37014				.37
10. Women's role		.72162			.56
11. Right to abortion		.71737			.52
12. Layoff women first		.61236			.41
13. Homosexuals as teachers		.48348			.37
14. Discrimination law		.47355			.39
15. Gender discrimination systemic		.40238			.48
16. Minorities and job guarantee			.69232		.55
17. Equality for minorities			.59135		.59
18. Minority discrimination systemic			.52966		.57
19. Media and minorities			.52329		.47
20. Right to refuse to sell home			.48549		.31
21. Equality of opportunity or result				.73745	.51
22. Income similarity				.69489	.68
23. Quotas for women				.67146	.63
24. Quotas for minorities				.63119	.64
25. Income limit for rich				.57968	.56
26. Workers and say in jobs				.34345	.47
Eigenvalue	8.9098	1.9018	1.2093	1.1926	
Variance Explained	34.3%	7.3%	4.6%	4.6%	

*Oblique rotation with listwise deletion of missing cases.

concerns. This expanded agenda implies that there are more opportunities for generating political support for gender equality; but, as we shall see, it also implies increased potential for mobilizing political opposition.

The third factor or dimension pertains to 'Minorities', and it includes questions about the fair access of minorities to jobs, the importance respondents attach to achieving equality for minorities, whether discrimination about minorities is systemic, and how minorities are represented in the media. The five items contained in this factor tap orientations towards both specific minority groups (for example, blacks in the United States, Aborigines in Australia, and Maoris in New Zealand) as well as questions referring to 'minorities' in general. Furthermore, the questions probe orientations about the status of minorities in a variety of settings—in the workplace, the neighbourhood, and society at large. That these items cluster along a single dimension suggests that respondents had little difficulty in recognizing 'minority issues' regardless of whether those issues take particular or generalizable forms. But significant too is the fact that respondents do not 'confuse' minority issues with matters of gender. Even though women and minorities historically have both been marginalized groups when it comes to social status or access to economic and political power, and despite the fact that politicization of both groups has been inspired by the same goal—to redress those historic imbalances—minority and gender issues nonetheless emerge as distinct dimensions in the belief systems of respondents.

The final dimension to emerge from the factor analysis taps attitudes towards 'Equality'. Arguably, the government, feminism, and minority dimensions all relate to equality in one way or another (Verba and Orren, 1985). The common theme linking the fourth set of items, however, is clearly the tension between equality of opportunity and equality of result. The appropriate balance between equality of opportunity/result is an old dilemma, one often associated with debates about the welfare state (Wilensky, 1975). What is significant and unexpected in this instance is that questions relating to the equality of opportunity/result did *not* load onto the government factor, but emerged instead as an analytically distinct line of cleavage in the belief systems of youth elites.

Debates about the welfare state have revolved around the extent to which the state should provide *generalized* benefits, entitlements applying to all by virtue of citizenship. What appears to underlie the equality dimension, however, is the question of whether specific, targeted, remedies are called for to alleviate adverse conditions confronting particular disadvantaged groups, groups that have not been caught by the welfare state's safety net—a gender underclass and a minority underclass as well as an economic underclass. Thus the fourth factor combines orientations towards equality of opportunity/result with questions about whether quotas shculd be used to help women and minorities gain access to educational institutions and to the workplace. For our youth elites at least, equality of opportunity/result is not simply a recasting of an old welfare-state issue; rather, it is entangled with a post-welfare-state agenda, one with different reference points and one that envisions quotas as instruments for achieving a measure of equality for uniquely burdened groups.

The factor analysis puts into place the tools we need to compare cross-nationally the political belief systems of youth elites in the Anglo-American democracies. Before taking up those tools, however, it is useful to step back from the details of the factor analysis and consider some of its more general implications. Broadly viewed, the data capture the general flavour of political discourse in the five countries, and provide some clues about why some of the ideological battles of the 1980s decade were so fierce. They suggest, for instance, why 'getting the government off the backs of people' and 'the evils of big government' proved to be such effective lightning rods for public debate. These phrases were not just the whimsical musings or erratic flourishes of leaders with idiosyncratic agendas; they were well-aimed ideological salvos that struck at the very heart of the most divisive issue of the day. Of all the questions incorporated in the factor analysis, 'size of government' was the single most important item, the one capping the most powerful dimension structuring political attitudes.

The emergence of the feminism and minority dimensions as the second and third most important factors is a clear indication of the advance of new issues onto the public agenda. In precise terms, matters of gender and minority equity are old issues. The point is, however, that both issues have gathered momentum in the course of the last two decades, and both have changed form and scope. The abortion issue in particular added a new and potent dimension to the gender debate. With respect to the minorities dimension, matters of racial equality were explosive political issues in the 1960s, at least in the United States. It is significant, though, that our factor analysis, which worked with pooled data, shows that concerns about minorities are not unique to American respondents; they are shared by youth elites in all five states and reflect, perhaps, the significance of the profound changes that have taken place in all the Anglo-American democracies, changes that were sketched out in Chapter 1. The equality of opportunity/result dimension achieved salience more recently as well. It captures controversies about meritocracy versus quotas, or affirmative action for particular underclasses. For most of the Anglo-American democracies, quotas are relatively novel weapons in battles for equality.

Common Structures, National Variations

By identifying the substantive issue domains underpinning the political belief systems of our youth elites, the factor analysis has revealed which common attitudinal cleavages were relevant to those ideological worlds. But to say that respondents organized their attitudes according to the same four dimensions—government, feminism, minorities, and equality of opportunity/result—does not mean that youth elites in the five countries agreed with each other on those issues. A much clearer picture of national ideological similarities and differences can be obtained by comparing the scope of agreement and disagreement across each of the four dimensions. To undertake those comparisons we require first some yardstick that summarizes respondent orientations towards each of the issue domains identified by the factor analysis. Following standard practice, simple additive factor scales were developed from the items contained in each factor. Respondents' answers to question items loading into each factor were weighted and then summed (see Appendix D); that procedure produced four factor-scale scores for every respondent, with each score reflecting the respondent's position on the dimension revealed by the terminal factor solution. Standard tests (Cronbach's Alpha) show that the resulting four scales are robust. Thus we can proceed to examine the national patterns of agreement and disagreement, and remain confident that the scales provide reliable indicators of each of the factors produced by the factor analysis. Our analysis begins with national similarities and differences on the government dimension.

The kinds of predictions that might be made about how different national groups are likely to be oriented towards government intervention in society and the economy depend on how much importance is attached to such factors as historical tradition. If the government dimension measures commitment, or opposition, to the welfare state, then unquestionably a very strong historical case can be made for anticipating that British youth elites will be the most likely to favour 'more government'. After all, Britain's exposure to industrialism was deep and sustained, and the comparatively early and complete development of its welfare-state apparatus indicates a historical readiness to adopt state-sponsored, collectivist remedies in response to the social divisions activated by deep industrialism. Following the same reasoning, we might expect American youth elites to be the most likely to favour less government; they inherit a tradition of rugged individualism, one that is reflected in a historical aversion to government intervention. Similarly, we would expect the Australian, Canadian, and New Zealand cases to take up the middle ground. Historically, all have been more ready than the United States to use the state as an instrument for achieving collective goals, while none experienced the kind of industrial social malaise that inspired Britain's expansive welfare state.

Expectations drawn from historical traditions, however, have to be balanced against other considerations, including the kinds of experiences encountered first-hand by this generation of youth elites. American youth elites of the 1980s, for example, approached political maturity not in an era of unsullied free enterprise, but during a period in which *laissez-faire* capitalism had been superseded by the mixed economy of the welfare state. Significantly, evidence clearly shows that this generation, more than any other, supported an expanded welfare-state effort (McCloskey and Zaller, 1984). Meanwhile, precisely the same generation of British youth elites was exposed to vigorous attacks on 'big government' and 'collectivism', the culprits responsible for 'the British disease' (King, 1985). Although systematic cross-national evidence of intergenerational differences in attitudes towards government is sketchy at best and far from conclusive, a strong case can be made that youth elites of the 1980s were not merely uncritical vessels of received wisdom on matters relating to government intervention in the economy.

Before turning to examine national distributions across the government dimension, it is useful to get a feel for cross-national differences by looking at respondent reactions to the nine questions making up that dimension. Table 2.3 summarizes national responses through a simple agree/disagree format. The first four questions in the table, the questions that load most powerfully onto the government dimension, all explicitly deal with attitudes about government and can be considered together. Question 1 presents respondents with a trade-off between downsizing government and losing government services. A slim majority of British respondents plump for 'smaller government' and Americans tend to lean in the same direction, but Australians, Canadians, and New Zealanders lean the other way. Generally, though, substantial segments of all national samples occupy the middle ground and, with the possible exception of the British and New Zealand respondents, the national samples are fairly evenly divided. The second question probes attitudes towards government and employment, and a clear majority of respondents in *every* national setting believes that 'government should see to it that everyone has a job'. There is also cross-national consensus in response to Question 4; a substantial majority of respondents in all five countries agree that 'the government should work to reduce substantially the income gap between the rich and the poor'. On both Questions 2 and 4, British respondents turn out to be most emphatic about government intervention as a tool for promoting employment and for redistributing wealth. When it comes to government regulation of business (Question 3), national differences are more pronounced. About two in three Americans think that 'the country would be better off if business were less regulated', and a majority of British and Canadian respondents agree with them, but New Zealanders and Australians clearly do not.

The national distributions across the first four questions are uneven, and when we compare national responses to the remaining five questions the results are also mixed. A clear majority of respondents in every country believes that social-welfare benefits should be restricted to the old and the handicapped (Question 5) and that 'taxing those with high incomes to help the poor is only fair' (Question 7). Nor is there any question that most respondents disagree with the idea that 'trade unions have too much

Table 2.3 Questions Included in the Government Scale

QUESTION		AUSTRALIA	BRITAIN	CANADA	NEW ZEALAND	UNITED STATES
1. In general, government grows bigger as it provides more services. Do you favour smaller government?	% Agree*	31.8	52.7	30.1	28.1	36.1
	% Disagree	43.8	34.9	44.5	45.5	34.9
2. The /government (Aus., Brit., N.Z.)/federal government (Can.)/ government in Washington (U.S.)/should see to it that everyone has a job.	% Agree*	54.8	70.6	54.4	57.3	60.3
	% Disagree	29.0	18.5	30.2	26.6	28.4
3. The country would be better off if /there was less government control over business (Aus., Brit., N.Z.)/business were less regulated (Can., U.S.).	% Agree	47.1	57.4	51.4	41.4	66.0
	% Disagree	52.9	42.6	48.6	58.6	34.0
4. The government should work to reduce substantially the income gap between rich and poor.	% Agree	68.3	78.2	60.1	65.1	64.0
	% Disagree	31.7	21.8	39.9	34.9	36.0
5. All except the old and the handicapped should have to take care of themselves without social welfare benefits.	% Agree	68.2	91.8	65.8	78.3	74.3
	% Disagree	31.8	8.2	34.2	21.7	25.7
6. The private enterprise system is generally a fair system for working people.	% Agree*	34.0	42.1	30.3	29.3	40.4
	% Disagree	47.0	32.8	48.3	47.0	41.5
7. Taxing those with high incomes to help the poor is only fair.	% Agree*	57.6	75.6	57.3	52.4	64.2
	% Disagree	28.0	14.1	27.0	32.1	18.6
8. Businessmen have too much power for the good of the country.	% Agree	56.6	47.4	39.4	43.6	61.7
	% Disagree	43.4	52.6	60.6	56.4	38.3
9. Trade unions have too much power for the good of the country.	% Agree	30.4	42.4	27.7	37.6	28.0
	% Disagree	69.6	57.6	72.3	62.4	72.0

*Percentages do not add to 100% because mid-points on these 7-point scales are omitted.

power for the good of the country' (Question 9). We can point to a cross-national consensus in responses to these three questions, but we also have to take note of substantial national variations within that consensus. For example, the more than 90 per cent of British respondents believing that social-welfare benefits should be limited to the old and handicapped amounts to a virtual national consensus. At the same time, more than one-third of the Canadians disagree with that point of view. Similarly, British respondents are most enthusiastic about taxing the rich to help the poor (Question 7). But the Australians (28 per cent), Canadians (27 per cent), and New Zealanders (32 per cent) are about twice as likely as Britons (14 per cent) to think that such a redistributive effort is not fair.

Not only are there significant variations within a consensus, but we can also see cross-national divisions in the responses to Questions 8 and 6. Americans and Australians generally agree with the view that 'businessmen have too much power for the good of the country' (Question 8) while Britons, Canadians, and New Zealanders generally disagree. And, finally, Britons are slightly more inclined than any other set of respondents to believe that the private-enterprise system is fair for working people (Question 6).

An overview of these summary data suggests substantial areas of cross-national agreement on many issues and minor national differences on others. At the same time, *these data provide no indication of clear or consistent national polarities*. It would seem that British respondents are different from other national samples in their responses to about five of the nine questions. The differences, however, do not run through the entire gamut of questions, nor is there any single national respondent pool that is consistently at odds with British responses. Thus while Table 2.3 provides a starting point, it does not reveal the net or additive impact of minor and sometimes contradictory national differences. For this we must turn to the scales derived from the factor analysis.

Figure 2.4 portrays the distributions of the national samples across the government scale. Each bloc is anchored by the mean score of the national sample, with the width of the blocs indicating the 'spread' of responses measured by standard deviations within each national sample. (As before, no significance should be attached to the height of respective blocs.) As the figure shows, the five sets of respondents share much common ground. All national samples straddle the mid-point of the government scale; in no instance does the mean location of any group lie outside of the spread of the other national samples; and the majority of respondents in all five countries fall between the mid-point and the 'more government' segment of the scale. But significant national variations are also evident. British youth elites, for example, appear to have inherited an 'active state' tradition; they are most inclined to favour government intervention, and their scores across the government scale are significantly different ($p<.05$) from those of respondents in the other four countries. More surprising, perhaps, are the relative orderings of the other national samples. Canadians, and not their American counterparts, are most likely to gravitate towards the 'less government' pole. Indeed, Figure 2.4 indicates that Canadian, New Zealand, and Australian youth elites are all less enthusiastic than their American counterparts about government intervention, in society and the economy. But even in the group most inclined to favour less government, the Canadian sample, there is no chorus demanding 'roll back the state'. The mean location of that group (38.1) corresponds almost precisely with the mid-point of the scale (38.0). Figure 2.4 also shows that the Canadian and New Zealand samples are least divided (have the smallest standard deviation) on the matter of government intervention, while Australian and United States respondents are most deeply divided—a finding that supports other evidence regarding the vitality of the government-intervention cleavage in those societies (Graycar, 1983; Verba and Orren, 1985; Bean and Kelley, 1988).

Figure 2.4: National Locations on the Government Scale

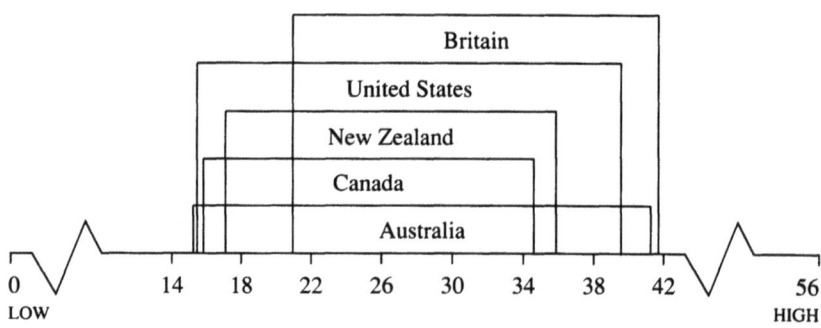

Our primary concern is not just with what proportions of youth elites support or oppose government intervention; it is with broader questions about the structure of attitudes and with what those structures can tell us about the larger ideological worlds of this political generation. If left and right work as meaningful ideological signposts, then they should provide reliable guides to respondents' positions on those issues that are central to political belief systems. How well, then, does left-right self-location capture or reflect orientations towards the government dimension among youth elites in the Anglo-American democracies? By exploring that question we can start to fill in the substantive meanings of left and right in the five national settings. Moreover, because the government factor was derived from pooled data, we can be reasonably certain that when we compare the ability of left-right location to predict positions on the government scale, we are comparing ideological apples with ideological apples.

Correlations (r's) between left-right self-placement and respondent scores on the government scale provide convincing evidence that views about government intervention in society and the economy are very much a part of the ideological worlds of youth elites in all of the Anglo-American democracies. Not surprisingly, the strength of correlation varies somewhat depending upon national setting. Left-right location is an extremely powerful predictor of orientations towards government in the British (r = .79) and Australian (r = .75) settings, slightly less so in the cases of New Zealand (r = .68) and the United States (r = .66), and weakest in the Canadian sample (r = .51). By conventional standards all of these correlations are unusually strong. Simple correlations, though, can obscure significant national differences. For instance, the correlations might be strong in the Australian case because left-identifiers uniformly favoured more government or in the American case because right-wingers uniformly opposed it. To disentangle similarities and differences between and among five national lefts and rights and to see how those differences and similarities are reflected in, or distorted by, party loyalties, we need to examine these data more closely.

The pursuit of social and economic justice through state intervention in society and the economy has been a consistent ideological thread uniting the lefts in all of the Anglo-American democracies throughout much of the post-war period. But if genuine ideological sea changes did in fact take place during the 1980s, if the historical coherence of the left unravelled and was replaced by a coherent right championing free enterprise, then we would expect to find evidence of a substantial anti-government consensus among this generation of right-identifiers in the five national samples. Alternatively, we may find an emergent ideological consensus on the right coupled with the persistence of ideological cohesion on the left.

The results of the comparison-of-means tests presented in Figure 2.5 shed some light on these issues. First, it is plain that regardless of national location, *all* left-identifiers are more inclined to support greater government intervention, just as all right-identifiers are more likely to oppose it. But is there more consensus within the rights or within the lefts when it comes to orientations towards government? On this issue the comparison-of-means matrix unmistakably points to *greater ideological consensus within the five national rights*. Indeed, the scope of that consensus is sufficiently expansive as to include those American respondents who place themselves at the mid-point of the left-right scale. Furthermore, the complete consensus within the right is broken only by a statistically significant difference between the most forceful opponents of big government, the Australian right, and the 'wetter' British right. The national lefts, by contrast, share less common ground, with the Canadian and

Figure 2.5: Comparison of Means of Left, Centre, and Right Identifiers on Government Scale

NATIONAL LEFT-RIGHT IDENTIFIERS	1	2	3	4	5	6	7	8	9	10	11	12	13	14	15	GOVERNMENT SCALE MEAN SCORES
1. Australia Right																17.2
2. United States Right																18.3
3. Canada Right																18.8
4. New Zealand Right																19.7
5. United States Centre																22.1
6. Britain Right	*															22.3
7. New Zealand Centre	*															23.9
8. Australia Centre	*	*														24.9
9. Canada Centre	*	*	*	*												26.0
10. Canada Left	*	*	*	*		*										28.1
11. Britain Centre	*	*	*	*	*	*	*									30.0
12. United States Left	*	*	*	*	*	*	*	*	*	*						32.7
13. New Zealand Left	*	*	*	*	*	*	*	*	*	*						33.7
14. Australia Left	*	*	*	*	*	*	*	*	*	*	*					34.9
15. Britain Left	*	*	*	*	*	*	*	*	*	*	*	*	*	*		39.2

* represents pairs of left-right identifiers with Government Scale mean scores significantly different at $p < .05$

British lefts constituting significant outliers. The position of the Canadian left on the government scale is statistically indistinguishable from that of

British mid-identifiers, but is significantly different (less interventionist) from those of the American, New Zealand, Australian, and British lefts. The British left is ruggedly interventionist, and uniquely so. Indeed, it is interesting to note that the mean score for the Canadian left is closer to that of even the extremist Australian right than it is to that of the British left. Thus while all left-identifiers support 'more government', it is plain that they are more likely than their right-wing counterparts to disagree about how much, or how little, government intervention there should be.

Within the broad themes of consensus within the right and fragmentation within the left, Figure 2.5 also provides evidence of significant national differences in the relative locations of ideological subgroups across the government scale. Given the cross-national similarities in the self-placement of respondents along the left-right scale (Figure 2.1) and considering the strong correlations between left-right self-placement and government-intervention scale scores, we might reasonably expect all national lefts to prefer more government, all rights to favour less government, and the mid-identifiers to take up the middle ground. However, when we track the rankings of ideological subgroups down the government scale, significant national discontinuities emerge. The expected pattern is consistently broken by ideological subgroups from the British sample, and in that sense British respondents routinely appear to be 'out of step'. Regardless of whether they are on the left, in the middle, or on the right of the left-right scale, British youth elites are significantly more likely than their subgroup counterparts to favour 'more government'. Thus, for example, the British right outflanks American mid-identifiers towards the 'more government' pole of the scale, and British mid-identifiers are more supportive of government intervention than is the Canadian left. The very substantial difference between the British left and all other lefts with respect to orientations towards government intervention underscores that same theme; it also clearly illustrates the extent to which the British left is also a deviant case—a 'rogue left'.

Together, these findings imply that, in the British case, national setting is significant at least as far as the government dimension is concerned. For this generation of youth elites, Australian, Canadian, and New Zealand respondents of both the left *and* the right have more in common with their American counterparts, and with one another, than with their British counterparts. In that sense, the evidence points not to American exceptionalism but to British exceptionalism.

Partisanship

Although the findings to this point are suggestive with respect to both national convergence and exceptionalism, they tell only part of the story. As we have seen, political parties are key players in linking individuals to the state and in shaping public policy. What happens, then, when we take partisanship into account, when we move from ideological self-placement on the left-right scale to how respondents locate themselves in the 'real' world of party politics, where the partisan options are limited and where the ideological dispositions of parties may be ambiguous? Are the patterns in Figure 2.5 faithfully reproduced when party identifications are considered? Or are they amplified, muted or distorted? Is there a consensus among partisans of the left in the five Anglo-American democracies? Or do partisans of the right have more in common when it comes to government intervention?

We pointed out in the previous chapter that for much of this century, Anglo-American governments grew faster when left-wing parties were in power. But we also noted that parties of the left confronted a variety of dilemmas during the 1980s. Traditional left-wing constituencies eroded, partisan identifications weakened, publics became more issue-driven, agendas expanded, government intervention was forcefully challenged, and publics appeared to be less certain that 'big government' could provide contemporary solutions to such concerns as social and economic justice. Moreover, the resolve of left-wing parties to support an expanded state weakened just as the opposition of right-wing parties to government intervention—or at least their rhetoric—became more vehement. But is there evidence of such ideological fragmentation among our *partisan* respondents? Are the dispositions of the national lefts and rights towards government intervention reflected in partisan positions on the government scale, or is there significant movement?

A comparison of Figures 2.5 and 2.6 is revealing on a number of counts. Predictably, partisans of the left tend to support 'more government', while partisans of the right oppose it. Furthermore, the extent to which the partisan rights accurately reflect the positions of their counterpart right-identifiers on the government scale is truly impressive. For example, Australians placing themselves on the right of the left-right scale have a mean score of 17.2 on the government scale (Figure 2.5), with Australian Liberals averaging 17.7 (Figure 2.6). The scores for the British right-identifiers and Conservatives are exactly the same (22.3) on the government scale. The consensus within the national right-identifiers on this dimension is almost precisely matched by the partisan rights. Moreover, the single exception to a total consensus within the right, the significant difference between the Australian right and the British right (Figure 2.5), remains an exception where the *partisan* face of the right is considered. British Conservatives are significantly less interventionist than Australian Liberals (Figure 2.6).

The cohesiveness of these Anglo-American rights is a particularly intriguing finding in the light of long-standing and vigorous debates about the similarities and differences between the Canadian and American ideological landscapes. It has been claimed, for instance, that the Canadian right is basically different from its American counterpart because it lacks 'the American aura of rugged individualism' (Horowitz, 1966). The

Figure 2.6: Comparison of Means of National Party Identifiers on Government Scale

NATIONAL PARTY IDENTIFIERS	1	2	3	4	5	6	7	8	9	10	11	12	GOVERNMENT SCALE MEAN SCORES
1. United States Republican													17.0
2. Australia Liberal													17.7
3. Canada Conservative													19.7
4. New Zealand National													21.4
5. Britain Conservative		★											22.3
6. Canada Liberal	★	★	★										25.5
7. New Zealand Labor	★	★	★	★	★								28.3
8. Britain Liberal-SDP	★	★	★	★	★	★							31.3
9. Canada New Democrat	★	★	★	★	★	★							31.6
10. Australia Labor	★	★	★	★	★	★	★						32.1
11. United States Democrat	★	★	★	★	★	★	★						33.0
12. Britain Labour	★	★	★	★	★	★	★	★	★	★			40.9

★ represents pairs of party identifiers with Government Scale mean scores significantly different at $p < .05$

data, however, provide no evidence of such a difference; at least for this generation of respondents, the anti-government inclinations of the American right and Republicans are indistinguishable from the *laissez-faire* attitudes of the Canadian right and Progressive Conservatives. If the Canadian and American data were viewed in isolation, it would be tempting to speculate that such a finding indicates ideological spillover, a uniquely North American and continental ideological convergence. Clearly, though, that hypothesis quickly runs into trouble when all the data are brought into play; it is geographically too modest because it fails to account for the even more striking similarities between the Australian and American rights.

A comparison of Figures 2.5 and 2.6 is also revealing when we turn to consider the lefts. The relative fragmentation of left-identifiers is reflected in ideological disagreements about government intervention within the partisan lefts. But unlike the rights, the latter *do* show significant movement—shuffling—in their ordering. In other words, the location of the national lefts is not a consistently strong predictor of the positions of their counterpart partisan lefts. For example, Figure 2.5 shows that New Zealand left-identifiers share common ground with the Australian and American lefts on the government scale. But New Zealand Labor is *not* the New Zealand left with a party label; there is a substantial discrepancy between where the New Zealand left and New Zealand Labor sit on the government scale. New Zealand Labor's location on the government scale is substantially different from that of either Australian Labor or American Democrats; it has 'drifted away', as it were, towards the centre. Unlike other partisan lefts, New Zealand Labor supporters do not appear to consider government intervention an entrenched policy platform. The Canadian data, by contrast, present a mirror image of the New Zealand pattern. As a group, Canadian left-identifiers share little common ground with their Australian, New Zealand, and American counterparts (Figure 2.5) but New Democrats, a subset within the Canadian left, turn out to be indistinguishable from left-wing partisans in Australia, Britain, and the United States.

The British data provide perhaps the most intriguing evidence of fragmentation within the left. We noted earlier that British left-wingers appear to share so little in common with the other Anglo-American lefts that they can be characterized as a 'rogue left'. Figure 2.6 clearly shows that the Labour party provides that rogue left with a partisan home. The distance between Liberal/SDP supporters and Labour partisans on the government scale is noteworthy too; it indicates residues of the ideological tensions that racked the Labour party following its decisive electoral defeat in 1979, a defeat that ultimately resulted in the formation of the SDP in 1981. Historically, the British Labour party may well have served as the ideological reference point, even beacon, for left-wing parties in other old Commonwealth states, but there is no evidence that it continues to play such a role for these respondents. It is Liberal/SDP partisans, not Labourites, along with Australian Labor, Canadian New Democrats, and United States Democrats, who form the ideological mainstream of left-wing partisans among the new elites in these old states.

The analysis to this point has aimed to shed light on whether, and the extent to which, partisanship modified the left-right ideological worlds of our youth elites on matters relating to government intervention. For that reason we have compared partisan and left-right locations on the government scale in order to highlight the independent effects of both variables. But we know that the dynamics of ideology are complex, and that left-right thinking and partisanship are not independent; they are thoroughly entangled, and each works to reinforce the other. Individuals employ left-right markers to find their bearings in the larger ideological world just as political parties employ left-right cues to claim and solidify public support. If left-right identification and partisanship reinforce each other, then we should be able to provide a much more comprehensive picture of national similarities and differences by seeing how those interactions work to structure respondents' orientations towards the deepest ideological cleavage, that concerning the appropriate role and extent of government intervention.

Figure 2.7 locates party identifiers in two-dimensional ideological space defined by scores on the horizontal left-right axis and the vertical government axis. In doing so, it illustrates the net effects of interactions between partisanship and ideological self-location. Clearly, the impact is substantial; the interactions sort partisan groups into three identifiable clusters while highlighting the ideological uniqueness of British Labour supporters. Isolated by their deep commitment to government intervention, British Labour identifiers appear to represent a vestige of the old left. More surprising, however, is the extent to which the interactions spatially distribute the other three clusters.

Figure 2.7: Parties in Government-Left/Right Space

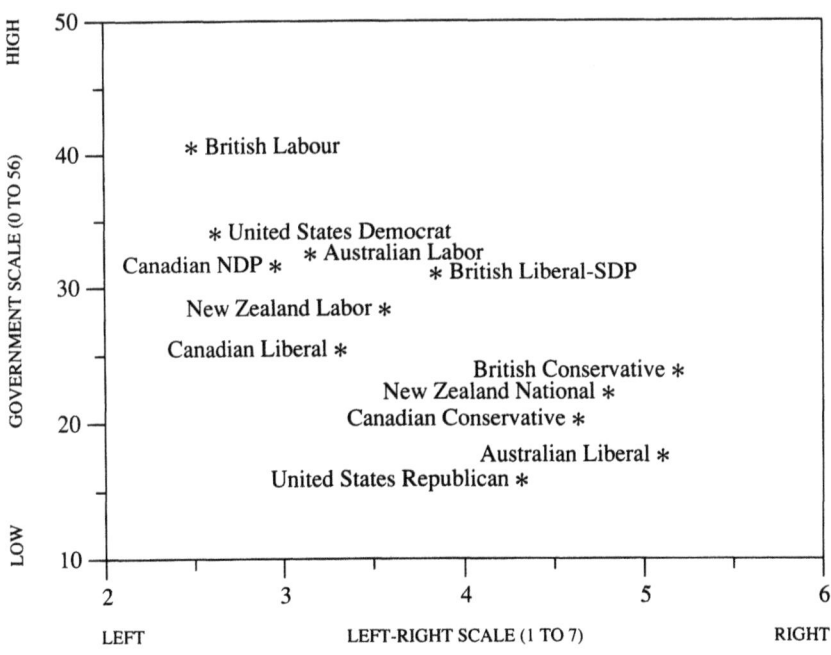

The distributions presented in Figure 2.7 underscore the extent to which the partisan rights form a single ideological cluster. That cluster is not especially tightly knit, but it is a single cluster nonetheless; it represents a single ideological family without orphans. As for the lefts, interactions produce two distinct ideological groupings, both of which sit apart from the British Labour outliers. Significant here is the membership of those groupings and the line of fragmentation within the partisan lefts. American Democrats, Canadian New Democrats, and Australian Labor clearly form a single, tightly knit cluster. Indeed, they are so closely aligned that the differences between them can only be considered negligible. If that group constitutes the ideological core of the partisan left for this political generation, it is a core that excludes supporters of major left-wing parties in two of the five Anglo-American democracies, Britain and New Zealand. British Liberal/SDP supporters, New Zealand Labor, and Canadian Liberals form a second identifiable cluster within the left, but it is a loosely knit group that orbits the core of the partisan left at some distance. Clearly, too, New Zealand Labor supporters are much more ambivalent about government intervention than are supporters of the traditional left-wing parties with which they are usually compared. But that finding is not so surprising when the policy record of the Lange Labor government is considered, a record that resembles in some important respects the free-enterprise agenda usually associated with the new right.

Conclusions

We have started to flesh out the political belief systems of our youth elites by exploring attitudes towards government intervention from a variety of different angles. That analysis drew attention to national variations. But, like a fugue, those national variations elaborate and underscore the same common theme—attitudes about government intervention in society and the economy are deeply embedded in the left-right thinking of respondents. That finding, in itself, is not surprising. Indeed, it would be more surprising if no differences between left- and right-identifiers were detected. Two aspects of the evidence, however, are very impressive: the cross-national consistency of the results and the sharpness of the differences between the lefts and rights. Regardless of national setting, left and right consistently carry the same conceptual freight; they mean the same things for each set of national respondents. In all of the Anglo-American democracies, to be 'on the left' unequivocally means to favour more government and to be 'on the right' emphatically means to favour less. While there are differences within the national lefts and rights regarding the extent of support for, or opposition to, an expanded state, there is no ambiguity about the general finding. No national left 'drifts' into ideological space occupied by its own, or any other, national right. To that very considerable extent, national setting does *not* impose a unique meaning upon 'left' and 'right'. Furthermore, the partisan face of that basic ideological difference reproduces only a slightly modified version of the same pattern. As it turns out, left-right self-location works as a slightly better predictor of attitudes about government intervention than does partisanship,[6] but regardless of which indicator is employed, the resulting patterns of distribution are essentially the same.

When we step back from the particular and assemble the broad findings, three general conclusions emerge from the preceding analysis: the left-right ideological cleavage runs deep; left-right self-placement tells us more (indeed, much more) about individual preferences than does nationality; and these preferences are efficiently captured by partisanship. But are battles over the role of the state in society and the economy among these youth elites likely to be just as intense in each national setting? Do they have the same flash-point? And are these conflicts equally likely to trigger disputes along the left-right fault-line?

Whether disagreement about government intervention will spark left-right divisions depends upon a variety of factors. Many of these have already been explored: namely, the salience of left and right as ideological signposts and the linkages between attitudes towards government intervention and conceptions of left and right. But it also depends upon how those factors combine with the configuration of respondents' attitudes about the nine items that together make up the government scale; upon whether responses to those nine items were tightly organized (strongly intercorrelated) or relatively incoherent (weakly intercorrelated). Other things being equal, disagreements about the role of the state in the economy and society would be more likely to animate left-right cleavages when attitudes about government intervention are more tightly clustered. Most of our attention has been focused on the cross-national distributions of attitudes across the government factor scale because our main goal has been to identify national similarities and differences along *common* factors. It should be recalled however, that the original factor scale was developed from pooled data. To search for systematic national differences in how tightly items within the government scale are clustered, these pooled data have to be disaggregated.

The data presented in Figure 2.8 indicate that there are indeed significant national differences in the clustering of attitudes about government intervention. The figures within the circles ($\overline{x}_r$'s) are mean inter-item correlation coefficients; the higher the scores, the tighter the clustering of attitudes. The lines linking the circles to the left-right box indicate the correlations between the government and left-right scales. The more powerful the correlations, the closer the circles are to the left-right box. The strong inter-item correlation coefficients for the British, Australian, and American samples indicate that these youth elites organize their attitudes about government intervention quite coherently; attitudes to one aspect of government intervention are closely connected to other attitudes in the same domain. That finding, coupled with the powerful correlations between the government and left-right scales, suggests that disagreement about *any* aspect of government intervention in society and

Figure 2.8: Government Scale Mean Inter-Item Correlations
($\bar{X}_r$) And Left-Right Pearson Correlation (r)

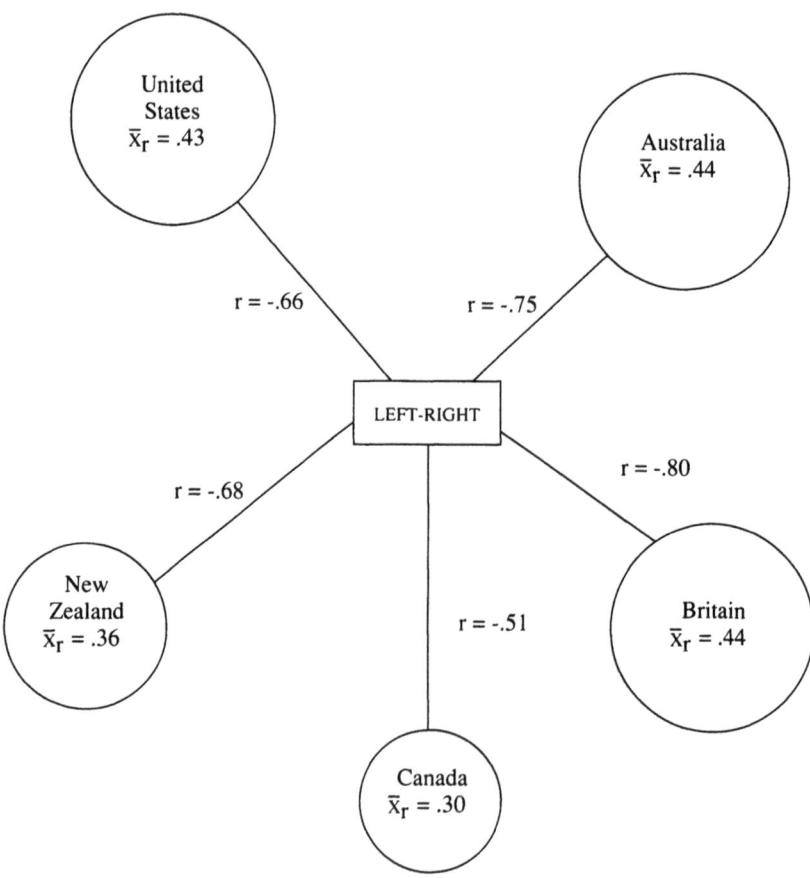

the economy would very quickly precipitate left-right ideological disputes. The Canadian data clearly paint a very different picture. The correlations between the state-intervention items are substantially weaker, disagreements about such issues as income redistribution turn out to be relatively independent of concerns about the size of government, and disagreements about these issues, either singly or together, are much less likely to trigger debates along the left-right divide. Thus the Canadian ideological climate appears to be relatively benign when compared with that of Australia, Britain, or the United States, at least as far as attitudes about government intervention are concerned.

The New Zealand data, again, are rather intriguing. Clearly, left and right provide meaningful ideological benchmarks, for correlations between the government intervention items and left-right self-location are strong (r = −.68), stronger even than for American respondents (r = −.66). But the inter-item correlation coefficient also shows that the linkages *among* the items within the government factor are quite weak ($\bar{x}_r$ = .34), in fact, almost as weak as in the Canadian case ($\bar{x}_r$ = .30). In other words, disputes about *any* aspect of the role of the state in the economy would likely spark left-right debates, but the chances that those debates would turn into a broad defence of, or attack upon, the role of the state in society and the economy would appear to be relatively slim.[7]

In summary, we have travelled a considerable distance in this chapter. We moved from a qualitative commentary about the broad ideological changes that seem to have swept across all of the Anglo-American democracies during the last two decades to a much more focused analysis of a matched sample of new elites in these states. The first stage of that analysis served a general purpose: it identified four primary dimensions within the political belief systems of these youth elites—government intervention, feminism, minorities, and equality of opportunity/result. The second stage involved a much more detailed analysis of respondent orientations towards the government dimension, and presented evidence showing (1) that orientations towards government operate as the deepest ideological divide among youth elites in all five states; (2) that 'left' and 'right' self-locations are powerful indicators of orientations towards government in all five states; (3) that there is greater ideological consensus among the five national rights than the five national lefts as far as government intervention is concerned, and, further, that this pattern holds when partisanship is taken into account; and (4) that attitudes about government intervention are most coherently organized among Australian, British, and American respondents, and most weakly organized among Canadian respondents.

These findings are illuminating and significant in their own right, but the task before us is to provide a more comprehensive picture of the political belief systems of youth elites. In order to do that we cannot rely only upon an analysis of respondent attitudes towards a single dimension. To reveal the *structure* of attitudes we have to examine how *all* of the major dimensions of ideological thinking are connected and how they fit together. The evidence we have presented about government intervention is our first building-block. We turn now to our second building-block, and consider attitudes towards the role of women in society and the economy.

NOTES

[1] The terms 'liberal' and 'conservative' are sometimes seen as more relevant ideological labels for American publics. We note, however, that research evidence

indicates that 'left' and 'right' are becoming increasingly familiar, especially to young and well-educated segments of the population (Laponce, 1970; Klingemann, 1979). For the purposes of cross-national comparability, the same left-right self-anchoring terminology was used in all of the national surveys, and we note that the US response rate to the left-right question was as high (93 per cent) as that obtained in any of the other national samples.

[2] Whether individuals regard themselves as 'on the left' because they identify with 'left-wing' parties or vice versa remains an unresolved puzzle. Our data indicate that respondents were more likely to place themselves on the left-right scale (89 per cent) than to report identification with a political party (78 per cent), but there were significant national variations in this regard:

NATIONAL SAMPLE	% PLACEMENT ON LEFT/RIGHT	% RESPONDENTS IDENTIFYING WITH PARTY
Australian	86.9	69.6
Britain	92.6	84.3
Canada	88.5	90.2
New Zealand	84.0	70.6
United States	92.9	95.6

[3] The Scheffe test is used as a conservative *post hoc* test for making statistical comparisons between scores of groups; it tells us whether the mean scores of groups are statistically different (Tabachnick and Fidell, 1989). The test uses an adjusted critical F, which is calculated by multiplying the table value of F (with (k-1) degrees of freedom in the numerator where (k-1) is the degrees of freedom for the effect, and the degrees of freedom associated with the error term in the denominator) by (k-1).

[4] While left-right location provides the best *single* indicator of ideological orientations, no one measure can adequately reveal the entire operational range of political belief systems. Belief systems are multi-dimensional attitude structures, whereas left-right works in only one dimension at a time. By interpreting orientations towards a variety of political issue positions side by side in a single plane, left-right in effect 'flattens' ideological space.

[5] The idea that the working classes and the poor are the only, or even primary, beneficiaries of the welfare state has been persuasively challenged. For example, Goodin and Le Grand (1987) have argued that the middle classes benefit extensively from the welfare state, that they have 'infiltrated' programs designed to benefit the poor and 'will defend those elements of welfare state programs from which they see themselves as benefiting . . . while supporting reductions in those parts from which they do not' (1987: 202). Middle-class interests, they argue, derive from the fact that they are the suppliers as well as large-scale consumers of some benefits (e.g., education) provided by the state, and, more than the working classes, are effective lobbyists in the protection of those interests. That logic provides the explanation for the Le Grand and Winter (1987) finding that in

Britain 'the Conservative government of 1979-1983 favoured government services which were more extensively used by the middle classes' (1987: 166).

[6] As it turns out, a more detailed statistical analysis shows that left-right is a slightly more accurate predictor. The average standard error of the left-right scale is 0.3657 compared with 0.3786 for party identification. Further, when the small number of respondents who locate themselves at the extremes of the left-right scale are dropped from consideration, left-right self-location becomes a much more powerful predictor of government intervention than party identification. (The average standard error is then 0.2234.)

[7] Inter-item correlation coefficients are used to indicate attitudinal coherence, but other strategies produce similar results. For example, we repeated the initial factor analysis using national samples rather than the pooled data. In all instances government intervention emerged as the most powerful factor. It explained 37.4 per cent of the total variance in Australia, 37.8 per cent in Britain, 25.6 per cent in Canada, 30.7 per cent in New Zealand, and 39.7 per cent in the United States.

CHAPTER THREE

Gender and Feminism

As a political and social movement, feminism is of particular interest to the present analysis. In part, this interest springs from the fact that feminist movements in the five countries have been closely entwined. If we look back at women's struggle for the franchise in the early decades of this century, it is clear that suffragettes in the five countries drew from overlapping pools of ideas, leaders, rhetoric, and tactics. Women in the five Anglo-American democracies received the vote at approximately the same time, and in all five cases the extension of the franchise to women was closely tied to the impact of the First World War and the temperance movement. (The Women's Christian Temperance Union was a vigorous proponent of female suffrage, believing that because women and mothers were the primary victims of alcohol abuse, they would be more likely than men to support the prohibition of alcoholic beverages.) All five countries went through similar and profound transformations during the Second World War as women entered the paid workforce in massive numbers, and as gender-based employment restrictions crumbled in the face of wartime necessity. The war experience shattered many myths, held by both women and men, about the gender divison of labour. More broadly, it also challenged traditional views about the larger role of women in society.

If we turn our gaze to more recent times, it is equally apparent that contemporary feminist movements in the five Anglo-American democracies have shared, and continue to share, many of the same symbols, rhetorical devices, and spokeswomen while pursuing similar objectives. In the late 1960s and early 1970s, for example, Germaine Greer was not simply an Australian feminist, nor was Betty Friedan simply an American feminist; both spoke to and for a much broader feminist constituency, and symbolized the aspirations of countless women across the Western world. It should not be surprising, of course, that women share much in common regardless of their nationality, and thus that the feminist movement tends to ignore national boundaries. In the case of the five Anglo-American democracies, moreover, women also share a common language, a common mass culture, and roughly similar economic and social environments. As a consequence, it is relatively easy for leaders and publications to move across national boundaries; feminists not only speak the same language, but are also able to employ the same symbols, experiences, and examples.

As we noted in the first chapter, feminism has emerged as an important and at times potent political force across the Anglo-American democracies. It is a force, moreover, that has assumed common characteristics across the five countries as women confront an essentially similar economic and social environment (see Table 3.1). Powerful lobby groups, such as the National Organization for Women (NOW) in the United States, the National Women's Coordinating Committee (NWCC) in Britain, and the Women's Electoral Lobby in Australia, have successfully promoted national legislation addressing such topics as equal pay for work of equal value, equal opportunity, and public support for day care. All five Anglo-American democracies have put into place either legislative or constitutional protections against gender discrimination—with the gender-equality provisions of the Canadian Charter of Rights and Freedoms going perhaps the furthest—although as Norris (1987: 3) notes, there may be a massive gap between *de jure* and *de facto* protection. At the interface of the private and public spheres, women's organizations across the board have addressed a variety of common concerns including abortion legislation, family law, and family violence. In short, while the claims of feminists have by no means gone uncontested, there is no question that feminism has moved to the centre of the political stage, and it was entirely appropriate that the United Nations declared 1975-1985 to be the official Decade of Women.

What is not clear, however, is the extent to which feminism occupies

Table 3.1 The Gender Environment

	AUSTRALIA	BRITAIN	CANADA	NEW ZEALAND	UNITED STATES
Date of franchise for women	1901	1928	1919	1893	1920
% Women in labour force (1988 est.)*	58.7	63.7	66.9	63.2	66.8
% Women in legislatures (lower houses) (late 1980s)	5	4	4	9	5
% Women enrolled in third-level education (1985)	47.5	43.7	52.5	45.5	51.2

*OECD Labour Force Statistics, 1989

the same ideological space across the five Anglo-American democracies. American and Australian women might well position themselves at different points on the feminist spectrum, as might American and Australian men. Feminism may be more closely tied to the left-right ideological organization of political beliefs in Britain than may be the case in Canada, and New Zealand feminists may have found a champion within the national party system that their counterparts in the four other countries lack. Here it should be noted that images from the popular culture and institutional realities alike suggest that feminists, and indeed their opponents, operate within nationally distinct political environments. For example, and only for example, images of the Australian popular culture have a masculine edge that is less evident in Canada, while Canadian women now have been assured of constitutional protections for gender equality that are not present in the other four countries. One might expect, then, that gender-related issues would take on a different political twist or spin in different countries despite underlying similarities in their economic and social environments.

In short, we find in feminism a broad, transnational social and political movement that is operating within similar yet subtly distinctive national arenas. The data at hand enable us to explore just what impact, if any, those national differences might have on the way in which youth elites integrate their support for or opposition to feminism into more sweeping ideological perspectives on the political world. We can ask if it makes any difference whether students happen to reside in Melbourne rather than in Boston, in Auckland rather than Montreal, as they try to weave feminism into a broader ideological response to a rapidly changing economic, social, and political environment. Does national location affect the contribution of feminism to the fabric of ideological beliefs? If there is an impact, is it greater for women than for men? For example, might it be the case that women share a roughly common perspective regardless of where they happen to live, while the perspectives held by men are conditioned more by the idiosyncratic features of their national environment?

The Measurement of Feminism

To address such questions, we need to be able to measure respondent orientations towards 'feminism', broadly defined. As we noted in Chapter 2, the initial factor analysis isolated six survey questions that clustered around feminist themes. When responses to these six questions were combined in an additive scale, they produced a coherent and stable measure of feminist orientations among respondents in the five countries. (See Appendix C for details of the scale construction.) In the analysis that follows, this scale will be referred to as the *feminism scale*, although in adopting this simplified terminology we recognize and wish to stress that the scale does *not* embrace the full spectrum of issues, values, and concerns conventionally embraced by the term 'feminism'.

A respondent falling towards the feminist or high end of the scale would

- support more laws aimed at eliminating differences in the treatment of men and women;
- disagree that if a company had to lay off part of its labour force, the first workers to be laid off should be women whose husbands have jobs;
- agree that it is the right of a woman to decide whether to have an abortion;
- believe that lesbians and homosexuals should be able to teach in schools;
- believe that discrimination makes it almost impossible for most women to get jobs equal to their ability; and
- believe that women would be better off if they had careers and jobs just as men do.

A respondent falling towards the more traditional end of the scale would hold the opposite set of opinions; he or she would oppose more laws aimed at eliminating differences in the treatment of men and women, disagree that it is the right of a woman to decide whether to have an abortion, and so forth.

Before turning to a detailed analysis of the feminism scale, it is useful to note a number of points. First, although the feminism scale met conventional statistical standards of reliability for both male and female respondents, the scale was somewhat more robust for male respondents than it was for female respondents. Put somewhat differently, the opinions of males across the six scale items clustered together more tightly than did the opinions of female respondents. This is an important point, to which we will return in the conclusion to this chapter.[1] Second, it may appear on face value that the question dealing with lesbian and homosexual teachers tapped a dimension of public morality quite distinct from feminism *per se*, even though the factor analysis placed this question squarely within the feminist domain. It is, perhaps, the leading reference to lesbians that explains this finding, for there appears to be a tendency within segments of the public to identify or associate the radical edge of feminism with a particular sexual preference, an identification that we are in no position to confirm or refute.

The third point concerns a reaction that many readers may have to some of the statements embedded within the feminism scale, a reaction along the lines of 'Well, surely everyone would agree . . . .' It might be expected, for example, that most of our respondents, who after all were young college students with rather strong vocational opportunities, would agree that 'women would be better off if they had careers and jobs just as men do'. It is thus interesting and somewhat surprising to note that 49 per cent of the Australian student respondents were either undecided on this issue or felt that 'women would be better off if they stayed at home and raised families'. When respondents were asked whether they agreed or disagreed with the statement that 'if a company has to lay off part of its labour force, the first workers to be laid off should be women whose husbands have jobs', 31 per cent of the British respondents agreed, as did 30 per cent of the Australians, 21 per cent of the Canadians, 19 per cent of the Americans, and 17 per cent of the New Zealanders. The point to stress is that despite their youth, university experience, and career opportunities, our student respondents were by no means overwhelmingly supportive of the feminist position. Although traditional responses were less common than feminist responses, they were by no means unknown.

National Differences

Figure 3.1 shows that nationality has some bearing, although not a marked one, on how students locate themselves with respect to the feminist agenda. British, Canadian, and New Zealand students are statistically indistinguishable from one another in their mean placement on the feminism scale. Thus, for example, knowing that a respondent lives in New Zealand rather than in Britain or Canada provides no predictive assistance in locating that individual on the feminist scale. However, the Australians students, who display the most traditional orientations towards the feminist agenda, stand apart in a statistical sense from their Commonwealth counterparts in Canada and Britain, but not those in New Zealand. More dramatically, the American sample stands apart from all four Commonwealth samples, a difference that holds not only for the more remote comparisons with Australian and New Zealand students, but also for the comparison with Canadian students. Thus geographic proximity seems to be a factor in one case but not in the other; although New Zealand and Australian students are indistinguishable from one another in their placement towards (although not at) the traditional end of the feminism scale, Canadian and American students do not share a common perspective.

Composite scales such as the one employed here can pose a problem when one attempts to interpret national differences. For example, the overall difference between Australian and American students in their mean scores on the feminism scale could, at least hypothetically, be generated in a number of quite different ways. It could be that American students are *systemically* more supportive of women's issues and more concerned about the status of women, that across each of the scale items American respondents manifest greater support for the feminist position than do Australian respondents. Conversely, national differences could have more *idiosyncratic* roots; there could be specific but isolated questions that generate the overall national differences in scale scores. American students, for example, could be much more supportive of a pro-choice position on the abortion issue, but indistinguishable from Australian students with respect to the other five items comprising the scale.

Figure 3.1: National Locations on Feminist Scale

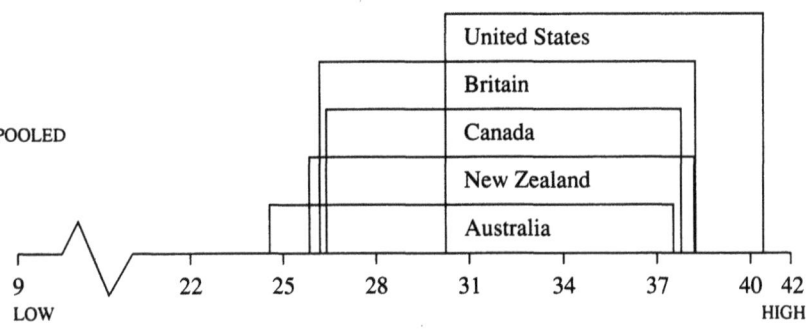

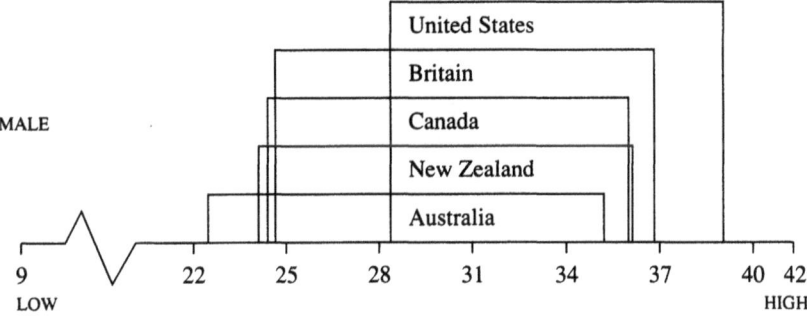

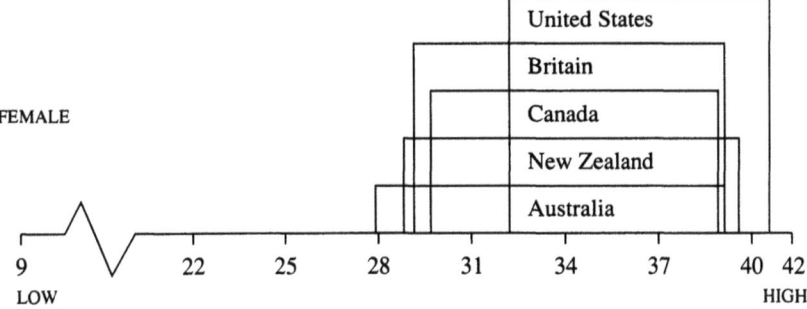

A closer examination of the data indicates that in this instance, the distinctiveness of American students tends to be systemic, although the questions on abortion, job discrimination, and the need for more laws to combat gender discrimination are more influential than the other three in pushing American scores towards the feminist pole. For example, among American students 91 per cent agree that 'it is the right of a woman to decide whether to have an abortion', an opinion shared by 87 per cent of the British respondents, 80 per cent of the Canadians, 79 per cent of the Australians, and 76 per cent of the New Zealanders. (The national differences are even more pronounced if we look only at the percentages of students who *strongly* agree that it is the right of a woman to decide; 80 per cent of the American students strongly agree, compared with 71 per cent of the British students, 61 per cent of the Australians, 60 per cent of the Canadians, and 57 per cent of the New Zealanders.) Furthermore, 61 per cent of the American students support the passage of the Equal Rights Amendment, while only 44 per cent of the Canadian students, 40 per cent of the British students, 35 per cent of the Australian students, and 28 per cent of the New Zealand students support 'more laws aimed at eliminating differences in the treatment of men and women'. Here it should be stressed, however, that the political battle over the passage of the Equal Rights Amendment was highly publicized at the time of the American survey, whereas there was no corresponding politicization of the gender-equality issue at the time of the survey in the four Commonwealth countries.[2] To this limited extent, then, the national differences in Figure 3.1 may not reflect any inherent national difference in predispositions towards feminism. Rather, they may reflect a temporal difference in the political climate, a difference carried into the feminism scale by the political debate in the United States over the Equal Rights Amendment.

Gender Differences

Up to this point, we have discussed national scores on the feminism index irrespective of the gender of respondents. However, it would be only reasonable to assume that gender 'should' have some impact on respondent scores. After all, men and women do not face the same objective circumstances; they are, for example, disproportionately concentrated in different sectors of the economy (see Table 3.2), and they face different obligations in the private sphere. Thus women can be expected to have a quite different instrumental orientation towards the issues on the feminist agenda. Here it should also be noted that there is an important redistributive element to the feminist movement, an element that seeks to redress not only the existing balance of power between men and women but also the existing allocation of economic costs and benefits. Although it would be inappropriate to view the feminist movement entirely as a zero-sum game, in which every gain for women is a loss for men, gender trade-offs are involved. To argue, for instance, that 'there should be more laws which aim at eliminating differences in the treatment of men and women' is surely to imply that the existing differences are inequitable, and that 'more laws' would lead to a situation where, at least in a relative sense, women would get more and men would get less.

Thus it is not surprising to find in Figure 3.1 that, in each of the five

Table 3.2 Economic Position of Women in the Anglo-American Democracies

	AUSTRALIA	BRITAIN	CANADA	NEW ZEALAND	UNITED STATES
Average female earnings as % of male earnings	82	72	50	72	66
% Women in part-time employment	79.0	94.3	72.0	78.7	70.3
% Female labour force in					
Primary	3.8	1.1	2.9	4.8	1.4
Secondary	13.8	16.8	13.4	10.2	15.7
Tertiary	82.4	82.2	83.8	85.0	82.9
Female over-representation in clerical work*	1.82	1.65	1.90	2.01	1.83
Female under-representation in administration*	0.65	0.23	0.75	0.24	0.72

*These figures represent the proportion of women in the occupation divided by the proportion of women in the labour force.

countries, female respondents have significantly higher scores on the feminism scale than do males. It is interesting to note, however, that the initial pattern of national differences remains essentially intact when we control for gender; women shift towards the high end of the feminist scale and men towards the low end, but the *pattern* of national differences among women is essentially the same as that among men. It is also important to note that there is a substantial degree of overlap between male and female scores on the feminism index. Although men are more traditional in their orientation than are women, the gender difference is one of degree rather than one of kind. Put somewhat differently, males may be more ambivalent and less enthusiastic in their support of feminism than are women, but they are not radically different in the kinds of policy options that they are willing to support.

For example, female respondents are more likely than male respondents to favour freedom of choice with respect to abortion. Across all five national samples combined, 86 per cent of the women but only 78 per cent of the men agreed that 'it is the right of a woman to decide whether to have an abortion'. A somewhat more pronounced gender difference emerges if we look at those who *strongly* agreed with the statement; 72 per cent of the women did so, compared with only 57 per cent of the men. The point to stress, however, is that on balance both women and men supported *the same policy option*; women were simply more emphatic in their support. To take a second example, 30 per cent of the men but only 16 per cent of the women agreed with the statement that 'lesbians and homosexuals should not be allowed to teach in schools'. Here again, we have a clear gender difference and yet a situation in which the great majority of both women and men would support the same policy position.

Overall, the national differences in Figure 3.1 are relatively inconsequential when compared with gender differences. There are, for example, no statistically significant differences among Australian, British, Canadian, and New Zealand female respondents, just as there are no significant differences among Australian, New Zealand, and Canadian male respondents. Thus, the national location of respondents is of little importance in predicting male or female scores on the feminism scale; the male subsamples tend to cluster together irrespective of nationality, as do the female subsamples. If you knew that a specific respondent was a woman, your ability to predict her score on the feminist scale would not be enhanced if you also knew whether she lived in Australia, Britain, Canada, or New Zealand.

At the same time, however, we can also identify a number of wrinkles to this overarching pattern. First, female respondents in the United States stand apart from all other respondents, including both their American male counterparts and female students in the four Commonwealth countries, in their emphatic support for the feminist position. To the extent that an extreme feminist outpost exists in our survey of youth elites, it is to be found among female university students in the United States. The second wrinkle comes from the scale location of American males. With respect to their average score on the feminist scale, American men clearly stand apart from their male compatriots in the four Commonwealth countries. Perhaps of even greater interest, there are no statistically significant differences between American men, on the one hand, and Commonwealth women, on the other.

To recast this point slightly, American men and American women are the outliers in Figure 3.1; they are 'out of step' with their Commonwealth counterparts in their more emphatic support for the feminist position. Apart from this American exceptionalism, there are no national differences among the Commonwealth women and, with the exception of the statistically significant difference between male students in Australia and Britain, there are no national differences among the Commonwealth men. In part, of course, this reflects the findings in Figure 3.1, where American respondents, irrespective of gender, could be distinguished from Commonwealth respondents by their more pronounced support for women's issues. Here we should also note that within their respective gender groups, both Australian males and Australian females demonstrate the weakest support for the feminist position. Both findings point to the conclusion that national location is not irrelevant to the way in which individuals position themselves on feminist issues; it simply and not surprisingly plays a subordinate role to that of gender.

When controls for nationality are brought into play, the policy divergence between men and women becomes somewhat more pronounced. For example, while 86 per cent of all female students and 78 per cent of all male students support the right of women to decide with respect to abortions, support for this position is highest among American females (94 per cent) and lowest among New Zealand males (69 per cent). To take a second example, 85 per cent of all female respondents, but only 67 per cent of all male respondents, agree that 'there should be more laws which aim at eliminating differences in the treatment of men and women'. When this relationship is controlled for nationality, agreement ranges from 90 per cent for American females to only 60 per cent for Australian males—a sizeable difference indeed. In both examples, however, the majority of women and the majority of men in each country share a common policy preference; gender and national differences are matters of nuance, enthusiasm, and degree.

The Linkage to Left-Right

With the preliminary examination of the feminism scale now in place, we can move on to a somewhat more complicated set of questions. More specifically, we can ask: To what extent are respondent outlooks on feminism woven into more general ideological perspectives on the political and social world? If we know how a respondent stands on issues relating to the status of women, does that stance provide any insight into how the same respondent views such things as government intervention in the economy, or legislative measures designed to protect minority rights? Conversely, does knowledge about such issues shed useful light on how the same respondent might view issues relating to feminism? We can also ask to what extent our answers to such questions must be conditional on the gender and national location of the respondent; do the same ideological linkages come into play for men as for women, or for Canadians as for Australians?

Perhaps we should begin by stating that in general terms, moving beyond gender-related issues to embrace a broader array of social and economic concerns, it is not clear that men and women bring radically or even substantially different perspectives to the political world.[3] It is worth noting, for example, that the massive infusion of women into Western electorates following the end of the First World War, when women acquired the right to vote under the same terms and conditions as men, had at best a modest impact on public policy (Hansen, Franz, and

Netemeyer-Mays, 1976; Abzug and Kelber, 1984; Norris, 1985). Although there was a short-term impact on electoral support for the prohibition of alcohol, and although social feminism played an important role in energizing the larger Progressive movement in its pursuit of pure food and drug laws, prison reform, minimum-wage legislation, and increased support for public education (Lemons, 1973; Kealey, 1979; Prentice et al., 1988), the entry of women into the electorate did not alter the fabric of public policy as much as supporters of the suffrage movement had hoped, or as much as opponents had feared.

There are, of course, many explanations that one might offer for why this quantum leap in participation produced little qualitative shift in the character of public policy. It could be that for many issues, and particularly for those of an economic character, newly enfranchised women brought a set of policy preferences to political affairs that was very similar to that held by the men who shared their lives and class positions. In addition, the small size of the state in the decades immediately following the First World War—the very limited intrusion of the state into economic and social affairs—meant that many issues of particular concern to women were neither aggressively nor adequately addressed through political action. The relatively constrained 'night watchman' state kept the concerns of women off the political agenda, and thus restricted political discourse to those matters in which gender differences were less likely to appear. Political discourse was also limited in this respect by the failure of party organizations to mobilize newly enfranchised women, and indeed by their ongoing indifference to the mobilization of women decades after the franchise had been extended to all persons (Bashevkin, 1982; 1985). As a consequence of the above, women exhibited lower levels of political participation than did men, and displayed less interest in things political (Campbell et al., 1960; Goot and Reid, 1975; Hansen et al., 1976; Evans, 1980; Fulenwider, 1981). Perhaps of greatest significance, the achievement of the vote was a hollow victory in the short run; enfranchisement did not immediately, or even quickly, propel significant numbers of women into positions of economic, social, and political power.

Over the last several decades, the historical difference in the political participation rates of men and women has eroded to the point where it has all but disappeared (Hansen at al., 1976; Evans, 1980; Abzug and Kelber, 1984). At the same time, there has been increased interest (Welch and Secret, 1981; Abzug and Kelber, 1984; Klein, 1984; Brodie, 1985; Zipp and Pulzer, 1985) in the emergence of a *gender gap*, a term used to describe a significant difference between men and women in various forms of political behaviour, including voting and competition for office. The gender gap received its first pronounced attention during the 1980 presidential election in the United States (Abzug and Kelber, 1984; Klein, 1984; Mansbridge, 1985; Norris, 1985), and has since been the subject of considerable speculation in other Western democracies (Christy, 1985; Norris, 1986).

In essence, the gender gap implies that gender counts in things political, *that men and women bring to the political world significantly different values, beliefs, and policy preferences*, and that these in turn result in gender differences in political choice and political behaviour. In determining whether in fact men and women have different orientations toward the political world, the left-right scale provides a useful point of departure. The utility of the scale stems partly from its comprehensive character; of greater utility is its capacity, amply demonstrated in the last chapter, to tap ideological orientations towards state intervention in the economic and social order. This ability is important because the expansion of the feminist movement closely paralleled and in part contributed to the growth of the welfare state following the Second World War. Not coincidentally, it was when the state expanded that the concerns of women began to climb the political agenda and feminism became more politicized. As the parameters of the modern welfare state expanded beyond the narrow domain of the 'night watchman' to embrace a broader range of social and economic issues, they expanded into the traditional domain of women. Concerns about education, child support, and family violence all came under the wing of the welfare state.

Moreover, and perhaps more importantly, an expansionist state proved to be an essential ally for women pushing claims of equality in the broader social and economic order. State intervention was imperative if women were to overcome traditional barriers to social and economic equality. Hence the quest for legislative proclamations of and protection for gender equality, a quest that spilled over into the constitutional arena in Canada (successfully) and the United States (unsuccessfully). For all of these reasons, therefore, feminist claims were easily grafted onto the programmatic agenda of the left, and onto the left's pursuit of an expanded state. Not surprisingly, feminist claims were vigorously promoted by the left from the earliest days of the Fabian tractarians. (Note, for example, G.B. Shaw's *The Equality of Women*.)

It should be stressed, of course, that feminism as a political movement has both distinctive roots and a distinctive political agenda. Feminists are not simply using a new vocabulary and a new arena to rehash the longstanding left-right debate over the appropriate size and scope of the modern state. At the same time, there are a number of reasons to expect feminism to be interwoven with older lines of ideological cleavage in Western societies. At least in the short run, the equality aspirations of women are tied to an expansionist state, and any significant contraction of that state will have implications for the pursuit of gender equality in the social and economic spheres. To take one example, employment-equity programs rely heavily not only on the moral suasion of governments but also, and ultimately, on the coercive power of the state and on the willingness of the state apparatus to use that power in the pursuit of gender equality. (An example here would be the necessity for firms and public institutions conducting business with the national government to comply with the provisions of employment-equity programs.) Thus we should expect to find a rather close relationship between left-right orientations, on the one hand, and orientations towards feminism on the other.

Table 3.3 shows that there is indeed a strong linkage between respondents' orientations toward feminism and their location on the left-right scale. The correlational relationship, moreover, is consistent in direction and remarkably consistent in strength across the five national samples. In all five cases, and for both women and men, respondents who locate themselves on the left side of the ideological divide are noticeably more supportive of feminism than are respondents who locate themselves on the right. The farther respondents move to the right, the weaker their support becomes for feminism, and the farther they move to the left, the stronger their support. Only in the Canadian case is the relationship relatively weak, although even there the general pattern holds; feminists fall to the left and more traditionally oriented respondents fall to the right.

Table 3.3 Pearson Correlations between Feminism and Left-Right by Nationality and Gender

NATIONALITY	ALL	MALE	FEMALE
Australia	−.47	−.49	−.39
Britain	−.49	−.56	−.37
Canada	−.31	−.33	−.31
New Zealand	−.42	−.35	−.46
United States	−.47	−.49	−.47

Figure 3.2 presents, in a graphic form, the correlational findings from Table 3.3. The figure also presents the mean inter-item correlations for the feminism index. For example, in the top-right corner of the figure two important pieces of information are presented. First, the feminism/left-right correlation for Australian students is a robust −.47, indicating that the farther such students fall towards the right end of the ideological scale, the less supportive they are of the feminist position. In terms of both direction and strength, this relationship is identical to the American sample, and virtually identical to the British sample. Second, the figure shows that the items comprising the feminism scale are strongly and positively correlated for Australian students. In this case, the Australian findings are nearly identical to those for Britain and New Zealand,

Gender and Feminism | 77

Figure 3.2: Feminist Scale Mean Inter-Item Correlations
($\bar{x}_r$) And Left-Right Pearson Correlation (r)

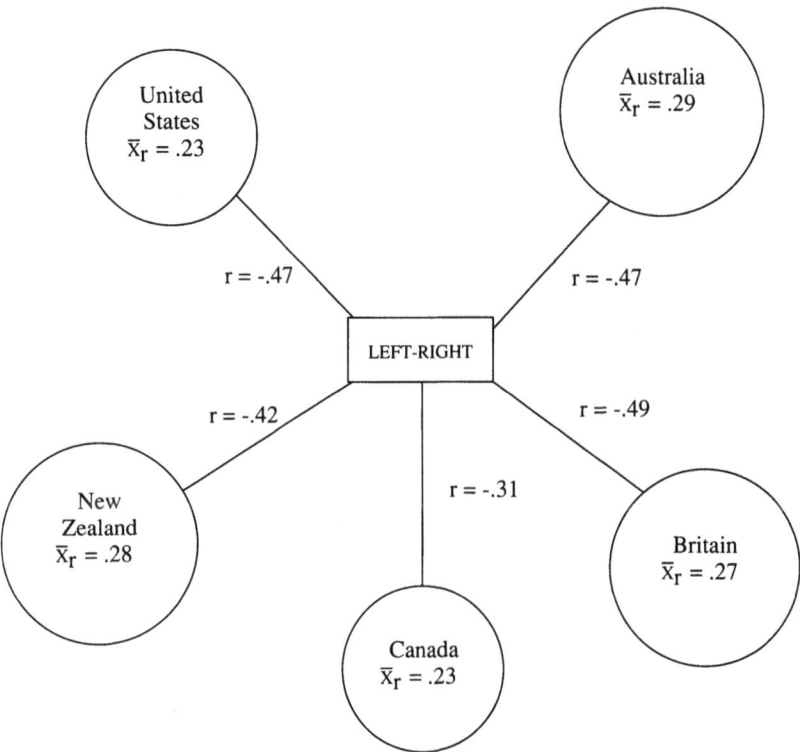

whereas the strength of the inter-item correlations is somewhat weaker for American and Canadian students. In qualitative terms, this means that the feminism index displays somewhat greater internal consistency in the case of Australia, Britain, and New Zealand than it does in the case of Canada and the United States, although it should be stressed that the national variation is not marked.

It is interesting and somewhat surprising to note that, with the exception of New Zealand, the correlations in Table 3.3 between the feminism and left-right scales are stronger for men than for women. Admittedly, these gender differences are modest and not altogether consistent, but they are interesting nonetheless because they are contra-intuitive. One might reasonably expect that orientations towards feminism would play a more central role in the political world of women than they would in the political world of men, if only because the public-policy stakes are much higher for women than they are for men. Given this assumption, scores on the feminism index should be more strongly correlated with left-right scores for women than for men. Put somewhat differently, one might expect that knowledge of how a woman stands on feminist issues would provide more insight into her more general political orientation than would similar knowledge about a man, if only because views on women's issues and the status of women often occupy a more central role in the belief systems of women than of men. However, Table 3.3 does not conform to this expectation, or at least fails to do so with respect to respondent scores on the left-right scale.

Here it is useful to note an important observation by Klein (1984: 126-7), who argues that men's support for feminism may be more abstract, more ideological than is the case for women:

> Though men and women share similar feminist views and are equally supportive of collective action, the women's movement, and the rise of protest, men, *who come to feminism out of abstract ideas* [emphasis added], are not conscious of feminism in the same way as women, who hold these views because of personal experience.... Men's support for feminist protest... derives from a general ideology about rights and attitudes toward a broad set of social issues rather than the specific plight of women.

Klein's point is central to the analysis unfolding in this chapter. Because the outlook of men towards feminism is less grounded in the reality of personal experience, a reality that may convey very complex and often contradictory messages to women, men find it easier to incorporate their outlook on feminism into more sweeping and comprehensive ideological packages, *or to derive their outlook on feminism from such packages*.

Before we turn to a detailed examination of more comprehensive ideological packages, it is useful to take a careful look at some of the national nuances in the relationship between the feminism and left-right scales. Figure 3.3 presents the results of a comparison-of-means test for fifteen sets of respondents—those locating themselves on the left, right, or centre of the left-right scale in each of the five countries. The upper-left quadrant of the figure shows that with respect to scores on the feminism scale, there are no significant differences among the five national 'rights'. Once you know that an individual defines his or her ideological location as right of centre, then the ability to predict the respondent's score on the feminism index is not improved by knowing in which country he or she lives. Essentially the same relationship holds on the left; the lower-right quadrant of Figure 3.3 shows that respondents on the American, Australian, British, and New Zealand left are indistinguishable from one another with respect to scores on the feminism index. Only between the American and Canadian lefts does a statistically significant gap emerge.

Figure 3.4 reproduces the same style of analysis, only this time respondents are grouped on the basis of partisan identification rather than

Figure 3.3: Comparison of Means of Left, Centre, and Right Identifiers on Feminism Scale

NATIONAL LEFT-RIGHT IDENTIFIERS	1	2	3	4	5	6	7	8	9	10	11	12	13	14	15	FEMINISM SCALE MEAN SCORES
1. Australia Right																27.8
2. Britain Right																29.1
3. New Zealand Right																29.7
4. Canada Right																30.0
5. New Zealand Centre																30.2
6. United States Right																30.4
7. Australia Centre																30.9
8. Britain Centre	★															31.6
9. Canada Centre	★															32.2
10. Canada Left	★	★	★	★	★											33.5
11. Australia Left	★	★	★	★	★											34.0
12. United States Centre	★	★	★													34.7
13. Britain Left	★	★	★	★	★	★	★	★								34.9
14. New Zealand Left	★	★	★	★	★	★	★	★								35.1
15. United States Left	★	★	★	★	★	★	★	★	★	★						36.4

★ represents pairs of left-right identifiers with Feminism Scale mean scores significantly different at $p < .05$

ideological self-location. In broad detail, and in most specifics, Figure 3.4 replicates the findings in Figure 3.3. Parties conventionally identified

80 | New Elites in Old States

Figure 3.4: Comparison of Means of National Party Identifiers on Feminism Scale

NATIONAL PARTY IDENTIFIERS	1	2	3	4	5	6	7	8	9	10	11	12	FEMINISM SCALE MEAN SCORES
1. Australia Liberal													28.6
2. Britain Conservative													28.8
3. New Zealand National													29.7
4. Canada Conservative													30.5
5. United States Republican													31.5
6. Canada Liberal	★	★											31.9
7. Britain Liberal-SDP	★	★											32.6
8. Australia Labor	★	★	★	★									33.0
9. New Zealand Labor	★	★	★	★									33.1
10. Canada New Democrat	★	★	★	★									34.7
11. Britain Labour	★	★	★	★	★	★	★						35.3
12. United States Democrat	★	★	★	★	★	★	★	★	★				36.4

★ represents pairs of party identifiers with Feminism Scale mean scores significantly different at p < .05

with the political left (the Labour parties of Australia, Britain, and New Zealand, the Canadian New Democratic Party, and the American Democratic Party) are grouped towards the feminist end of the scale, and parties conventionally identified with the political right (the American Republicans, the Australian Liberals, the British Conservatives, the Canadian Progressive Conservatives, and the New Zealand Nationals) are grouped toward the traditionalist end of the feminist scale. Of perhaps greater surprise and importance, and as the upper left quandrant of Figure 3.4 shows, there are no significant *national* differences in feminism scores among respondents identifying themselves with the five right-of-centre parties. Significant national variation is also rare among left-of-centre parties, although in this latter case the lower-right quandrant of Figure 3.4 shows that American Democrats are significantly more supportive of the feminist position than are respondents who identify with the Australian or New Zealand Labor parties. Overall, Figure 3.4 demonstrates that orientations towards feminism are related in a direct and relatively powerful fashion to partisan identification. Yet the figure also shows that once it has been established that an individual identifies with a party lying on the right or left of the ideological spectrum, little additional predictive information is gained by knowing in which of the five countries the respondent lives. Without exception, partisans of the right share a common perspective on feminism, as do partisans of the left with the partial exception of American Democrats.

To this point we have discussed, first, the relationship between feminism and ideological self-location on the left-right scale and, second, the relationship between feminism and partisan identification. Figure 3.5 pulls this discussion together by simultaneously locating partisan groups on both the feminism and left-right scales. In the bottom right-hand

Figure 3.5: Parties in Feminism-Left/Right Space

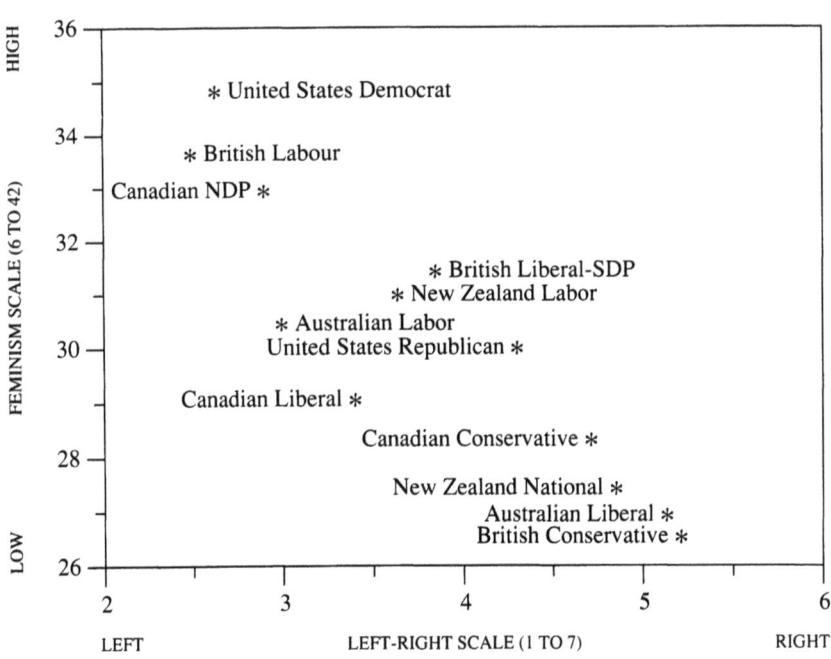

corner of the figure we find respondents identifying with the the American Republicans, the Australian Liberals, the British Conservatives, the Canadian Progressive Conservatives, and the New Zealand Nationals. The five groups of respondents share, albeit to varying degrees, a similar right-of-centre ideological location and a relatively traditional orientation towards feminism. In the top left-hand corner of the figure we find respondents identifying with the Labour parties of Australia, Britain, and New Zealand, the Canadian New Democratic Party, and the American Democratic Party. These five partisan groups share, albeit again to varying degrees, a left-of-centre ideological location and a stance relatively supportive of feminist positions. The polar extremes in Figure 3.5 come from American Democrats, on the one hand, and British Conservatives/ Australian Liberals on the other.

The Broader Ideological Environment

We have suggested that, historically, the expansion of the state under the political leadership of the left carried with it large and important implications for the improved status of women in society. In Chapter 2, we also demonstrated that the preference for a large and expansionist state is strongly linked to the left-right idelogical location of our contemporary respondents. Furthermore, the analysis to this point in the chapter has demonstrated a strong relationship between respondent orientations towards feminism and the ideological self-location of respondents on the left-right scale, a relationship that is consistent across the five national samples. (The Canadian case is somewhat of an exception with respect to the strength, but not the direction, of the relationship.) In Figure 3.6 we bring these relationships together by presenting, for each of the five countries, the correlations among the feminism, government, and left-right scales.

At first glance, Figure 3.6 may strike the reader as alarmingly complex. Keep in mind, however, that most of the information in the figure has already been brought into play. The mean inter-item correlations for the government index, contained within the broken circles, have already been discussed in Chapter 2, as have the correlations between the government and the left-right scales. In a similar fashion, the mean inter-item correlations for the feminism index, contained within the solid circles, have already been discussed in reference to Figure 3.2, as have the correlations between the feminism and left-right scales. Thus the new information in Figure 3.6 is restricted to the correlations between the government and feminism scales.

In the case of Australian, British, and American respondents, those correlations are robust indeed. Although the relationship weakens somewhat in the case of New Zealand and Canadian respondents, it is still of moderate strength and in the same direction as the former cases. (When controlled for gender, the national differences here closely parallel those

Figure 3.6: Combined Government and Feminist Scale Mean Inter-Item Correlations ($\bar{x}_r$) and Left-Right Pearson Correlation (r)

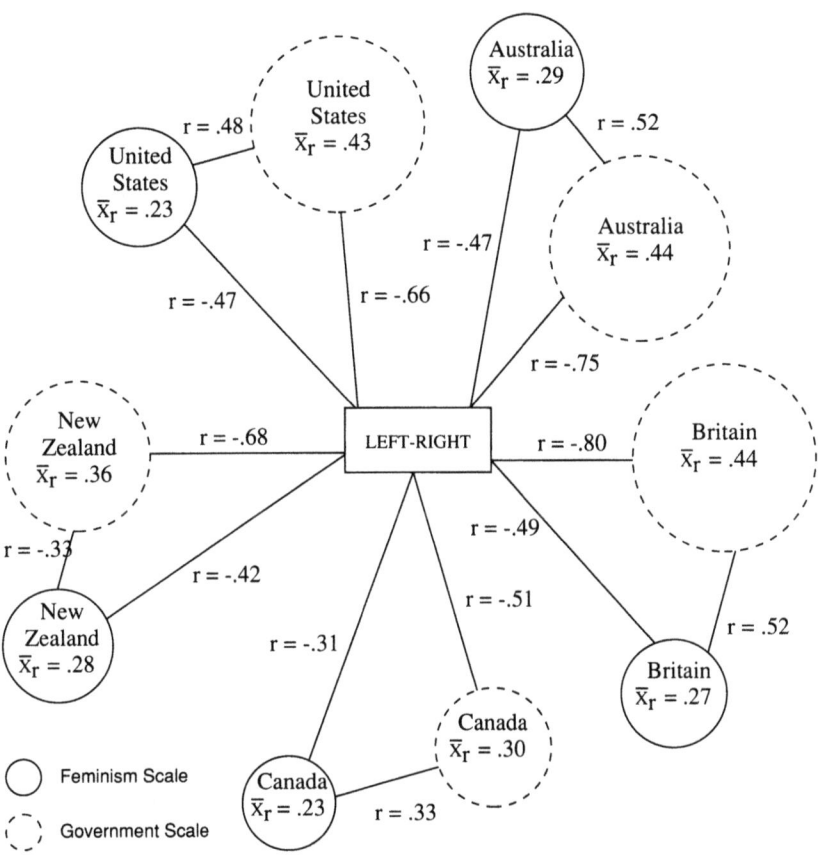

noted in Table 3.1; the relationship is stronger for New Zealand women than it is for New Zealand men, and weaker for Australian and British women than it is for their male counterparts.) In more qualitative terms, Figure 3.6 demonstrates that *pro-feminist respondents are considerably more supportive of government intervention* in the economic arena, and indeed in the broader public and social domain, than are respondents with a more traditional stance regarding feminist issues. This relationship should not be surprising, for government intervention has been an important and quite likely essential tool for women pursuing equity within the workplace. Any ideological enthusiasm for deregulation, for a weaker government presence within the economic environment, thus poses a potential threat to employment-equity programs depending on government suasion, incentives, and legislation.

Nonetheless, it is important to reiterate and underscore the basic finding presented in Figure 3.6. For the youth elites embraced by this study, *orientations towards feminism are thoroughly integrated into broader ideological frameworks*, frameworks that draw their organizing principles from the classical distinction between left and right, and that extend to cover the more specific ideological domain of government intervention in and regulation of the economy. In this sense, feminism is not a free-floating ideology, nor is it one that cuts across pre-existing ideological frameworks. At least for new political elites, feminism is firmly anchored in more conventional and more over-arching ideological perspectives. While this anchor is slightly more firmly affixed for men than it is for women, the gender gap in this instance is one of nuance only.

Conclusion

This chapter has not only explored the new feminist dimension of the contemporary ideological world, but has also sought to position that dimension relative to more conventional ideological structures. The findings are straightforward. First, both women and men have reasonably coherent perspectives about the range of issues embraced by the term 'feminism'. Second, women and men differ systematically and predictably in their perspectives on feminism, although this conclusion should by no means imply that women consistently support the feminist position, for they do not, or that men consistently oppose the feminist position, for they do not. Third, outlooks on feminism are strongly and consistently linked to ideological self-location on the left-right scale, and to more specific respondent beliefs concerning government regulation of and intervention in the economy. Fourth, national differences across the board are modest at best. Although American respondents stand apart to some degree, the differences are not pronounced. Among Commonwealth respondents, national differences pale to insignificance. What remains to be seen is the extent to which perspectives on feminism are linked to even broader ideological structures, ones that reach beyond the conventional domains of left-right and government economic intervention. It is to that task that we now turn.

NOTES

[1] The standardized alpha coefficient for the feminism scale was .68 for all male respondents, and .61 for all female respondents. The national alpha scores for men and women respectively were .69 and .63 (Australia), .70 and .60 (Britain), .63 and .52 (Canada), .66 and .66 (New Zealand), and .65 and .55 (United States).

[2] For a comparison of the constitutional politics of gender equality in Canada and the United States, see Gibbins and Nevitte (1989).

[3] For an expansion of this argument, see Gibbins and Nevitte (1989).

CHAPTER FOUR

Minorities on the Ideological Landscape

We began the last chapter by noting that feminism constitutes a broad, transnational movement, the social and political dynamics of which are roughly similar across a wide range of national settings. We also noted that women in the five countries included in the present study share a common language (with the exception of Canadian francophones), a common mass culture, and essentially similar economic and social environments. As a consequence of both factors we found that, *regardless of national location*, feminism occupies roughly the same ideological space within the belief systems of youth elites. While national differences were by no means absent in Chapter 3, the observed variations were matters of nuance and degree. We found that in all five countries, respondent orientations towards feminism were strongly linked to the conventional ideological rubric of left and right, and to the debates over government intervention in the economy that have followed the historical evolution of the welfare state.

The absence of more pronounced national variation is an important finding to keep in mind as our analysis shifts in the present chapter to ideological perceptions of minority rights. In the case of minority rights, the demographic and sociological backdrop is radically different than it was in the case of feminism; broadly similar national patterns are replaced with idiosyncratic national circumstances. Whereas Australia, Britain, Canada, New Zealand, and the United States have, for all practical purposes, identical gender compositions, they differ significantly in their ethnic and racial circumstances. Yet, surprisingly, these rather striking national differences in objective circumstances generate rather modest ideological differences in the belief systems of youth elites.

Methodological Backdrop

Although the national populations of the five Anglo-American democracies remain overwhelmingly white and of European descent, all five have become *multicultural* and *multiracial* to a significant and increasing degree. This transformation has been brought about by radical shifts in patterns of immigration. Take, for example, the Canadian case. Between 1946 and 1960, immigrants to Canada from Africa, Asia and Latin America constituted only 4.0 per cent of the Canadian total. During the 1960s this proportion climbed to 19.6 per cent, and then it jumped to 51.5 per cent during the 1970s. By the early 1980s, two-thirds of the immigrants to Canada were arriving from African, Asian, and Latin American countries, with Asian immigrants alone making up more than half of the Canadian total. In this respect the Canadian case is by no means atypical. In Australia immigration from Asia has increased from less than 15 per cent of the Australian total in the mid-1970s to over a third by the late 1980s. In Britain post-war immigration from New Commonwealth countries (including Pakistan) has increased the number of ethnic minorities to about 5.0 per cent of the total population (Anwar, 1986).

Changing patterns of immigration have produced a noticeable convergence among the Anglo-American democracies; all have become multi-racial to a significant degree, and all confront, to at least some extent, attendant public-policy disputes on such issues as multiculturalism and linguistic assimilation. At the same time, however, interesting national variations persist. Take, for example, national differences in the character of aboriginal populations. Of the five democracies only Britain lacks a racially distinct aboriginal population, whereas the four 'settler nations' all have racially distinct and politically salient, albeit numerically small, aboriginal populations. Those populations, however, have little in common apart from their aboriginal status and a weak collective identity as Fourth World communities. Although many of the Native Indian communities of North America span the Canadian-American border, these internally diverse communities share very little in common with Aboriginal communities in Australia, and the latter have a frail connection at best with Maori communities in New Zealand. Thus with the qualified exception of Canada and the United States, the five Anglo-American democracies are distinct and idiosyncratic with respect to aboriginal populations.

Any Canadian-American similarity on the aboriginal front is overshadowed by a much more important national difference stemming from racial divisions within the United States. There is no parallel in the Canadian historical record for the experience of American blacks, or for the more general American experience with racial conflict. (Although Canada was the terminus for the 'Underground Railway' carrying slaves out of the American south, the evolution of Canadian social and political life was largely unaffected by the experience.) There has been no Canadian history of slavery, no civil war fought in large part on the issue of emancipation, no Reconstruction period following civil war, no civil-rights movement, and no 'civil-rights vision' analogous to that which has reshaped American public policy over the past three decades (Sowell, 1984). The pre-eminent minority in Canada has been linguistically rather than racially defined, and the position of francophones in Canada bears little resemblance to that of blacks in the United States. Francophones comprise a quarter of the national population, compared with approximately 10 per cent for the American black population. Francophones are strategically critical to the achievement of majority governments in Canada, and thus exercise a degree of electoral power seldom matched by American blacks. Francophones, moreover, constitute 80 per cent of the population of Quebec, and thus control the government of Canada's largest province in size and second largest province in population. They also exercise a great deal of influence in the party organizations that have dominated Canadian political life, and their contribution to the political leadership of the country has included Prime Ministers Wilfrid Laurier, Louis St Laurent, and Pierre Elliott Trudeau.

All this, of course, is not to suggest that the Canadian experience has been exemplary; Canada's racial relations copybook has been blotted many times. One has only to look at the treatment of Chinese immigrants in British Columbia during the latter part of the nineteenth and first half of the twentieth centuries, the expulsion of Japanese Canadians from the west coast during the Second World War, and the ongoing social marginalization and economic destitution of Canada's aboriginal peoples. (With respect to the economic and social conditions of aboriginal peoples, the Canadian situation closely parallels that in Australia and in New Zealand.) These experiences, however, are not comparable in either their scale or their impact on the national consciousness to the sustained politicization of racial issues within the American national community. In this respect the Canadian experience is much closer to that of Australia, Britain, and New Zealand than it is to that of the United States.

This discussion of Canadian and American differences brings a number of important points to the fore. The first is that the Anglo-American democracies differ not only in their current demographic composition, but also in their historical experience with minority groups. Simply knowing, for example, that approximately 10 per cent of the contemporary American population is black and approximately 1 per cent of the contemporary Australian population is Aborigine provides little useful leverage for understanding contemporary communal politics. One must also be aware of the backdrop provided by slavery and civil war in the United States, and by the very troubled historical relationship between white settlers and Aborigines in Australia. The past, then, casts a large shadow over the present. However, the question to be addressed in the present analysis is whether that shadow is still detectable in the belief systems of youth elites and, if so, whether it creates nationally distinct systems of political belief.

The second point to stress is that there are no prima facie reasons to assume that minority groups are simply interchangeable in the role they might play within ideological belief systems. We cannot assume, for example, that the perceptions an American might have about Vietnamese or Mexican immigrants mimic those that he or she might have about American blacks, or that an Australian will respond to Aborigines in the same way as to Third World immigrants in Sydney or Greek immigrants in Melbourne. In short, and as common sense would dictate, all minorities are not alike simply because they are minorities. (Some 'minorities', as in the case of women, may even be majorities!) At the same time, when we shift focus and move away from the peculiarities of each national setting, the existence of significant minorities, regardless of the uniqueness of their composition, raises a common set of concerns with respect to such issues as political representation, institutional recognition, and integration into dominant patterns of political culture. In other words, the political interplay between minority and majority interests in different countries may well have significant points of commonality even though the specific character of minority groups may vary considerably. Thus we might ask: Do such commonalities prevail in the structure of political belief systems, leading to roughly similar patterns across the five Anglo-American democracies, or are they overshadowed by national differences in the character of minority groups?

Third, we must recognize that the political dynamics surrounding minority rights and interests may vary substantially from country to country. Aboriginal issues in Canada, for example, do not compare in their political saliency with racial issues in the United States, or perhaps even with aboriginal issues in Australia. Minority interests may also be pursued within quite different institutional contexts, and thus with quite different results. For example, American blacks have far greater *constitutional* leverage on the political process than do Maoris in New Zealand or Aborigines in Australia, whereas the Maoris have entrenched *representational* leverage provided through special Maori seats in the New Zealand parliament. Similarily, the constitutional entrenchment of the Canadian Charter of Rights and Freedoms in 1982 has given a variety of minority groups—the new 'Charter Canadians'—greater constitutional leverage, and has given their claims greater political saliency, than was the case in Canada before 1982 and what may well be the case in the other three Commonwealth countries today. To take one more example, the existence of formal treaties in Canada, New Zealand, and the United States gives Native groups in those countries a form of legal and moral leverage on the political process that Australian Aborigines lack.

Fourth—and in contrast to the case with feminism—there is no overarching minority-rights ideology spanning the five Anglo-American democracies, an ideology that draws from a common pool of social experience and political leadership. The cross-national situation of minority groups is much less coherent, much more fragmented, and much more diversified in its political expression than is the case for women. Potentially, therefore, youth elites may be able to respond to minority groups' claims and aspirations in a more *ad hoc* and idiosyncratic fashion. In constructing comprehensive political belief systems, a student in New Zealand receives few environmental cues that he or she should react to

Maori claims in the same way that a student in Britain might react to the claims of racial minorities in that country. In other words, it is not clear that the experience in any one country necessarily provides an ideological model for other countries. Here it should also be noted that while the Anglo-American democracies may share an underlying liberal political culture, the focus of that culture on individual rights provides little guidance as to the appropriate resolution of conflicts rooted in group claims and intercommunal realities.

The more general point to stress is that youth elites in the five Anglo-American democracies confront quite different objective and historical realities in trying to make sense out of their political world. It would be very difficult for an American student in Detroit or New York to make comprehensive sense out of his or her political world without coming to grips with race relations in the United States, without adopting some position towards the conditions and aspirations of black Americans. Racial relations are simply too central in the American political experience to be ignored. It is less clear, however, that a student in Auckland, Perth, or Toronto would necessarily have to come to grips with aboriginal conditions, aspirations, and claims. It is at least conceivable that such a student could construct a broad, comprehensive political belief system within which aboriginal issues would be all but ignored. Given all of this, minority relations may play a nationally idiosyncratic role in the belief systems of youth elites. In marked contrast to the case of feminism, national differences in historical and objective circumstance might be expected to forge national differences in political belief systems.

At the same time, there are some threads that may lace together the five rather divergent national experiences, threads that may enable minority relations to play a similar ideological role in the five Anglo-American democracies despite significant national differences in historical and objective circumstances. In the five countries, minority groups of all stripes have become increasingly vocal and sophisticated in launching claims against the broader society, and those claims have climbed rapidly up the political agenda. There is nothing new about this in the United States, of course, but the change in the Commonwealth countries has been quite dramatic. In all five countries, minority groups have deployed roughly similar legislative and judicial strategies to pursue their claims upon the broader society, and in all five countries national visions are now routinely painted in multiracial and multicultural tones. Finally, we would argue that youth elites across the board face a future in which minority claims and aspirations will play an increasingly important role. While their grandparents and parents may have been able to construct models of social and political reality within which minority rights and minority groups played a marginal role at best, our respondents confront a very different world. How, then, do youth elites weave outlooks towards minority rights and minority groups into broader ideological fabrics?

The Measurement of Minority Orientations

In order to measure respondents' orientations towards minority groups and rights, we draw upon a set of five questions that emerged from the initial factor analysis discussed in Chapter 2, questions that are worded in a similar yet not identical fashion in the five national surveys. Ideally, question wording should be standard in cross-national research, as indeed was the case in the last chapter's construction of the feminism scale. In the case of minorities, however, a standard terminology would have done considerable violence to quite divergent national circumstances; national differences in measurement terminology were therefore needed to reflect important national differences in the contextual definition of minority rights. Thus in some cases the component questions for the minority scale refer to generic 'minorities', while in other cases they refer to specific minority groups that are largely if not entirely idiosyncratic to the particular national community. In all cases, however, the questions began with the wording utilized in the American survey, which was the first to go into the field. Questions were then modified, if necessary, to fit the specific circumstances of the four Commonwealth countries. For example, the New Zealand questionnaire contained references to *Maoris* while the American questionnaire referred to *blacks*. Although differences in question wording were required to meet the differences in national circumstances noted above, we tried to minimize national variation by employing identical question formats and identical locations for the questions within the respective questionnaires.

The question that carried the greatest weight in scale construction asked American respondents to position themselves on a seven-point scale with respect to two polar statements: 'If blacks would try harder they could be just as well off as whites', and 'Social conditions make it almost impossible for most blacks to overcome poverty even if they tried'. In the British questionnaire the term *blacks* was replaced by *ethnic minorities*, in the Canadian questionnaire it was replaced by *racial minorities*, in the Australian questionnaire by *Aborigines*, and in the New Zealand questionnaire by *Maoris*. As Table 4.1 shows, these differences in wording coincide with, *but are not necessarily responsible for*, marked national differences in response. For example, New Zealand respondents are much more likely to attribute poverty among the Maoris to a lack of individual effort than are American respondents to make the same attribution for blacks. The unanswerable question in this specific instance is whether the differences in Table 4.1 reflect an underlying national attitudinal difference in outlook toward racial minorities, whether they reflect the technical substitution of terms, or whether they reflect national differences in the objective circumstances of minority groups.

The question carrying the next most weight in scale construction asked American respondents to rank 'achieving equality for blacks' relative to

Table 4.1 National Differences in Response to Minority Poverty Question

	PERCENTAGE ANSWERING				
	AUST	BRIT	CAN	NZ	US
If blacks/racial minorities/ethnic minorities/Aborigines/Maoris would try harder, they could be just as well off as whites (score = 1, 2, or 3)	30.1	19.4	22.5	45.6	16.4
Mid-point on the scale (score = 4)	13.8	18.0	25.0	15.7	14.1
Social conditions make it almost impossible for most blacks/racial minorities/Aborigines/Maoris to overcome poverty even if they try (score = 5, 6, or 7)	56.1	62.7	52.6	38.8	69.5
Mean score	4.5	4.8	4.5	3.8	5.0

nine other national goals including such things as curbing inflation, reducing unemployment, and maintaining a strong military defence. Once again, in the British survey *ethnic minorities* became the operative term, while in Australia it was *Aborigines*, in Canada it was *racial minorities*, and in New Zealand it was *Maoris*. In all five countries, respondents were asked whether they agreed or disagreed with the statement: 'The news media pay too much attention to minority groups.' Here agreement rates ranged from 46.2 per cent of the New Zealand respondents and 44.2 per cent of the Australians to 35.7 per cent of those in Britain, 27.6 per cent of those in the United States, and 25.8 per cent of those in Canada.

The fourth question in the set asked American respondents whether they agreed or disagreed with the statement: 'If blacks are not getting fair treatment in jobs, the government should see to it that they do.' For Australian respondents the operative term was *Aborigines*, for British respondents it was *ethnic minorities*, for Canadians it was *racial minorities*, and for New Zealand respondents it was *Maoris*. Across all five countries, there was a very high level of support for government intervention. The proportion of respondents agreeing strongly with the statement ranged from 57.9 per cent in the United States to 30.6 per cent in New Zealand; the proportion who agreed either strongly or moderately ranged from 91.3 per cent in Britain to 76.5 per cent in New Zealand.

The final question in the set asked American respondents whether they agreed or disagreed with the statement: 'White people have the right to refuse to sell their homes to blacks.' The parallel question in the Australian questionnaire referred to *Aborigines or other racial minorities*, in the British questionnaire to *coloured people*, in the Canadian questionnaire to *racial minorities*, and in the New Zealand questionnaire to *Maoris and Pacific Islanders*. In all five countries, the level of agreement with the statement was low but not negligible; agreement, either strong or moderate, ranged from 30.0 per cent in the American sample to 17.8 per cent in the Canadian sample.

Despite the considerable national variance in question wording noted above, the five questions performed in a remarkably similar fashion. When the global factor analysis discussed in Chapter 2 was replicated in turn for each of the five national samples, in each case the five questions loaded on a single factor in every instance. In four of the national samples, the questions were strongly correlated with one another (see Figure 4.2). The exception came in the Canadian case, where the mean inter-item correlation coefficient was relatively modest.

The five questions have been used to construct a *minority scale* measuring respondent orientations towards minority issues. A high value on the scale indicates support for minority rights, claims, and aspirations. More specifically, respondents with relatively high scores on the scale tend to agree that social conditions make it almost impossible for minority groups to overcome poverty, that achieving equality for minority groups should be a relatively high national priority, and that the government should see to it that minority groups get fair treatment with respect to employment. Conversely, such respondents disagree that the media gives too much attention to minority groups, and disagree with the statement that whites have the right to refuse to sell their homes to members of minority groups. In all five national samples, the minority scale met conventional tests of reliability.[1]

National Differences

Figure 4.1 presents the sample distributions on the minority scale. As the figure indicates, Australian and New Zealand students have the lowest mean scores on the scale, although the very substantial overlap among the five national samples should also be noted. The comparison-of-means test reveals that there are no statistically significant differences in mean scores among the American, British, and Canadian respondents, and that there is no significant difference between the Australian and New Zealand means. However, there are significant differences between the American, British, and Canadian means, on the one hand, and the Australian and New Zealand means, on the other.

Here the difference between absolute and relative scores is critical. The fact that respondents from the Antipodes are *relatively* hostile to minority rights and aspirations does not mean that they are also hostile in an *absolute* sense. Thus we find, for example, that 84.5 per cent of Australian students and 76.5 per cent of New Zealand students agree

Figure 4.1: National Locations on the Minority Scale

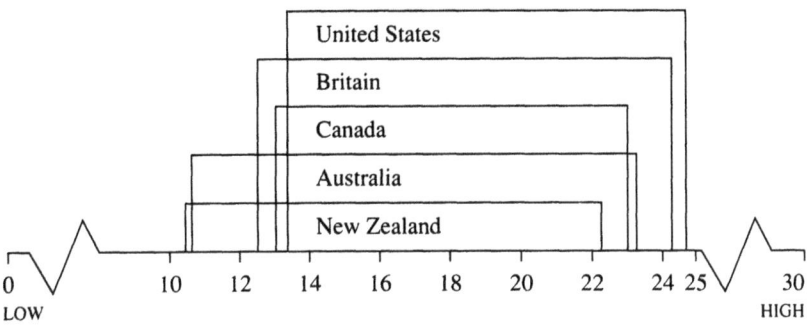

that the government should 'see to it' that Aborigines and Maoris get fair treatment in jobs. It is also interesting to note, albeit problematic to interpret, that among the four Commonwealth countries, the two cases with the lowest mean scores on the minority index are also the two where the scale questions had the most specific minority-group reference; while British and Canadian respondents were asked about generic racial and ethnic minorities, the questions to Australian and New Zealand respondents were framed with reference to very specific minority groups, the Aborigines and Maoris respectively.

The Linkage to Left-Right

Figure 4.2 shows that scores on the minority scale are strongly and negatively correlated to the left-right scale. In more qualitative terms, the farther respondents place themselves to the left on the left-right scale, the more supportive they tend to be of minority rights, claims, and aspirations. Conversely, those respondents who locate themselves on the right side of the ideological divide tend to be much less supportive of minority rights, claims, and aspirations. Thus in four of the five national samples, the left-right scale is indeed a powerful predictor of minority orientations, and one that applies with virtually the same force across the four countries. In the Canadian case, however, the relationship between the minority and left-right scales is *much* weaker. Not coincidentally, the internal cohesion among the five questions comprising the minority scale is also much weaker in the Canadian case, as evidenced by the mean inter-item correlations reported in Figure 4.2. Canadian respondents tend to have a less coherent outlook on minority issues, and tend to anchor that outlook less firmly to the left-right scale.

Figure 4.3 replicates an earlier form of analysis that, in this case, can be used to determine two things: first, whether respondents on the right

Figure 4.2: Minority Scale Mean Inter-Item Correlations
($\bar{x}_r$) And Left-Right Pearson Correlation (r)

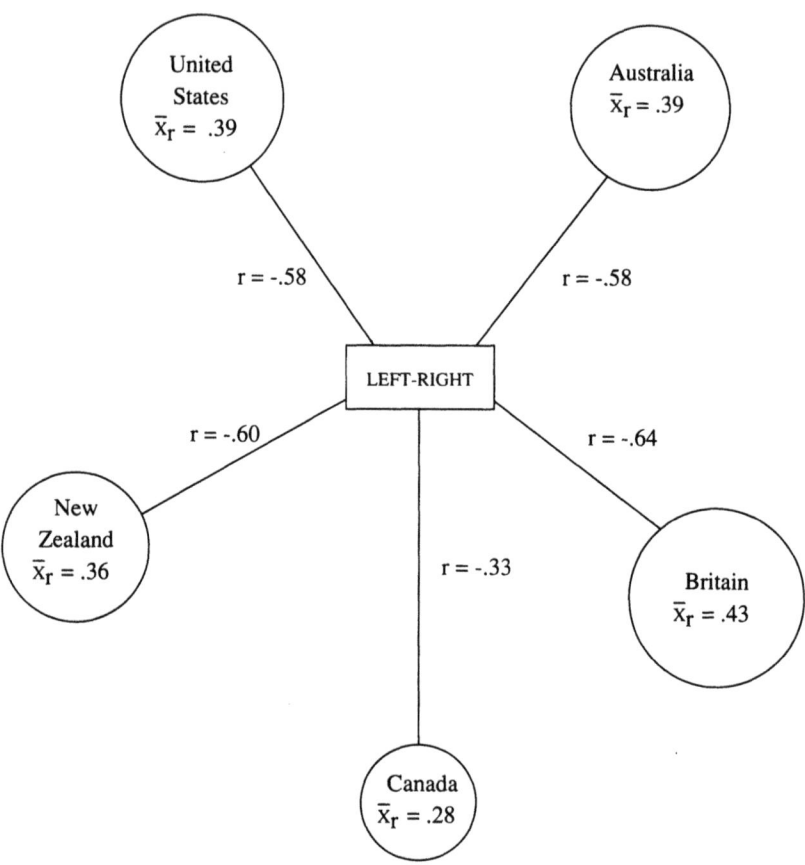

consistently differ from respondents on the left, irrespective of their national location; and second, whether significant differences exist *among* the five sets of national lefts, and *among* the five sets of national lefts. The lower left quadrant of Figure 4.3 addresses the first issue and shows that, in each and every case, respondents locating themselves on the right side of the ideological divide differ significantly from those respondents locating themselves on the left side of the divide. In no case do the lefts of one country share a common location on the minority scale with the rights of another country. Respondents locating themselves on the mid-

Minorities on the Ideological Landscape | 95

Figure 4.3: Comparison of Means of Left, Centre, and Right Identifiers on Minority Scale

NATIONAL LEFT-RIGHT IDENTIFIERS	1	2	3	4	5	6	7	8	9	10		MINORITY SCALE MEAN SCORES
1. New Zealand Right												12.8
2. Australia Right												13.0
3. United States Right												13.8
4. Britain Right												13.9
5. New Zealand Centre												14.2
6. Canada Right												15.1
7. United States Centre												16.8
8. Australia Centre	★	★										16.8
9. Britain Centre	★	★	★	★	★	★					11 12 13 14 15	18.7
10. Canada Centre	★	★	★	★	★	★						18.8
11. Canada Left	★	★	★	★	★	★						18.9
12. Australia Left	★	★	★	★	★		★					20.4
13. New Zealand Left	★	★	★	★	★		★					20.6
14. United States Left	★	★	★	★	★	★	★					20.7
15. Britain Left	★	★	★	★	★	★	★	★	★	★		21.5

★ represents pairs of Left-Right identifiers with Minority Scale mean scores significantly different at $p < .05$

point of the left-right scale generally fall to the centre of the minority scale. In all five national samples, however, there are no significant differences between the respective rights and those respondents falling on the mid-point of the left-right scale, while in three cases (Australia, Britain, and New Zealand) those at the mid-point were significantly less supportive of minority rights than were their respective lefts. Thus in a relative sense, mid-point respondents tend to cluster with those on the right rather than with those on the left.

Figure 4.3 also shows that the five national rights, boxed together in the upper left-hand corner of the figure, are statistically indistinguishable from one another. To put this finding in more qualitative terms, once you know that a respondent locates himself or herself on the right side of the left-right scale, you would be no better off in predicting the respondent's location on the minority scale if you also knew in which country the respondent lived; knowledge about whether the respondent lives in Australia or Britain, Canada or New Zealand is superfluous. With one exception, these national similarities also hold for the five national lefts, boxed together in the lower right-hand corner of the figure. The exception is that respondents on the British left have significantly higher scores on the minority scale than do respondents on the Canadian left. Overall, and as the previous figure would predict, Figure 4.3 shows that ideological self-identification with respect to the left-right scale is a powerful organizer with respect to predispositions towards minority groups. Moreover, once that self-identification is in place, nationality is virtually irrelevant.

Figure 4.4 repeats the same form of analysis, only in this case respondents are grouped by party identification rather than by their self-location on the left-right scale. In the upper left-hand corner of the figure we find respondents identifying with the Liberal party of Australia, the British Conservative party, the Canadian Progressive Conservative party, the New Zealand Nationals, and the Republican party of the United States, all parties conventionally associated with the political right. In keeping with the national differences observed in Figure 4.1, it is not surprising that the supporters of the right-of-centre parties in New Zealand and Australia have the lowest scores on the minority index. However, there are few statistically significant differences among the right-of-centre party mean scores on the minority index; only the Canadian Progressive Conservatives stand apart, and then only from the Australian Liberals and New Zealand Nationals. If we look at respondents identifying with parties conventionally associated with the political left—Australian and New Zealand Labor, British Labour, Canadian NDP, and the US Democrats—significant national differences are again rare. Respondents identifying with the British Labour party stand apart from their Labor compatriots in Australia and New Zealand, and from Liberal-SDP identifiers in Britain, and American Democrats stand apart from New Zealand Laborites. Otherwise, identifiers with the parties of the conventional left are undifferentiated by their scores on the minority scale.

Table 4.2 shows the degree of spread between left-wing and right-wing partisans in each of the five countries. The table is derived from Figure

Minorities on the Ideological Landscape | 97

Figure 4.4: Comparison of Means of National Party Identifiers on Minority Scale

NATIONAL PARTY IDENTIFIERS		MINORITY SCALE MEAN SCORES
	1 2 3 4 5 6	
1. New Zealand National		12.4
2. Australia Liberal		12.8
3. United States Republican		14.1
4. Britain Conservative		14.4
5. Canada Conservative	★ ★	15.9
6. Canada Liberal	★ ★ ★ ★ 7 8 9 10 11 12	18.1
7. New Zealand Labor	★ ★ ★ ★ ★	18.2
8. Britain Liberal-SDP	★ ★ ★ ★ ★	18.8
9. Australia Labor	★ ★ ★ ★ ★	19.5
10. Canada New Democrat	★ ★ ★ ★ ★	19.5
11. United States Democrat	★ ★ ★ ★ ★ ★ ★	20.6
12. Britain Labour	★ ★ ★ ★ ★ ★ ★ ★ ★	21.9

★ represents pairs of party identifiers with Minority Scale mean scores significantly different at $p < .05$

4.4 and simply reports, for each country, the difference between the minority-scale mean scores for the right-wing and left-wing parties. As the table shows, there is greater spread in the British sample between Conservatives and Labourites than there is in any other national sample. The smallest spread is found in the Canadian case, where only 3.6 points separate the mean scores of Progressive Conservative and NDP respondents. Given that the Canadian Liberals are wedged in between the

Progressive Conservative and NDP 'extremes', it appears that Canadian parties differ little with respect to minority rights.

Table 4.2 National Differences in Partisan Mean Scores on Minority Scale

NATIONAL SAMPLE	PARTISAN L-R POLARITY	DIFFERENCE IN MEANS
Australia	Labor-Liberal	6.7
Britain	Labour-Conservative	7.5
Canada	NDP-Progressive Conservative	3.6
New Zealand	Labor-National	5.8
United States	Democrat-Republican	6.5

A quick comparison of Figures 4.3 and 4.4 brings two interesting, albeit perhaps not surprising, findings to light. The first is that self-identification on the left-right scale produces a somewhat more sharply defined clustering of respondents than does party identification. The five national rights and, with one exception, the five national lefts form coherent blocs within which significant national differences cannot be detected. Conversely, the clustering of the five right-of-centre parties and the five left-of-centre parties is not quite so neat. This finding stems from two factors. First, Anglo-American brokerage parties tend to be rather ambiguous ideological containers, whether by design or not. Although some major parties, such as the British Labour Party, have occasionally eschewed brokerage politics, and although left-of-centre parties have often experienced considerable internal debate over the appropriate weight to be given to political education and electoral success, ideological purity has rarely been pursued and never achieved. Second, the parties are, after all, national rather than international or cross-national organizations, and thus some degree of national differentiation is to be expected. In this sense, the surprising finding is that national variation among the five lefts and rights is not more pronounced in Figure 4.4.

The second finding to emerge from the comparison of Figures 4.3 and 4.4 is that the overall spread in mean scores among the partisan groupings in Figure 4.4 virtually equals the spread in mean scores among the ideological camps shown in Figure 4.3, and generated by the left-right scale. In other words, there is no tendency for partisan groupings to be pulled toward the middle of the minority scale—no tendency, for example, for *partisans* of the right to occupy a more moderate position than *ideologues* of the right. (Of course, there is a substantial overlap between ideological location and partisan identification.) Although parties may indeed be ambiguous ideological containers, this does not reduce the clear differentiation among party supporters with respect to orientations towards minority rights and issues.

The last figure in this section brings together party identification, self-location on the left-right scale, and mean scores on the minority scale. The polar groups in Figure 4.5 are formed by those respondents who identify with the British Labour party, on the one hand, and with the Australian Liberal party, on the other. The British Labour respondents are both the farthest to the left and the most supportive of minority-group rights, claims, and aspirations; the Australian Liberals are about as far right as the British Conservatives and about as unsupportive of minority rights, claims, and aspirations as are the New Zealand Nationals. The five right-of-centre parties cluster in a rather loose fashion towards the bottom-right corner of the diagram. The relative outliers come from the Canadian Progressive Conservatives, who stand somewhat apart in their relatively strong support for minorities, and the US Republicans, who are located to the left of their Commonwealth compatriots.

Figure 4.5: Parties in Minority-Left/Right Space

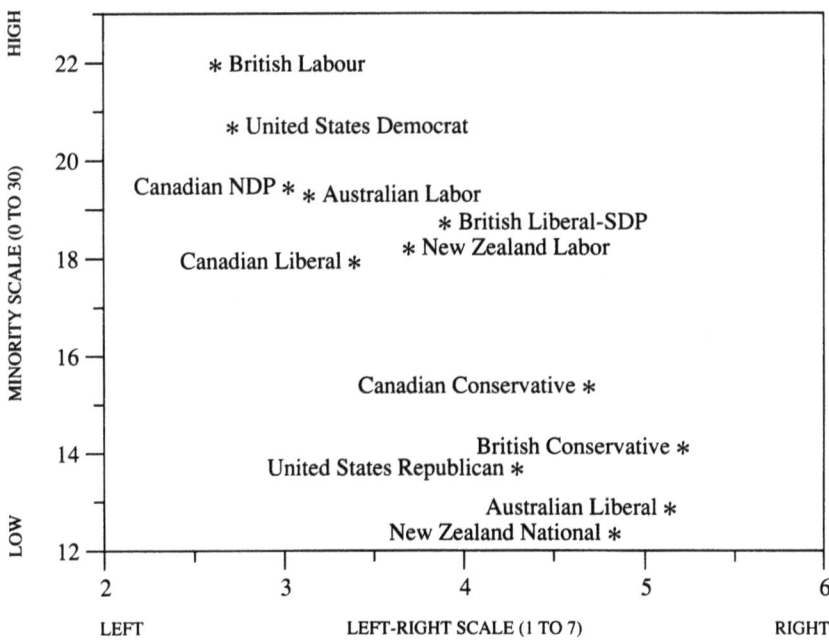

Four of the five left-of-centre parties form a tighter cluster in the upper-left corner of Figure 4.5. In this instance, the outlying case is composed of supporters of the New Zealand Labor party, who stand apart in both their middle-of-the-road ideological location and their relative lack of support for minority groups. Here note should also be made of the

Canadian Liberals and the British Liberals-SDP. Both occupy a very different ideological space than do the parties of the right, but both lie at the margins of the four-party left-of-centre cluster. Canadian Liberals are at the margin because of their relatively unsympathetic stance towards minorities, while the British Liberal-SDP supporters stand apart because of their more central location on the left-right scale.

In introducing this chapter, we asked to what extent orientations towards minorities are woven into broader, more all-encompassing ideological fabrics. With respect to the ideological cloth provided by the left-right scale, the answer is clear and emphatic; minority orientations are woven tightly into this particular ideological fabric. They provide detail, colour, pattern, and texture to the underlying but content-free concepts of left and right. Only in the Canadian case is the weave rather loose, as shown by the relatively weak correlational connection between ideological self-placement and scores on the minority scale. What remains to be seen is the extent to which minority orientations are linked to the other belief-system elements identified in this study. It is to the relationship between the minority scale, on the one hand, and the government and feminism scales, on the other, that we now turn.

The Broader Ideological Environment

Our discussion of the location of minorities on the Anglo-American ideological landscape begins with Figure 4.6, which positions the minority scale relative to the feminism, government, and left-right scales. In order to unravel and simplify this rather complex figure, it is useful to examine the ideological linkages within one national sample before turning to the cross-national comparison. Let us begin, then, with the ideological picture that emerges for American respondents, a picture captured in the upper left-hand corner of Figure 4.6.

In tackling the American panel in Figure 4.6, we should begin by noting that several of the important elements in the ideological landscape of American youth elites have already been put into place. The relationship among the feminism, government, and left-right scales, a relationship captured in the bottom portion of the panel, has been discussed previously (see Figure 3.6), as has the relationship between the minority and left-right scales (see Figure 4.2). However, two new elements have been added to the picture in Figure 4.6. The first is the robust, positive relationship between the minority and feminism scales; respondents who are relatively supportive of minority interests are also relatively supportive of feminism, a relationship that supports the oft-encountered depiction of women as a minority group. (Conversely, respondents who are relatively opposed to minority interests are also relatively opposed to claims for greater gender equality.) The second new element in Figure 4.6 is the *very* robust, positive relationship between the minority and government scales. Although the direction of this relationship is not unexpected, given that

Figure 4.6: Combined Minority, Feminism, and Government Scale Mean Inter-Item Correlations ($\bar{X}_r$) And Left-Right Pearson Correlations (r)

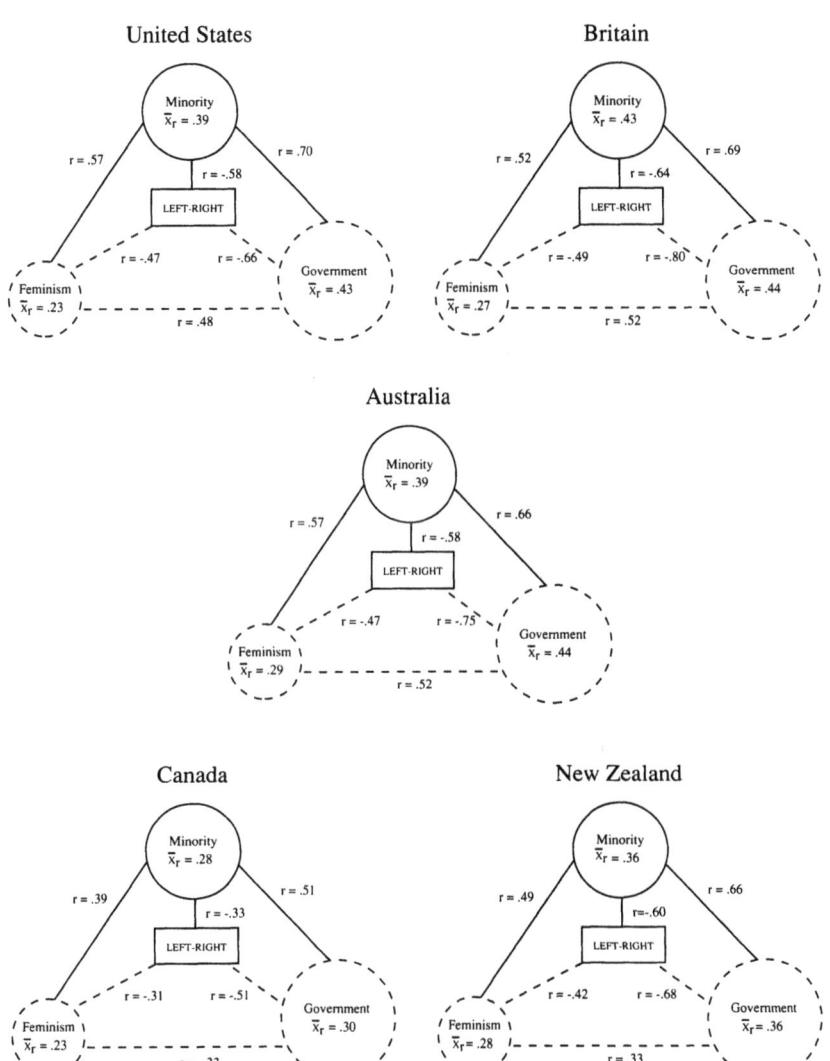

it reflects the relationship between the minority and left-right scales, the strength of the relationship is truly impressive nonetheless.[2]

The ideological relationship between the minority and government scales also reflects a compelling logical connection in the real world of public policy. State intervention in the economic and social orders has become an essential tool in the pursuit of minority-group claims. Given how poorly many minority groups fared in the more distant past, when the economic and social orders were relatively unencumbered by state intervention, it is difficult to reconcile minority interests with any substantial reduction in the role of government. Here the converse argument should also be stressed. Those who believe as a matter of principle in the reduction of state intervention will find it difficult to reconcile that principle with support for minority-group interests, rights, and aspirations. The modern interventionalist state is too important a vehicle for the pursuit of those claims, and thus the downsizing or dismemberment of that state poses an acute concern for those groups that have benefited to date from state intervention.

Figure 4.6 presents a useful summary sketch of the political belief systems that have emerged to this point within the sample of American youth elites. The figure shows a high level of integration among the various elements, and particularly between outlooks towards minority groups—in this case blacks—and government intervention. In the strong correlation between the minority and feminism scales, we see the ideological underpinnings of the 'rainbow coalition' that played such a prominent role in democratic politics during the 1980s. Throughout the figure, there is a great deal of connectedness and constraint; if we know where a respondent is located with respect to one element in the belief system, we have a reasonably good idea where he or she stands with respect to the other elements in the system. It should also be noted that orientations towards the rights, claims, and aspirations of black Americans play a very important role in the larger belief system, and indeed a more important role than orientations towards feminism. Finally, it should be noted that the bi-polar belief system is firmly anchored to the left-right scale. If we can locate an individual on the left-right scale, we can hazard a pretty good guess as to how he or she feels about feminism, minority rights, and government intervention. More specifically, respondents falling towards the right end of the ideological spectrum are relatively opposed to minority rights, feminism, and government intervention, whereas those falling towards the left end are relatively supportive of the same three elements. In this sense, the three more specifically defined elements in Figure 4.6 provide some flesh and bones to the meaning of left and right within the American political landscape.

The next question to address is whether the American pattern is unique—whether, for example, the strong linkages to the minority scale in Figure 4.6 reflect a singularly American preoccupation with racial issues. Are we faced with American *exceptionalism*, or is the American pattern similar to broader ideological patterns spanning the five Anglo-American democracies? In part, the answer to this question, and thus the rejection of American exceptionalism, has already come from Figure 4.2, which showed that the relationship between the left-right and minority scales was very similar across four of the five Anglo-American democracies, and that the exception was not the United States but Canada. If we return to Figure 4.6 and examine the linkage between the minority and government scales, we see once again that the relationship is virtually identical in the American, Australian, British, and New Zealand samples. Only in the Canadian sample does the relationship weaken to any appreciable degree. Substantively, it might be argued that the findings reflect the fact that multiculturalism has been a policy pursued by Canadian governments of both the left and right over the past thirty years.

If we examine the relationship between the minority and feminism scales, the American and Australian correlations are identical in direction and strength. The relationship weakens somewhat but not greatly in the British and New Zealand samples, and then weakens more substantially in the Canadian case. Here it is also interesting to note that in Table 4.3 the correlation between the feminism and minority scales is marginally stronger for men than it is for women. At the risk of overstating a relatively modest gender difference, Table 4.3 suggests that men are more likely than women to define women as a minority group, and to adopt an all-encompassing ideological position which incorporates both women and racial minorities. For their part, and perhaps not surprisingly, women are more prone to distinguish between the rights, claims, and aspirations of women, on the one hand, and those of minority groups, on the other. The assumption that they are 'all minorities' has greater currency for men than it does for women.

Table 4.3 Correlation between Feminism and Minority Scales (controlled for gender of respondent)

COUNTRY	MEN ONLY	WOMEN ONLY
Australia	.54	.53
Britain	.55	.42
Canada	.37	.32
New Zealand	.49	.41
United States	.63	.45

So what do we conclude about American exceptionalism? In some earlier work we published on American-Canadian differences with respect to minority issues (Nevitte and Gibbins, 1985), we argued that rather striking national differences stemmed from both the greater historical legacy and the contemporary saliency of race relations in the United States. In the following passage, for example, the *implicit* argument is one of American exceptionalism:

in the field of minority relations, the Canadian attitudinal world is quite different in character from the attitudinal world in the United States. Lacking the black experience and confronted by a smaller, more diverse, and less politicized minority population, the Canadian world is characterized by less consistency and by relatively weak linkages to other values which, at least logically, should be closely entwined with minority orientations. There has been no ready Canadian equivalent of the American black experience as an organizer of Canadian thought on minority relations (1985: 271).

In a demographic sense, one could easily substitute Australia, Britain, or New Zealand for Canada in the above paragraph. And yet it is clear from Figure 4.6, and the lesson learned from a broader set of cross-national comparisons, that Canada, *not* the United States, is the exception. In terms of the general strength and character of the relationships encompassed by the figure, there is little to distinguish the emergent ideological structure for American youth elites from that which emerges from the Australian, British, and New Zealand samples. It is the ideological structure of Canadian political beliefs that stands apart.

That Canada may be an exception, while the US certainly is not, is an important finding given that there are rather compelling reasons why we might expect the United States to stand apart from the four Commonwealth countries. The American historical experience with slavery and civil war has been unique, and there has not been even an approximate parallel to the American civil-rights movement in the Commonwealth countries. However, when we examine how respondents fold minority issues into broader ideological structures, American respondents do not stand apart. In at least a rough sense, a university student in New Zealand weaves his or her views towards Maoris into a more overarching belief system in the same way that an American student would do. The fact that the minority scale was based on somewhat idiosyncratic questions in each of the five national samples appears to have had little impact on the ideological structure of political beliefs. Minorities lodged in objectively different national environments appear to serve as functional equivalents for one another in the ideological belief systems of youth elites.

Conclusions

At this time it is appropriate to step back from the details of the data analysis and explore some of the broader patterns and implications. In so doing, the first point to stress is the important place that orientations towards minority rights occupy in the political belief systems of youth elites. Across all five Anglo-American democracies, the predispositions measured by the minority scale play a central role in respondents' organization of their ideological world. Strong and consistent correlational linkages exist between the minority scale and the other issue-related measures built into the study thus far, linkages demonstrating that orientations towards minority rights, claims, and aspirations are thoroughly woven into the broad ideological fabrics that youth elites use to make sense out of their political world. This demonstration is further strengthened by the linkages between the minority scale and the left-right scale.

The second point to stress is the continued centrality and power of the left-right scale as an organizer of political beliefs. We find that simply being able to locate respondents on the left-right scale tells us a great deal about their orientations towards minority rights, claims, and aspirations, and about a host of other beliefs to which such orientations are attached. The ideological structures modelled in Figure 4.6 provide ample demonstration of the power of the left-right scale in predicting a wide array of political beliefs and values. Although the historical and conceptual roots of *left* and *right* would suggest that the left-right scale would be particularly relevant for the study of attitudes towards government intervention, Figure 4.6 shows that the scale is equally relevant for the study of minority orientations. As the political agenda has expanded in recent times to incorporate minority claims and aspirations, the left-right scale appears to have experienced a concomitant conceptual expansion, allowing it to embrace the new politics of minority rights. In effect, the scale has been 're-loaded' for youth elites facing a political environment in which minority rights and claims have come to the fore.

The left-right scale not only picks up attitudinal differences of degree; it also registers differences of kind. Note, for example, the illustration provided by Table 4.4, where three sets of respondents are compared—those locating themselves on the right, left, and centre of the left-right scale. The three groups are compared with respect to their responses to a question on the media's coverage of minority groups. (In this case, the question wording was identical across the five national samples.) The differences between two of the three ideological camps—those on the left and those on the right—are not simply ones of nuance and degree;

Table 4.4 Left-Right Differences in Perceptions of Media Coverage

Percentage *agreeing* with the statement that 'the news media pay too much attention to minority groups'

COUNTRY	LEFT	CENTRE	RIGHT
Australia	23.7	44.8	65.0
Britain	17.8	30.9	61.5
Canada	19.7	22.3	41.8
New Zealand	20.5	61.0	67.6
United States	16.8	47.5	49.1

the two sets of respondents see the world in *very* different ways. We might also note parenthetically, with respect to Table 4.4, that respondents opting for the mid-point of the left-right scale do not consistently occupy an attitudinal mid-point between the lefts and rights. In two cases (New Zealand and the United States) mid-point respondents are indistinguishable from right-of-centre respondents, while in one case (Canada) they are indistinguishable from left-of-centre respondents.

Although there are very substantial differences between respondents on the left and those on the right, Table 4.4 shows that *national* variation is much more modest. The five national lefts are almost identical, while only Canadian and American respondents stand apart, and not radically so, on the right. This finding illustrates the third general point to be stressed, and that is the relative weakness of national variation compared to the much more substantial ideological variation across the left-right scale. Of course, statistically significant national variations have not been entirely absent in this chapter. Nonetheless, those differences have been greatly overshadowed by the differences between left and right, differences which have more or less held regardless of the national location of respondents. Despite very real national variation in historical and objective circumstance, and despite the consequent need to use different questions in the different national surveys, we observed *very modest national differences* in the political belief systems of youth elites. Thus a student in London trying to construct a comprehensive ideological map of the world, and trying to fit minority groups into that construction, does not come up with a radically different ideological picture than does a student in Boston or Perth. In the organization of political belief systems, nationally idiosyncratic features of the minority environment do not play a major role.

This suggests, in turn, that the historical past does not throw a large shadow over the political beliefs of contemporary youth elites. Although that shadow is detectable in the belief systems of youth elites, it does not create nationally distinct systems of political belief. This conclusion takes us back to the discussion of feminism, where we found that *regardless of national location*, feminism occupies the same ideological space within the belief systems of youth elites. The same finding prevails in the case of minority attitudes, but in this instance the finding is much more surprising given very considerable differences in national circumstances.

Although the summary picture presented in Figure 4.6 may initially seem rather complex, it should not obscure some very important general findings. In four of the five countries, youth elites manifest political belief systems that are strikingly similar. Those belief systems, moreover, are firmly anchored in the polar concepts of left and right. Knowing whether a student identifies with the left or right tells us a great deal about his or her political beliefs; knowing in which country the student lives tells us much less. To the extent that any one country stands apart from this general pattern, it is Canada; the ideological constructs of Canadian students seem in some ways to be a pale shadow of those prevailing elsewhere in the Anglo-American democracies. Before drawing any conclusions about Canadian exceptionalism, however, there is one further piece to be added to the ideological landscape of youth elites.

NOTES

[1] The alpha reliability coefficients for the minority scale are as follows: Australia (.76), Britain (.79), Canada (.67), New Zealand (.74), and the United States (.76). The weaker Canadian score reflects the relatively low inter-item correlations in the Canadian case.

[2] It should be noted that the strength of this relationship stems in part, but only in part, from a conceptual overlap introduced by the item in the minority scale that asked respondents, in the case of the American questionnaire, if they agreed or disagreed with the statement: 'If blacks are not getting fair treatment in jobs, the government should see to it that they do.'

CHAPTER FIVE

Equality: Of Opportunity or Result?

One striking finding that has emerged in the preceding three chapters is the extent to which different attitudinal domains overlap in the political belief systems of youth elites. In somewhat more technical language, there are strong correlations among student orientations towards the role of government, towards feminism, and towards minorities. A great deal of *constraint* is clearly evident in the belief systems of youth elites; the attitudinal components hang together in coherent structures that differ in detail, but not in design fundamentals, from one Anglo-American democracy to the next. Thus no matter where one chooses to penetrate those belief systems, the initial point of entry exposes a good deal of the larger system of political belief. For example, knowledge about how an individual feels towards feminism provides very useful clues as to how the same individual feels about minority rights and the role of government. While the degree of constraint is not so great that to know one thing is to know it all, it is nevertheless clear that a variety of quite different beliefs are bound together into well-packaged ideological wholes.

Given the character of our respondents, the existence of relatively cohesive and coherent political belief systems should not come as a complete surprise. After all, the senior university students will have spent their last three to four years in an environment where logical patterns of thought were encouraged, and indeed where marks were awarded in part according to the ability of students to make some sense out of a very complex world. On average, therefore, students bring to the political world a more sharply honed set of analytical tools than one would expect to find within the mass public, and thus we should expect to find a greater degree of ideological coherence within their systems of political beliefs than we should expect to find within the mass public (Converse, 1964).

Moreover, there are reasonably compelling logical arguments to explain the *individual* linkages among the component parts that have been discussed so far in the analysis. For example, in Chapter 3 we identified powerful correlational linkage between the government and feminism scales, and then went on to argue that government intervention in the social and economic orders can be seen as an important and perhaps indispensable tool for the pursuit of gender equality. As a consequence it is difficult, although certainly not impossible, to reconcile strong support for feminism with support for the extensive withdrawal of the state from the social and economic orders. In Chapter 4, a parallel argument was developed to explain the strong correlational linkage between the government and minority scales. Government intervention, it was argued, goes hand in hand with attempts to dismantle long-standing barriers of racial discrimination; at least in common parlance, government intervention has been seen as the means through which one pursues minority claims and aspirations. In summary, then, the high degree of connectiveness or constraint witnessed at the end of the last chapter makes logical sense; it seems like the reasonable product of young, well-educated individuals trying to make some holistic sense out of a complex political environment.

And yet we might also ask if the *coherence of the whole* goes beyond the logical linkages between and among the component parts. Is there some underlying concept or principle that explains the strong correlations among the government, feminism, and minority scales, something embedded not only within the three specific scales but also within the more global left-right continuum?

A clear candidate is the notion of *equality*, in all of its political, economic, and social guises. One could argue, for example, that feminism represents, on at least one level, the pursuit of greater equality of opportunity and result for women. Although the phrase *gender equality* does not circumscribe the entirety of feminism, it surely captures the central core. Minority rights, claims, and aspirations swirl around notions of equality; equal treatment in the pursuit of employment, equal standing within the social domain, and equal influence within the political arena. Much of the debate over the proper role of government and government intervention is also related to the use of such intervention to redistribute income, economic opportunities, and social status. Government intervention is seen to provide the means to overcome the inherent *inequalities* of the market system; the political debate centres upon the degree to which this is a desirable and/or achievable goal. Finally, the concepts of left and right can easily be grafted onto a debate over the degree of equality that should prevail within the economic, social, and political orders. Those on the left tend systematically to support a more equal distribution of income, status, and political influence; those on the right are more comfortable with, and at times supportive of, the inequalities that emerge from an unconstrained market economy and an unencumbered social order.

Thus equality may well be the underlying principle knitting together the political belief systems exposed in Figure 4.6 and preceding figures. At the very least, orientations towards equality are likely to form an important part of the ideological cluster that has been identified in Figure 4.6, and that has been systematically linked to the left-right continuum. In this chapter, then, we turn to the measurement of student orientations towards equality, and to the degree to which those orientations are woven into broader systems of political belief.

Measurement of Equality

The initial factor analysis discussed in Chapter 2 identified six survey questions that fall within the conceptual domain of equality, and that can be used to construct a reliable measure of respondent orientations towards equality. In contrast to the situation we encountered in the last chapter, the measurement of orientations towards equality is relatively uncomplicated by variance in question wording across the five national samples. In only one of the six questions did reference groups change in response to divergent national circumstances.

Two of the six questions dealt with the issue of income equality. In the first of the two, and the one that carried the greatest overall weight in the construction of the equality scale, respondents were asked to position themselves on a seven-point scale between two alternatives: 'Under a fair economic system, all people earn about the same', or 'People with more ability should earn higher salaries'. In the second question, respondents were asked to express their agreement or disagreement with the statement 'There should be a law limiting the amount of money any individual is allowed to earn in a year', a sentiment that attracted only minority support among youth elites. In both cases, the questions were identical across the five national surveys.

A second set of questions dealt with the issue of hiring quotas. In the first question, Australian, British, and New Zealand respondents were again placed in the context of a fair economic system, and were asked to position themselves on a seven-point scale between two alternatives: 'Firms should be made to increase the number of women in good jobs', or 'Job hiring should be based strictly on merit'. American and Canadian respondents were placed in the same context, but the first alternative had a slightly different wording: 'Quotas in job hiring should be used to increase the number of women in good jobs.' (The wording of the second alternative was consistent across the five national surveys.) In the second question, the emphasis shifted to quotas for racial minorities, and here the question wording varied across the five surveys. Respondents were asked to position themselves on a seven-point scale between the following alternatives:

> *American respondents*: 'Quotas in school admissions and job hiring should be used to insure black representation', or 'School admissions and job hiring should be based strictly on merit'.
>
> *Australian respondents*: 'Places should be reserved for Aborigines to ensure their representation in the professions (such as teaching, medicine, law)', or 'Admission to professional training should be based strictly on merit'.
>
> *British respondents*: 'Places should be reserved for ethnic minorities to ensure their representation in schools and the work place', or 'School admissions and job hiring should be based strictly on merit'.
>
> *Canadian respondents*: 'Quotas in school admissions and job hiring should

be used to ensure the representation of racial minorities', or 'School admissions and job hiring should be based strictly on merit'.

New Zealand respondents: 'Places should be reserved for Maoris to ensure their representation in the professions (such as teaching, medicine, law)', or 'Admission to professional training should be based strictly on merit'.

One of the alternatives confronting respondents was essentially the same across all five national surveys—that merit should prevail in decisions relating to educational admissions and hiring. Only the other alternative varied according to unique national circumstances.

The final two questions tapped somewhat different aspects of the equality domain. The first, which was identical across the five surveys, asked respondents to position themselves on a seven-point scale between two classical alternatives:

Here are two ways of dealing with inequality; which do you prefer? *Equality of opportunity*, giving each person an equal chance for a good education and to develop his or her ability, or *equality of results*, giving each person a relatively equal income regardless of his or her education and ability.

As Table 5.1 shows, the primary variance in the question comes from the *degree to which* respondents support 'equality of opportunity'. Very little support is evident for 'equality of result', a finding that is not surprising given that the universities are often perceived to be important vehicles through which equality of opportunity can be transformed by hard work and good grades into inequalities of result.

Table 5.1 Equality of Opportunity or Result?

	EQUALITY OF OPPORTUNITY	MID-POINT	EQUALITY OF RESULT
Australia	92.7%	4.0	3.3
Britain	87.0	4.3	8.7
Canada	93.7	2.2	4.1
New Zealand	91.5	4.6	3.9
United States	87.3	6.0	6.7

The final question in the set addressed the issue of equality within the workplace. Respondents were asked to position themselves on a seven-point scale between two alternatives: 'Workers should have more say in important decisions than they do now', or 'The important decisions should be left to management'. This question was worded identically across the five national surveys, and across all five a clear majority of respondents supported more say for workers in important decisions. (The proportion ranges from a low of 53.5 per cent among Canadian respondents to a high of 61.9 per cent among New Zealand respondents.) Here it would be interesting to know if the respondents' subordinate status within the university environment provides a short-term identification with 'the workers', an identification that may not persist once graduation has come and gone. (Certainly the complementary identification of the professoriate as 'management' would stretch the imagination in some cases!)

The *equality scale* was constructed by recoding all six component variables so that high scores registered support for greater equality. The component variables were assigned equal weight, and respondent scores were summed across the six variables. As Figure 5.1 shows, distributions of the national samples differ little. The American and British samples have identical standard deviations and means. (The boxes in the figure span one standard deviation on either side of the mean.) The New Zealand sample has the same central tendency but a smaller standard deviation. Statistical tests reveal no significant differences among the American, Australian, British, and New Zealand means, or between the Australian and Canadian means. However, the Canadian mean is significantly lower than the American, British, and New Zealand means. Thus apart from knowing whether or not a respondent is a Canadian, nationality has no bearing on respondent scores on the equality index.

Figure 5.1: National Locations on Equality Scale

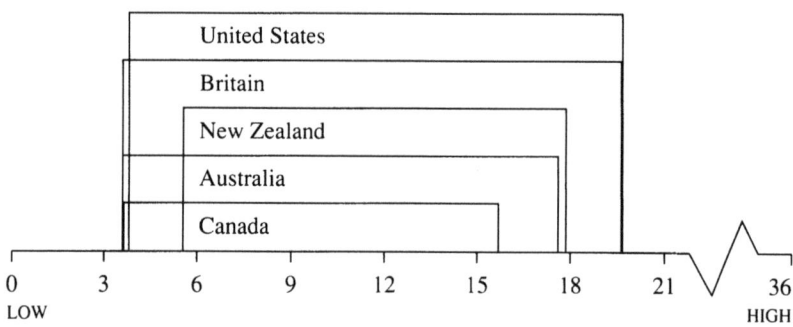

The Linkage to Left-Right

Figure 5.2 presents two important pieces of information. First, the figure shows the mean inter-item correlations for the six component questions of the equality scale. The six questions 'hang together' in a tight fashion for American and British respondents, in a slightly looser fashion for Australian respondents, and in a decidedly looser fashion for respondents from Canada and New Zealand. In qualitative terms, Figure 5.2 suggests that American and British students have a relatively coherent orientation toward the cluster of rather diverse concerns incorporated within the equality index. (To take but one example, how a student feels about the distribution of authority within the workplace imposes some constraint on how he or she feels about hiring quotas or income limitations.) American and British respondents do not stand apart in the *direction* of their beliefs, for, as Figure 5.1 has demonstrated, they are no more or no less 'pro-equality' than are their counterparts in Australia and New Zealand. As individuals, they simply manifest a more consistent outlook, be that outlook positive or negative. Conversely, Canadian and New Zealand respondents demonstrate much less consistency; the stance of a respondent towards any one of the elements embraced by the equality scale is less predictive of his or her outlook towards other elements. In more sweeping terms, Figure 5.2 suggests that orientations towards equality may play a more salient role in the political cultures of Britain and the United States than they do in the political cultures of the other three Anglo-American democracies, the assumption being that saliency will promote attitudinal coherency and consistency. In matters of little concern to our peers and significant others, our beliefs are free to wander with little constraint, but in matters of greater public concern, external constraints come more readily into play, generating attitudinal consistency in their wake.

The second piece of information to be derived from Figure 5.2 is the relationship between orientations toward equality, on the one hand, and ideological self-placement on the left-right scale, on the other. The figure shows very powerful relationships in four of the five national samples; as one moves from left to right, scores on the equality scale decline sharply. Put somewhat differently, self-placement on the left-right scale is a powerful predictor of respondent orientations towards equality. Conversely, the equality scale is a powerful predictor of ideological self-placement on the left-right scale. Only in the Canadian case does this relationship weaken, and it does so quite dramatically. The interesting point to note is that the relationship for New Zealand students is very much in line with the relationship for American, Australian, and British students, even though the mean inter-item correlation for the equality index is much weaker in the New Zealand case.

It is clear, then, that orientations towards equality are strongly linked to the global ideological constructs of left and right. More specifically, Table 5.2 shows that respondents on the left and right have sharply divergent perspectives on equality-related issues. The table draws upon four of the six questions used to construct the equality scale, and compares respondents positioning themselves to the left and right of the mid-point on the left-right scale; respondents positioning themselves on the mid-point have been excluded from the table.

Table 5.2 contains a wealth of information, and indeed far more than

Figure 5.2: Equality Scale Mean Inter-Item Correlations
($\bar{x}_r$) And Left-Right Pearson Correlation (r)

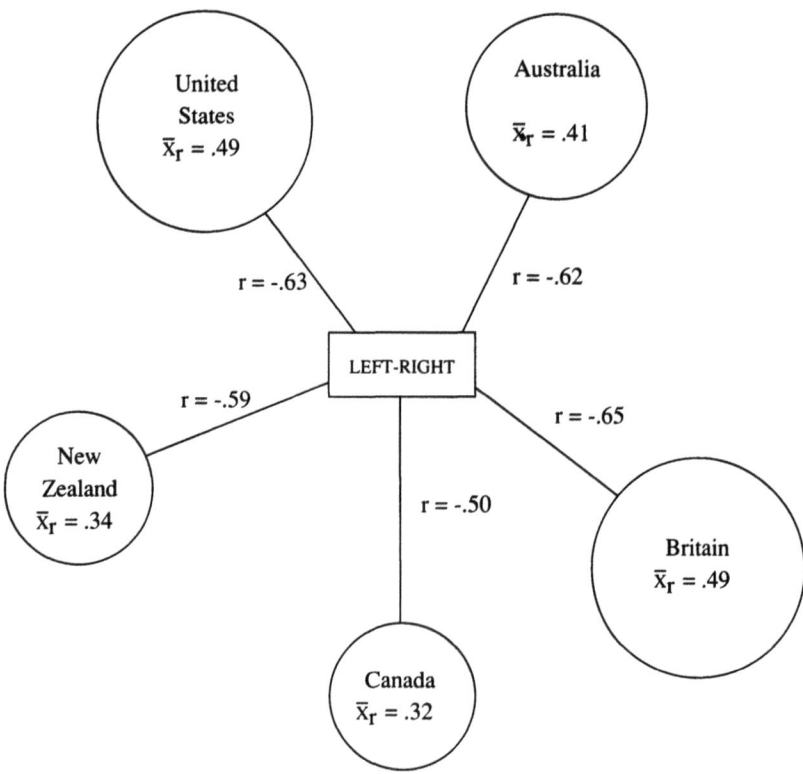

can be summarized in a few paragraphs. The table can be read both vertically (by columns) and horizontally (by rows). For example, take a close look at the second column from the left, the column for British respondents. By moving down this column, one can see how the British lefts and rights differ. Respondents on the British right are far more likely than those on the left to believe that people with more ability should earn more money, to oppose any limit on incomes, to believe that job hiring should be based strictly on merit, and to believe that important decisions should be left to management. In virtually every case, there is a very substantial gap between those on the left and those on the right. Note, for instance, that while a majority of those on the right agree that important decisions should be left to management, only one respondent in ten on the British left shares that opinion.

By moving across the rows in Table 5.2, it is possible to trace out the extent of national differences within the ideological camps of the left and

Table 5.2 Left-Right Differences in Orientations Towards Equality

		AUST.	BRIT.	CAN.	NZ	US
% agreeing that 'people with more ability should earn higher salaries'	Lefts	53.6	46.4	74.5	54.1	61.5
	Rights	90.5	93.3	93.8	89.6	96.5
% agreeing that 'there should be a law limiting the amount of money any individual is allowed to earn in a year'	Lefts	30.2	47.8	17.9	20.4	24.3
	Rights	3.8	8.7	9.3	3.3	6.8
% agreeing that, with respect to the hiring of women, 'job hiring should be based strictly on merit'	Lefts	52.0	53.4	73.1	23.5	44.6
	Rights	94.3	93.3	90.7	58.1	86.7
% believing that 'the important decisions should be left to management'	Lefts	7.5	10.3	21.1	8.6	17.2
	Rights	40.8	52.3	45.1	32.0	58.2

right. Note, for example, responses to the question regarding hiring policy. The table shows a great deal of agreement among the American, Australian, British, and Canadian rights; only the New Zealand rights stand apart in their relatively weak support for the merit principle. Among the lefts, both New Zealand and Canadian respondents stand apart; the former by the relative strength of their opposition to the merit principle, and the latter by their relative support for the same principle. To take a second example, Table 5.2 highlights how the British left stands apart with respect to support for laws limiting the amount of income earned by individuals. Overall, however, the table shows comparatively sharp differences between the left and right within each national sample, and relatively modest but by no means negligible cross-national differences between respondents identifying with the left and those identifying with the right.

National differences within the left and right are explored further in Figure 5.3, which compares the mean scores on the equality scale for fifteen ideological groupings derived from the left-right scale. Like previous figures of this type, Figure 5.3 identifies significant differences in paired sample means, in this case with reference to mean scores on the equality scale. The upper-left quadrant of the figure shows once again that there are no statistically significant national differences among the five 'rights'. Once you know that an individual depicts himself or herself as right-of-centre, knowing the individual's nationality provides no appreciable gain in predicting his or her score on the equality scale. Thus in this specific but important sense, the Australian right is indistinguishable from the British right, which in turn is indistinguishable from the Canadian right, and so forth. Here it is also interesting to note that respondents locating themselves on the mid-point of the left-right scale tend, on balance, to be closer to their respective national rights than to their respective national lefts in terms of their location on the equality scale. For example, American, Australian, and, with one exception, New Zealand mid-point respondents are statistically indistinguishable from right-of-centre respondents.

The situation on the left side of the ideological divide is only slightly more complex. As the lower right-hand quadrant of Figure 5.3 shows, left-of-centre respondents in the American, Australian, British, and New Zealand samples are indistinguishable from one another with respect to their mean scores on the equality index. However, respondents on the Canadian left, and only on the Canadian left, stand apart as a result of their relatively antagonistic stance towards equality. Moreover, respondents on the Canadian left do not only stand apart from their counterparts in the other four Anglo-American democracies; they are also statistically indistinguishable from respondents on the New Zealand right and from mid-point identifiers across the board. Yet with the exception of the Canadian left, Figure 5.3 presents a picture in which national differences fade almost to the point of invisibility. The mean scores on the right-hand border of Figure 5.3 demonstrate that ideological self-placement on the left-right scale has a dramatic impact on respondent orientations towards equality, whereas the boxed quadrants of the figure demonstrate that, apart from the Canadian left, national location is of hardly any relevance at all.

Figure 5.4 transforms the left-right discussion by examining the location of partisan groupings on the equality scale. In most important respects, Figure 5.4 replicates the earlier findings of Figure 5.3. The upper-left quadrant of the figure shows that supporters of the five conventionally labelled parties of the right cluster together, irrespective of nationality, and the lower-right quadrant shows that supporters of left-wing parties also cluster together, irrespective of nationality. In the latter case, however, respondents identifying with the British Labour party are an emphatic exception to the general rule; their extreme position on the equality scale places them apart from respondents identifying with the Labor parties of Australia and New Zealand, the Democratic party of the United States, and the New Democratic Party of Canada. Here it should also be noted that respondents identifying with the Canadian Liberal party are all but indistinguishable from respondents identifying with parties conventionally placed on the right, and that British Liberal-SDP respondents occupy a less ambiguous middle-of-the-road position.

Equality: Of Opportunity or Result? | 117

Liberal-SDP respondents stand apart from four of the five right-of-centre parties, including the British Conservative party, and from three of the five left-of-centre parties, including the British Labour party.

Figure 5.3: Comparison of Means of Left, Centre, and Right Identifiers on Equality Scale

NATIONAL LEFT-RIGHT IDENTIFIERS	1 2 3 4 5 6 7 8 9 10	EQUALITY SCALE MEAN SCORES
1. United States Right		5.5
2. Britain Right		5.9
3. Australia Right		6.2
4. Canada Right		6.2
5. United States Centre		7.0
6. New Zealand Right		8.1
7. Australia Centre		9.2
8. New Zealand Centre	*	9.8
9. Britain Centre	* * * *	10.5
10. Canada Centre	* * * * 11 12 13 14 15	10.6
11. Canada Left	* * * *	10.8
12. United States Left	* * * * * * * * * *	14.1
13. Australia Left	* * * * * * * * * *	15.1
14. New Zealand Left	* * * * * * * * * *	16.1
15. Britain Left	* * * * * * * * * *	16.2

* represents pairs of left-right identifiers with Equality Scale mean scores significantly different at $p < .05$

118 | New Elites in Old States

Figure 5.4: Comparison of Means of National Party Identifiers on Equality Scale

NATIONAL PARTY IDENTIFIERS		EQUALITY SCALE MEAN SCORES
1. United States Republican		5.5
2. Britain Conservative		6.1
3. Australia Liberal		6.6
4. Canada Conservative		7.1
5. New Zealand National		8.6
6. Canada Liberal	★	9.2
7. Britain Liberal-SDP	★ ★ ★ ★	10.5
8. Australia Labor	★ ★ ★ ★ ★ ★	12.8
9. Canada New Democrat	★ ★ ★ ★ ★ ★	13.0
10. New Zealand Labor	★ ★ ★ ★ ★ ★ ★	13.6
11. United States Democrat	★ ★ ★ ★ ★ ★ ★	13.8
12. Britain Labour	★ ★ ★ ★ ★ ★ ★ ★ ★ ★ ★	17.9

★ represents pairs of party identifiers with Equality Scale mean scores significantly different at p < .05

Finally, a comparison of mean scores in Figure 5.3 and 5.4 shows that respondents identifying with the British Labour party occupy a more extreme position on the equality scale than do respondents identifying with the British left. It is interesting to note, in fact, that the left-right scale in Figure 5.3 creates greater polarization than does the partisan alignment in Figure 5.4. In every case but one (US Republicans), partisan groups have a mean score closer to the overall mean than do their corresponding ideological groupings. For example, respondents identifying with the British Conservative party are closer to the population mean than are respondents identifying with the New Zealand left. Thus the partisan organization of political allegiance appears to blunt ideological cleavages within national samples of youth elites.

Figure 5.5 brings the partisan discussion to a close by simultaneously locating the twelve partisan groupings on the left-right and equality scales. In this figure, supporters of the British Labour party are the clear outliers, although they are set apart more by their mean score on the equality index than by their position on the left-right scale. The US Democrats, Canadian New Democrats, Australian Laborites, and New Zealand Laborites cluster together with respect to the equality index, but are spread apart by their relative location on the left-right scale. The Canadian Liberals and, to a lesser degree, identifiers with the British Liberal-SDP coalition, are set apart from the pack by their scores on both indices. Canadians Liberals, for example, stand clearly apart from the five left-of-centre parties with respect to the equality scale, and also stand clearly apart from the five right-of-centre parties with respect to the left-right scale. For their part, the five right-of-centre parties occupy a roughly equivalent but by no means identical ideological space in Figure 5.5.

Figure 5.5: Parties in Equality-Left/Right Space

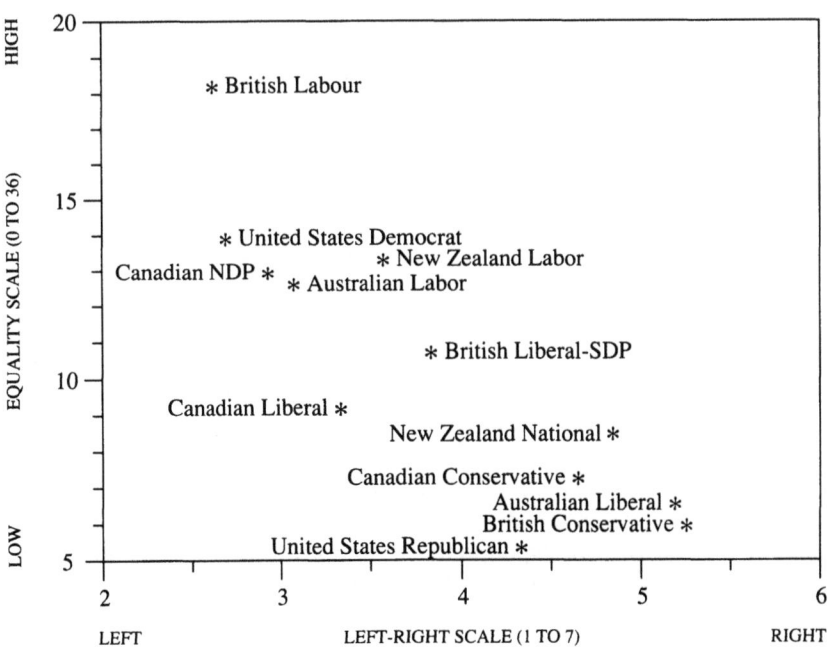

The Position of Equality in the Broader Ideological Firmament

The generally powerful relationship discussed above between the equality and left-right scales demonstrates that respondent orientations towards equality are linked to—and perhaps anchored in—more abstract ideological perspectives on the political world. The discussion now turns from the abstractions of the left-right scale to the linkages between the equality scale and the more specific political beliefs measured by the government, feminism, and minority scales. Our concern is to see how orientations towards equality are positioned with respect to the configuration of political beliefs described in preceding chapters. Conceptually, the analysis parallels that were encountered at the end of Chapter 4 when we examined the correlational linkages among the government, feminism, and minority scales. Diagrammatically, however, the situation becomes considerably more complex. As a consequence, this analysis begins with a detailed examination of the British case, and then examines the degree to which the other four national samples reflect, or at least correspond to, the British pattern.

Figure 5.6A presents, for British respondents, the correlations among the four attitudinal scales, and the correlation between each of the four and the left-right scale. As the reader will note, the diagrammatic presentation is considerably different from that utilized in the preceding chapters; the left-right scale has moved from the centre of the figure to form the outer shell. To appreciate this conceptual transformation, it is useful to consider a biological analogy. An organic cell has both an enclosing membrane and a nucleus composed of a number of protoplasmic elements that give the cell its definition, character, and role. Figure 5.6A is analogous to the organic cell; the left-right scale forms the enclosing membrane for the political belief system, a membrane that in turn encases a variety of more specific values, beliefs, and attitudes. The analogy is particularly appropriate given that the left-right scale, like the membrane of the cell, is content-free. Thus if we want to attach some policy content to the left-right scale—if we want to know, for example, whether self-placement on the scale shapes orientations towards gender politics—we must turn to the nucleus of the belief system, to the specific attitudinal scales that are correlated with the left-right scale. In Figure 5.6A and the following figures, the distance between any specific scale and the enclosing left-right 'membrane' is in inverse proportion to the strength of the correlation between the two scales; the stronger the correlation, the shorter the distance between the scale and the membrane.

Figure 5.6A summarizes a wealth of information, much of which has already been presented above in a more isolated fashion. The figure shows that for British respondents, all four attitudinal scales have strong negative correlations with the left-right scale. Although the correlational

Equality: Of Opportunity or Result? | 121

Figure 5.6A: Britain

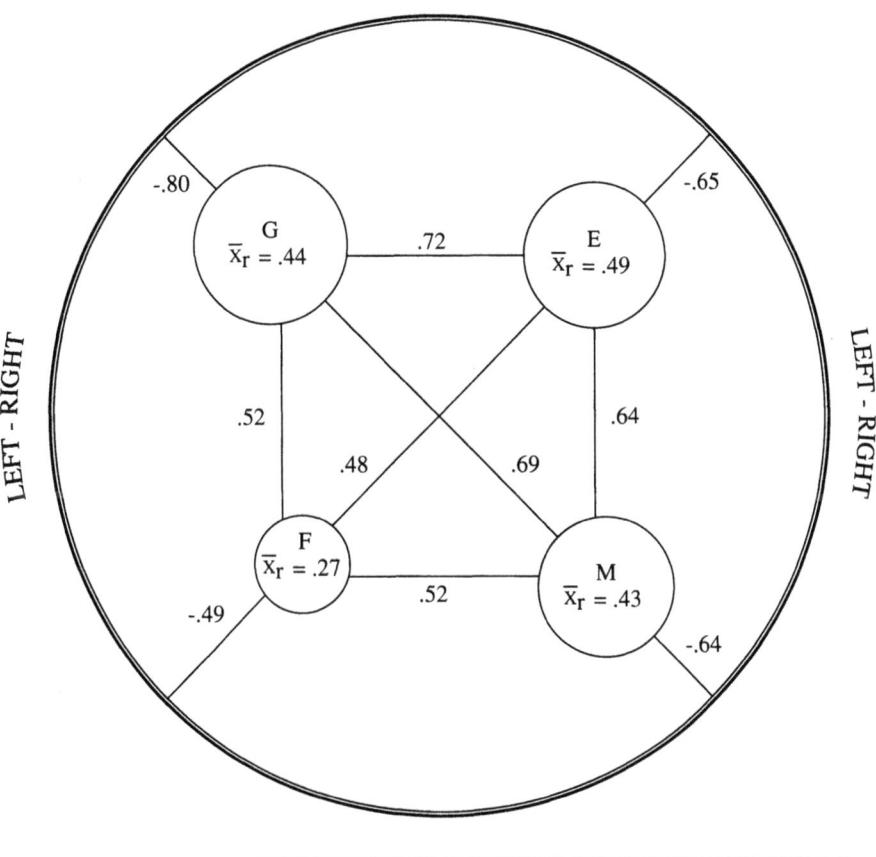

G = Government   E = Equality   F = Feminist   M = Minority

relationship is strongest in the case of the government scale, it is still robust even in the case of the feminism scale. Thus the location of respondents on the left-right scale provides a great deal of information about their views on government intervention in the economy, feminism, minority rights, and equality. Those views 'fill up' the left-right scale, transforming it from an abstract ideological perspective to a specific predictor of respondent perspectives across a wide range of political issues. This much, however, we already knew. The additional information in Figure 5.6A comes from the correlational linkages between the equality scale, on the one hand, and the feminism, government, and minority scales, on the other. Here the figure shows that for British respondents, orientations towards equality are strongly linked to respondent positions on the other three scales. Not surprisingly, respondents who support greater equality are also relatively strong supporters of feminism and minority rights. Perhaps of somewhat greater surprise is the very strong relationship between the equality and government scales. The relationship suggests that respondents who favour a greater degree of equality in the economic and social domains, see government intervention as the vehicle through which such equality can be attained. Conversely, respondents who support a reduction in government intervention are prepared to tolerate and perhaps even to welcome a greater degree of inequality as the consequence.

More generally, Figure 5.6A reveals a political belief system with a great deal of coherence and constraint. Both are first apparent *within* each of the four attitudinal scales; responses to the specific questions embedded within the four scales are strongly correlated with one another, although admittedly this is less so in the case of the feminism scale than for the other three scales. Second, both coherence and constraint are apparent in the correlational linkages between and among the four scales. Respondent views on minority rights are strongly tied to views on feminism, which in turn are tied to respondent positions on the government and equality scales. Even the weakest link in the chain—that between the equality and feminism scales—is still robust by conventional expectations for survey research. Third, both coherence and constraint are apparent in the linkages between each of the four scales and the enclosing left-right 'membrane'. The attitudinal domains encompassed by the four scales fit comfortably within the rubrics of left and right.

The question that can now be addressed is the extent to which the British pattern finds reflection in the other four Anglo-American democracies. For American and Australian respondents, the reflection is almost perfect, a finding that holds true for both the location of the equality scale and the more general ideological organization of political beliefs. As Figures 5.6B and 5.6C show, the location of the equality scale relative to the other three attitudinal scales is virtually identical in the American, Australian, and British samples. More generally, the *patterns* of political belief in the United States and Australia are also virtually identical to the British pattern. Remember, this does not imply that sample mean scores on any particular measure are identical across the three national samples. Thus, for example, the similarity of Figures 5.6A, 5.6B, and 5.6C should not suggest to the reader that, on average, American respondents have the same outlook on feminism as do respondents in Australia and Britain, for in fact this is not the case. However, the similarity of the three figures does show that there is a common *pattern* of political belief, that a number of specific components come together in an organized system of political belief that is all but identical for American, Australian, and British respondents. The differences that exist among the three figures are trivial at best. A close examination of any of the elements of the three figures, be it the relationship between specific attitudinal scales, the internal coherence of specific scales, or the linkages between specific scales and the left-right scale, shows that for these three sets of respondents, differences in nationality play no discernible role in the ideological organization of the political world.

Figure 5.6B: United States

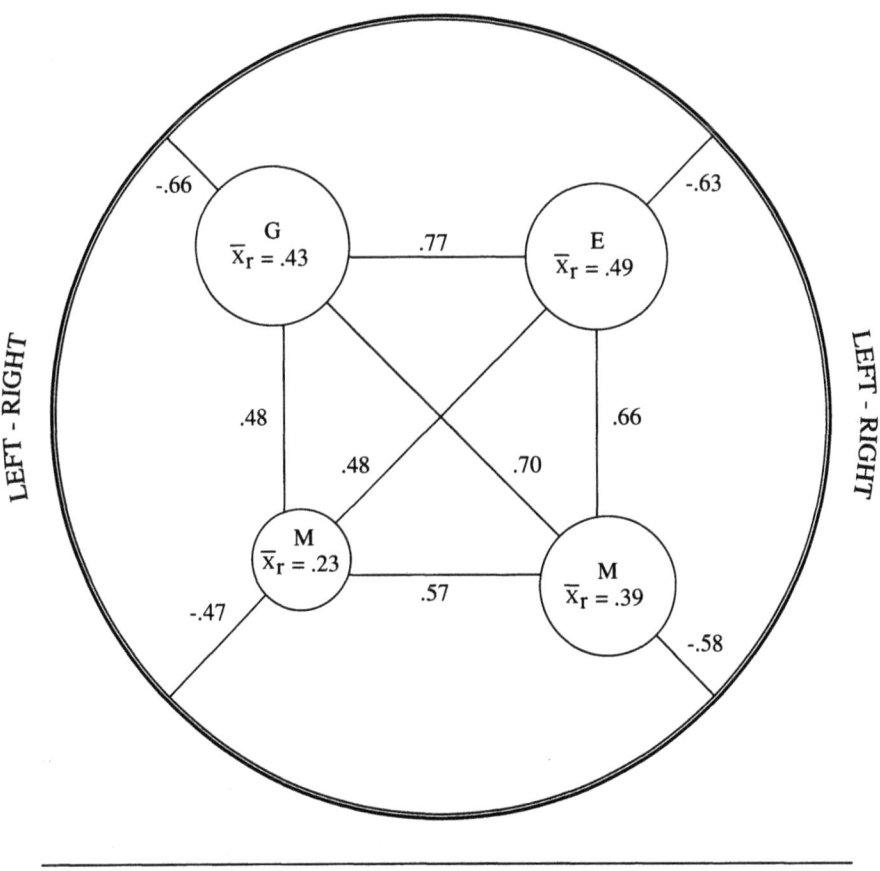

G = Government   E = Equality   F = Feminist   M = Minority

Figure 5.6C: Australia

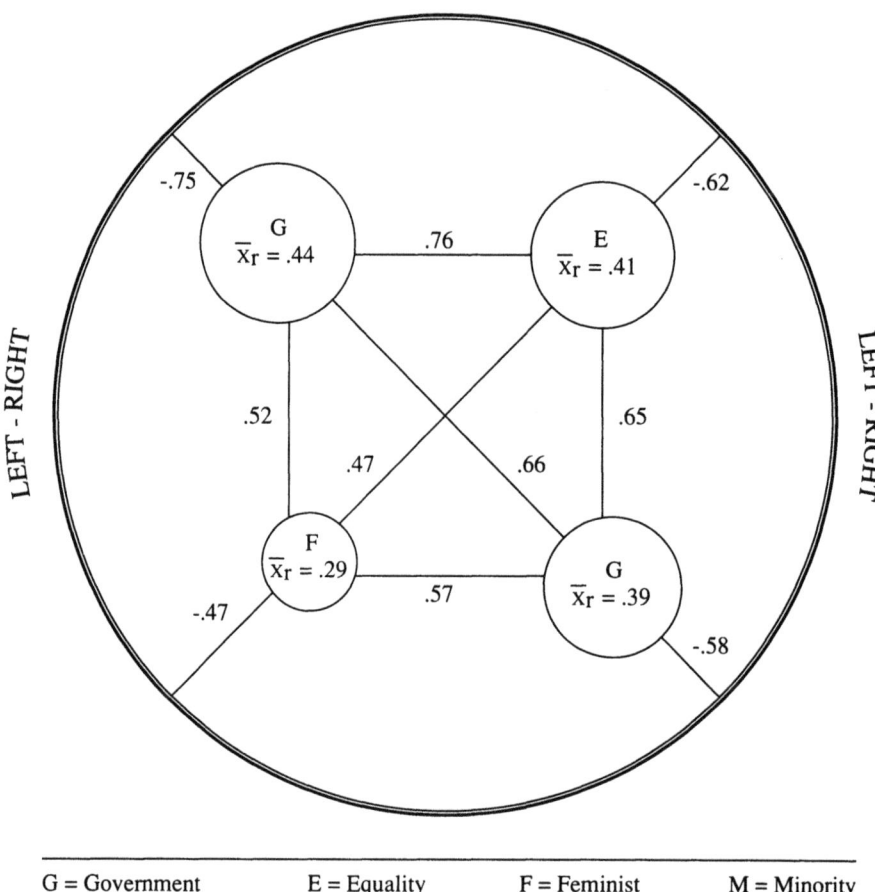

G = Government   E = Equality   F = Feminist   M = Minority

If we turn now to the case of New Zealand, Figure 5.6D shows that the British pattern is faithfully replicated in general design, but that the degree of internal coherence and constraint is significantly weaker. At the outset, the four attitudinal scales themselves display less internal coherence than is the case for American, Australian, and British respondents. Indeed, New Zealand respondents differ in this respect more than in any other. Partly as a consequence, the linkages among the four attitudinal scales are also weaker in the New Zealand case, although the difference is admittedly quite modest. Finally, the four attitudinal scales also have slightly weaker ties to the enclosing left-right scale or 'membrane'. Thus New Zealand respondents depart from the 'British' pattern primarily with respect to the robustness or internal rigour of their belief systems. However, in the general structure and design of their political belief systems, New Zealand respondents do not stand apart from their American, Australian, and British counterparts.

Figure 5.6D: New Zealand

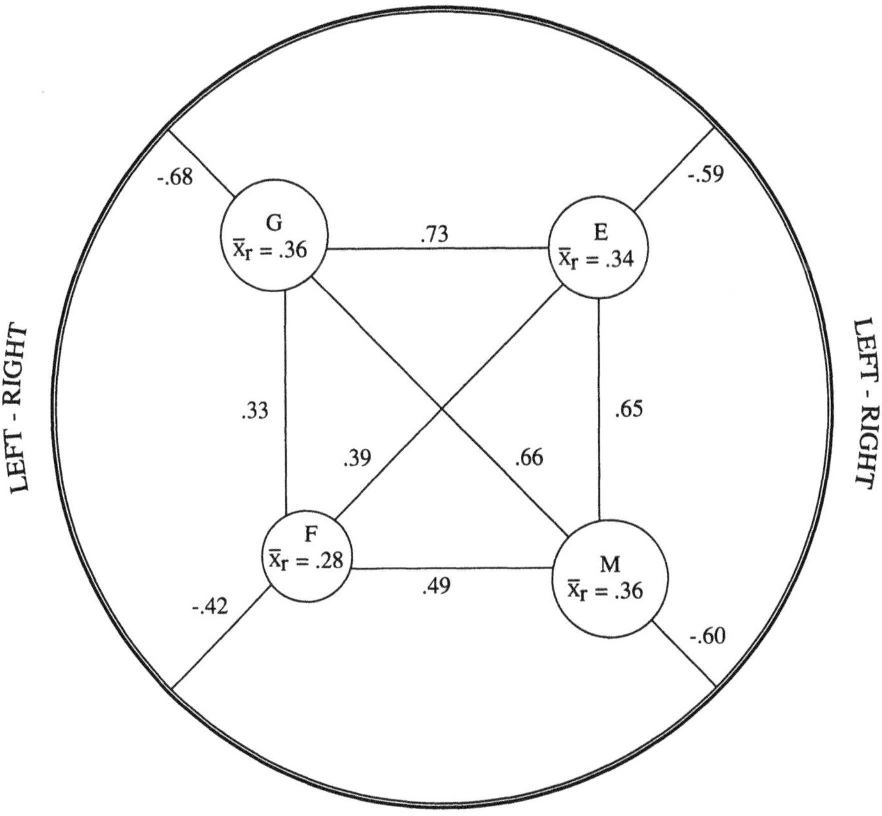

G = Government   E = Equality   F = Feminist   M = Minority

If we turn finally to the Canadian data, Figure 5.6E shows even greater departure from the internal coherency and constraint of the British results. The four attitudinal scales display even less internal coherence than we found in the case of New Zealand respondents. The correlations among the four attitudinal scales also diminish in strength, with an even greater decline evident in the correlations between each of the attitudinal scales and the left-right scale. Thus of the five sets of Anglo-American respondents, Canadians display the least ideological coherence and constraint in their political beliefs. Whether we direct our attention to specific attitudinal domains, as tapped by the various scales, or whether we direct our attention to the overall pattern among the five scales incorporated in Figure 5.6, Canadian respondents stand apart. If there is a clear case of exceptionalism in the data set, it emerges from the Canadian sample and not, as we might have initially expected, from the United States. There is indeed an 'Anglo-American' pattern of political belief and ideological organization, but one that leaves a relatively weak imprint on the Canadian political culture.

Figure 5.6E: Canada

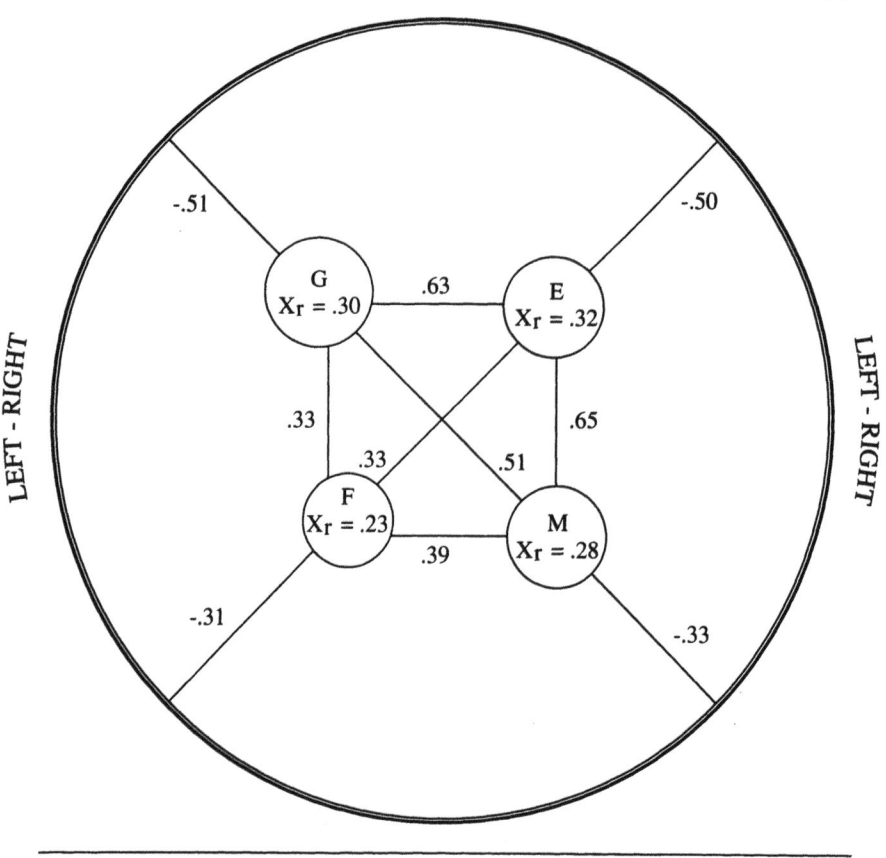

G = Government   E = Equality   F = Feminist   M = Minority

It is intriguing to note that the British pattern is most faithfully replicated in the two Anglo-American democracies where opposition in the popular culture to British norms and precedent is most vigorously asserted—Australia and the United States. In the two Anglo-American democracies where ties to Britain have been less contentious and less denied in the popular culture—Canada and New Zealand—there is considerably more discrepancy with respect to the British model. It is also interesting to note that a ready and conventional explanation for the Canadian departure from the British model is not supported by the data presented in this chapter. Before, one might have argued that Canadian exceptionalism springs from the proximity of Canada to the United States, that the very distinctive American political culture has slowly and inexorably dissolved those aspects of the Canadian political culture inherited from Britain. However, this argument becomes difficult to sustain given the virtually identical patterns of political belief among American and British respondents. At least in terms of our data set, to approximate the American pattern is also to approximate the British pattern. For similar reasons, it is difficult to argue that New Zealand respondents depart from the British model because of the ideological influence of neighbouring Australia. Such an argument would be much easier to sustain if there were any discernible differences between belief systems in Britain and Australia, differences that are not to be found in the data set under investigation here.

Conclusion

In drawing this discussion to a close, there is one further explanation for Canadian exceptionalism that should be pursued, albeit an explanation that offers no purchase on the more modest New Zealand departure from the British model. In some important respects, the Canadian political culture is a bi-national amalgam of British and French elements. Although the historic founding cultures of English and French Canada are of declining relevance in the contemporary world, the survival of a distinct society among the francophone population of Quebec, the Québécois, provides important social, institutional, and normative support for distinctive patterns of political culture. Could it be, then, that English Canadians are much closer to their compatriots in the other four Anglo-American democracies than the analysis to this point has suggested, and that Canadian exceptionalism can be accounted for by the existence of a distinctive French Canadian cultural element carried into the data set by francophone respondents?

Figure 5.7 offers some limited support for such speculation. In this figure, the analysis for all Canadian respondents contained in Figure 5.6E has been independently replicated for anglophone and francophone respondents. As Figure 5.7 shows, the isolation of the anglophone respondents does not result in any significant convergence with the British

Figure 5.7: English and French Canada

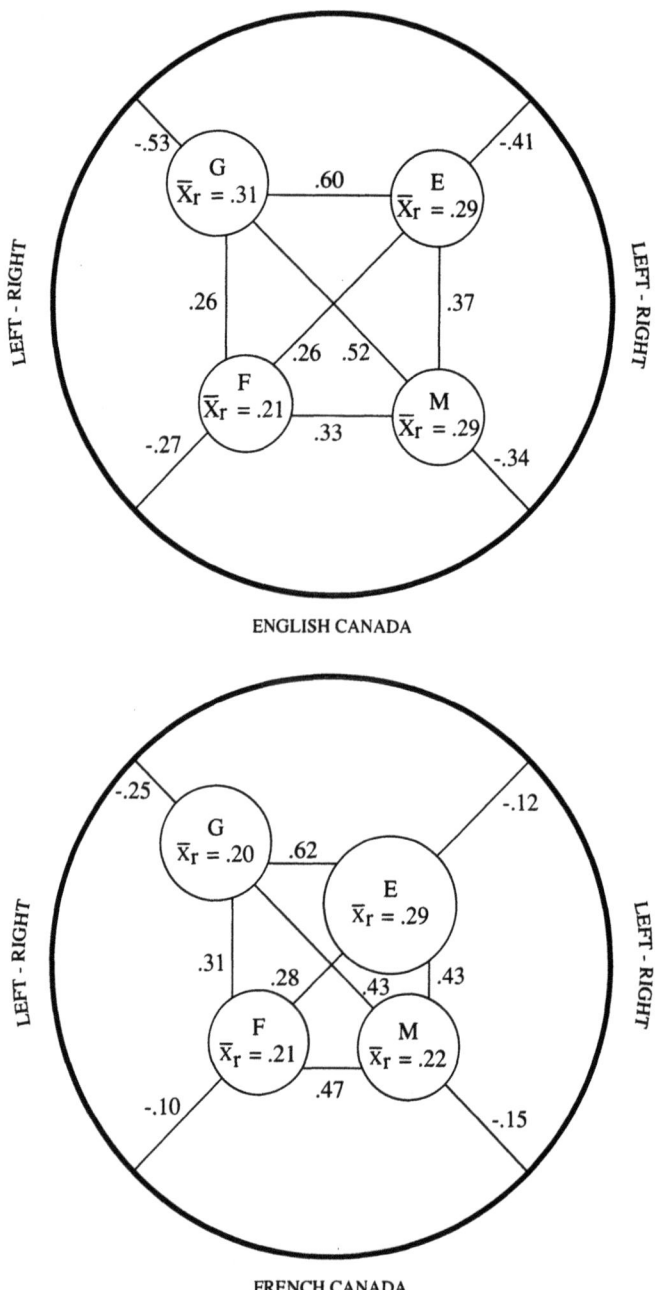

ENGLISH CANADA

FRENCH CANADA

G = Government   E = Equality   F = Feminist   M = Minority

model. By and large, anglophone Canadians look pretty much like all Canadian respondents; little if any movement towards the British norm can be detected. However, the isolation of francophone respondents reveals an interesting and indeed quite dramatic difference between the two sets of Canadian respondents. It is clear that the left-right scale, as a vehicle for ideological organization, has much less relevance for francophones than it has for anglophones. (It should also be noted that the internal coherency of the government scale is particularly weak for francophone respondents; it is this scale that is conceptually the closest to conventional depictions of left and right.) In fact, the analogy of the cell, in which the left-right scale provides an enclosing membrane for more specific attitudinal predispositions, breaks down for francophones. While francophone respondents draw basically the same linkages among the four attitudinal scales as do anglophones, those scales are not linked in turn to the left-right scale, as they are for anglophone Canadians. Thus it is with respect to the left-right scale that francophone Canadians truly stand apart, and it is in this respect that anglophone Canadians most clearly mimic the more general pattern of political belief in the Anglo-American democracies.

CHAPTER SIX

Ideology and Political Influence

Who Runs the Country?

We began the last chapter with the suggestion that views about equality may well provide a unifying theme for many of the findings that have emerged in the course of our analysis. The evidence presented in Chapter 5 adds weight to that interpretation. Orientations towards equality of opportunity/result clearly do structure the political world views of our respondents. Beliefs about equality of opportunity/result *are* connected to the other salient attitudinal structures we have identified—the government dimension, the gender dimension, and the minorities dimension, dimensions that also capture concerns about egalitarianism in one form or another. Furthermore, we have shown that each of the four dimensions structuring the political beliefs of our respondents are related, sometimes very powerfully, to self-placement on the left-right scale. To this point, though, our strategy has been to build, piece by piece, a picture of the internal structures of the ideological worlds of our respondents. In this chapter we climb outside of these structures to probe the issue of equality further. Our goal is to examine respondents' perceptions about the stratification of influence and about equality of influence. Two questions guide our analysis: How do youth elites believe influence is distributed in their societies? And, how would they prefer influence to be distributed?

In liberal democracies, the idea that individuals *should* have equal political rights is hardly challenged at all; it is fundamental to conceptions of democratic citizenship in all the Anglo-American states. As would be expected of this cluster of countries, there are broad similarities with respect to the configuration of political rights, their scope, and their content. The principle of 'one person, one vote', for example, underpins the right to participate, and in all instances universal suffrage is made meaningful because it is surrounded by a parcel of other protections such as the secret ballot, freedom of expression, and freedom of assembly. The right to vote is justified on a number of important normative grounds, not least of all because it gives concrete expression to the democratic ethos that in electoral matters all adult citizens should count the same. But voting has instrumental value as well. The opportunities to choose between representatives, to criticize, and to throw leaders out of office work together; they amount to a guarantee that citizens will have at least a minimum level of influence over governments. Voting, however, is but one aspect of influence. Indeed, it is not even clear that the occasional chance to vote is the most significant aspect of influence. Thus questions about 'who runs the country' have become the focus of casual debate as well as formal political analysis even though the struggle for universal suffrage in each of the Anglo-American democracies was settled more than half a century ago.

Speculations about 'who runs the country' raise fundamental questions about the discrepancies between the ideal of equality and the performance of liberal democracies, about the gap between formal rights and effective rights, and about the tension between the ethos of equality and evidence of systematic inequalities (Macpherson, 1977; Gutmann, 1980). Typically, those speculations do not revolve around voting or the influence of individuals; they focus on groups and the dynamics of influence in liberal democracies. At issue is the relative power of groups and how governments respond to pressures exerted by groups pursuing collective interests. If influence lies at the heart of political conflicts, if the battles for resources are determined by the distribution of influence, then groups are the gladiators and governments themselves increasingly have become the battlegrounds as states have assumed a larger role in society and the economy (Dahrendorf, 1959; Schattschneider, 1960; Miliband, 1969; Dahl, 1982).

Providing an unequivocal answer to the question 'Who runs the country?' is a tantalizing prospect, for it would undoubtedly tell us a great deal about the *real* workings of any political system. But nailing down such an answer has been a difficult business for a combination of reasons. First, the central ideas 'power' and 'influence'[1] are contested concepts. Political analysts working from a variety of perspectives employ very different assumptions about the precise dimensions of influence and how it works (Lukes, 1974). The differences between pluralists, elite theorists, political economists, and Marxists, for example, run deep on such crucial questions as: What forms does influence take? How is it expressed? And, what role does the state play? Consequently, sharply divergent views prevail about the extent to which, and how, public agendas are shaped by contests between groups (Bell, Edwards, and Wagner, 1969; Lindblom, 1977; Rae, 1977; Manley, 1983).

Second, and relatedly, analysts exploring influence have to grapple with the problem of measurement. Making empirical judgements about which groups have more influence and which have less implies that there is some agreed-upon standard against which influence can be measured. But there is no such standard. While many liberal societies have finely honed standards where such individual rights as voting are concerned—rights that bear on *individual* influence—they are virtually silent when it comes to matters of *group* influence. To be sure, placing limits upon financial contributions to election campaigns amounts to a ceiling, just as guaranteeing the electoral representation of minorities can be seen as a floor.[2] But these floors and ceilings are exceptions, not the rule, and they apply to the electoral domain, not to the broader field of play where the dynamics of group competition can decisively shape policy outcomes.

Third, values creep into debates about political influence. Attempts to answer the question 'Who runs the country?' cannot be easily disentangled from views about who *should* run the country. Indeed, there is every reason to believe that values about who should run the country represent yet another face of ideology (Form and Rytina, 1969; Hochschild, 1981). Thus the ideological divisions we have explored so far might well be reinterpreted as *stemming from*, or being *rooted in*, fundamental disagreements about the distribution of influence, about which groups have influence and which do not, about who should have more influence and who should have less. A preference for 'less government', for example, might be read as support for productive coalitions and a rejection of distributional (rent-seeking) coalitions. 'More government' generally plays into the hands of distributional coalitions, like unions, that aim to promote and secure such protections as a minimum wage, employment equity, and safety standards in the workplace. Similarly, support for 'feminism' or 'minorities' reflects a desire to give women and marginalized social groups more influence in society and the economy. On the other hand, those preferring 'less government' typically regard these goals as intrusive 'institutional rigidities'.

The size and role of government have been contentious issues in the equality debates during both the 1960s and the 1980s. In the 1960s, governments in all of the Anglo-American democracies pushed to raise economic floors and to expand an array of social and political rights. Group rights advanced as rights based on class, gender, and culture were promoted through the efforts of larger governments. In the United States, for example, Lyndon Johnson's Great Society programs aimed to achieve equality 'not just as a right and a theory but equality as a fact and a right' (Verba et al., 1979). Similar goals were pressed by Harold Wilson's Labour government and by like-minded governments in Australia, Canada, and New Zealand. In the 1980s, however, the pendulum swung the other way. Political leaders in all five countries wanted to reduce the role of government, to cut back on transfer payments, and to restore incentives to the economy. Publics were encouraged to be more resourceful, more self-reliant; citizens were invited to get on their collective bikes. Equality was still the theme, but it was equality for the individual that gained the upper hand. It was the form of equality that drew its inspiration from Fredrick Hayek, Irving Kristol, and Robert Nisbet, and not from the egalitarians of the 1960s, that gained ground (Steinfels, 1979). In the 1960s governments were the instrument for pursuing equality; in the 1980s they were the obstacle. Views about equality plainly are not fixed, and as

Daniel Bell (1972) suggests, the central problem of post-industrial society appears to be the redefinition of equality.

The role of governments is contentious because governments can and do shape the field of play. They can check the influence of some groups and set free the influence of others. The evidence to which we now turn explores two basic questions: How much equality of influence do respondents see between groups in society? How much equality of influence would they like to see? Or, to put the matter slightly differently, how much inequality of influence is acceptable? If influence lies at the heart of political conflicts about equality, and if debates about how influence is distributed cannot be neatly separated from beliefs about how influence *ought* to be distributed, then answers to such questions as 'who runs the country?' should reveal a great deal about the ideological similarities and differences among and between these Anglo-American youth elites and their lefts and their rights. But how to proceed?

Evaluating Influence

If we wanted to get a feel for how influence actually works in the Anglo-American democracies, it would be logical to start by sifting through the evidence that has accumulated from studies of power and influence in these five societies. Those findings could be scanned in a search for common themes and for exceptions. It is important to stress, though, that this is *not* our goal; we are not concerned with the conclusions that researchers have formed about influence on the basis of detailed investigations. Rather, our objective is to fathom the views of our respondents. We want to know how this particular generational cross-section of observers think influence is distributed and how they think it ought to be distributed in their societies. To that end, all respondents were asked the same battery of questions about influence (Figure 6.1).

Given the serious conceptual difficulties confronting empirical studies of influence, it is important to be clear about the logic of the approach followed here and to identify key methodological decisions explicitly. First, as can be seen from Figure 6.1, we explore attitudes about influence through the reputational approach, a strategy that calls for respondents to make judgements about the influence hierarchy. All approaches have limitations, and the adequacy of the reputational method has been questioned on the grounds that it measures only perceptions about influence; it does not measure influence itself. The relevant point to emphasize, though, is that the reputational approach is sufficient for our purposes because it taps precisely what we are interested in—*perceptions* about influence. We can only guess about the extent to which perceptions match reality, the extent to which they feed reality, and whether the judgements of our respondents really do reflect the *actual* influence hierarchies of their societies. We do not claim that our respondents' views about influence are entirely objective; we note only that the respondents are well-educated, likely well-informed and comparatively sophisticated observers whose judgements about the influence hierarchy were reached independently.

Figure 6.1 Measuring Influence

Question: We would like to know how much influence you think various groups *actually have* over [Australian, British, Canadian, New Zealand, American] life, and how much influence you think they *should have*. Here is a scale in which '7' represents 'very influential' and '1' represents 'very little influence'.

```
No
opinion    Very influential       In between        Very little influence
   |       L_____|_____J
   9              7                  4                        1
```

	ACTUAL INFLUENCE	INFLUENCE THEY SHOULD HAVE
Labour unions	_____	_____
Farm organizations	_____	_____
Business leaders	_____	_____
Media	_____	_____
Intellectuals	_____	_____
Banks	_____	_____
Consumer groups	_____	_____
Feminist groups	_____	_____
Leaders of minorities*	_____	_____
Political parties	_____	_____

*Aus: Aboriginal leaders   Brit: Leaders of minorities   Can: Leaders of minorities
New Zealand: Maori leaders   United States: Black leaders

Second, no single set of questions can expose the complexities of influence or reveal all of its nuances. But the issues of which questions to ask and how to ask them are particularly critical when dealing with slippery concepts like influence. We noted earlier that analysts disagree profoundly about the scope and dynamics of influence. But there is a large measure of agreement about a key conceptual issue that has important methodological implications: influence is *relational* and it comes into play in exchanges between actors. That being so, the influence that might be assigned to any one group necessarily is contingent upon which other groups are involved in the exchanges or are under consideration. From that perspective it is pointless to try to evaluate the influence of any one group in isolation. Figure 6.1 shows that our respondents were asked to rate the influence of ten groups. That list is far from exhaustive, of course, and choices had to be made, not least because there are practical limits to the number of items that respondents can reliably consider at the same time. The particular groups included in our battery of questions fall into three categories: (1) groups that traditionally represent the most powerful economic actors: land, labour, and capital—farming interests, trade unions, and businesses and banks; (2) 'mediating' groups (Verba and Orren, 1985)—political parties, intellectuals,[3] and the media; and (3) challenging groups (that is, those groups that recently have emerged to challenge the status quo)—consumers, feminists, and minorities. Because influence is relational, presentation is important. Respondents were simultaneously presented with the *entire* set of groups they were being asked to consider and the instructions made it clear at the outset that they were being asked to rate the actual and preferred influence of each and every group.

Third, and as with other aspects of the questionnaire, the cross-national comparability of the influence questions was another concern. Thus all the influence questions were asked in precisely the same way, the instructions were identical in each national study, and all questionnaires employed the same influence metric with the scale ranging from 'very influential' (7) to 'very little influence' (1). Furthermore, the groups were listed in exactly the same order and, with the single exception of the minorities item, which in some national settings was tailored to signify particular minorities,[4] all groups were identified in the same way. The uniformly strong completion rates across the entire battery of influence questions (Australia, 98 per cent; Britain, 98 per cent; Canada, 95 per cent; New Zealand, 97 per cent; and the United States, 96 per cent) suggest that few respondents had any difficulties either in following the instructions or in making judgements about where these groups should be placed on the influence scales.

Perceived and Preferred Influence

We start with the broad picture: How do respondents perceive the distribution of influence in their respective societies? Figure 6.2 presents a great deal of information, but we can wade our way through it if we track the positions of the same groups across the five columns. After repeating that procedure for each group we find that the common themes turn out to be far more striking than the national differences. Three are of particular note.

First, there is a remarkable degree of consensus about which groups are most influential. Respondents were not explicitly asked to rank order the groups but, for interpretive purposes, we can consider the *relative* placement of groups as a form of ranking. From that standpoint we can see that, without exception, media, business, political parties, unions, and banks rank at the top end of the influence scale in all five countries. Furthermore, within that cluster the media consistently rate as the most influential group of all.[5] From the perspective of traditional analyses of

136 | New Elites in Old States

Figure 6.2: Perceived Influence in Society

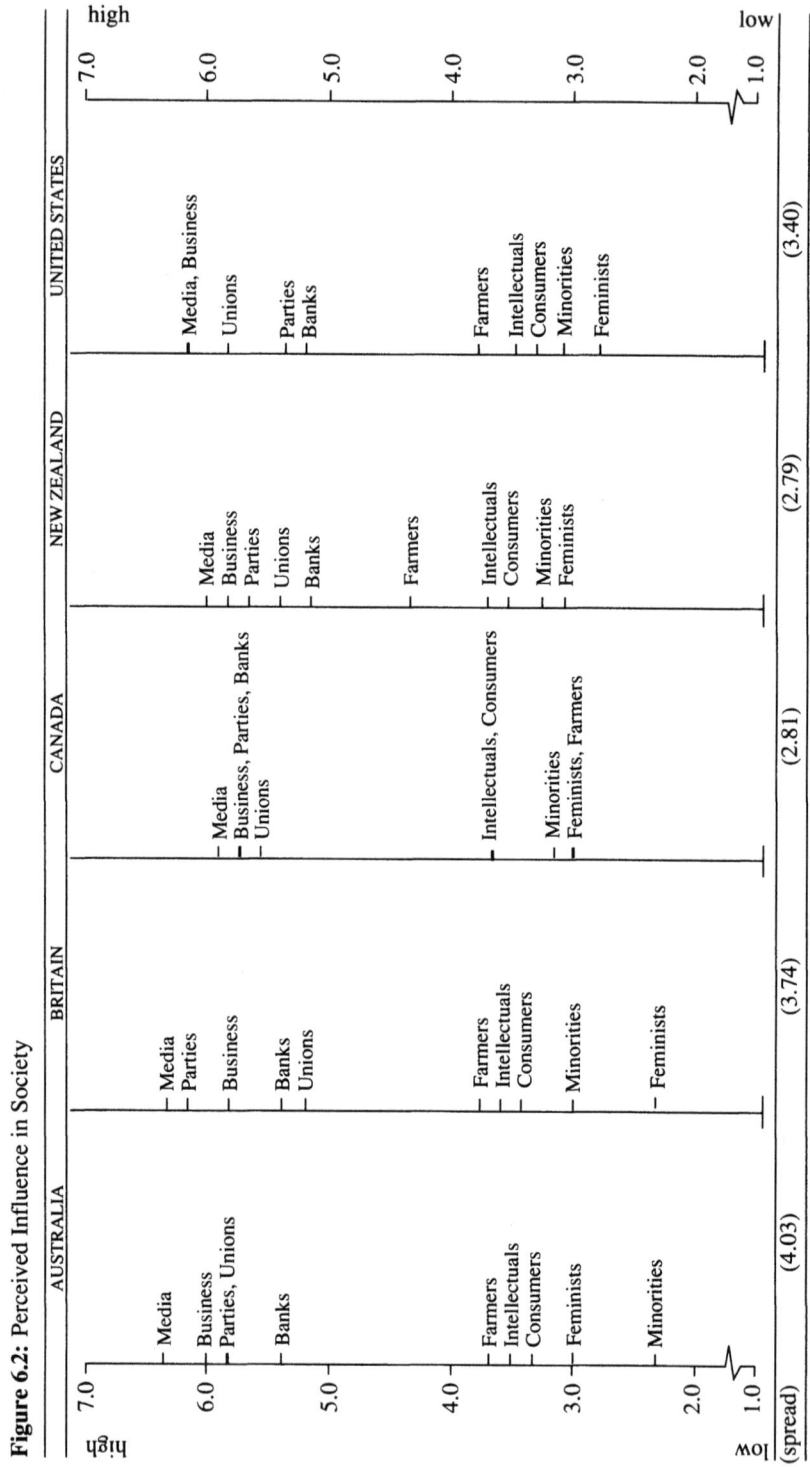

power, studies that dwell on the primacy of economic interests in liberal societies, that finding is somewhat surprising. But it is not isolated; recent studies probing the attitudes of mass publics in a variety of industrialized states have reported similar results (Verba et al., 1987), results that might be explained in terms of the information explosion that took place in the 1970s and 1980s. As Rothman (1979) has argued, recent technological changes have resulted in a sudden massive increase in the capacity to generate and exchange information. Those changes place a premium on the ability to manage, sort, and give order to a huge volume of information. In that sense, the media are strategically placed to make sense out of a seemingly increasingly complex world. There is considerable disagreement about who controls the media, whether it 'takes sides', and the extent to which it supports or undermines the status quo. Less contentious, though, and on this point our respondents seem to concur, is the media's *capacity* to be a gatekeeper, its *potential* to feed and shape public opinion, to put 'spin' on the public events of the day. Next to the media, business is typically rated as very influential, but after that national variations come into play.

The second noteworthy theme to emerge from these data has to do with youth elite perceptions about which groups fall to the bottom end of the influence hierarchy. The cross-national consensus about the five most influential groups necessarily means, of course, that there is also agreement about which five groups occupy the lower rungs of the influence ladder. There are striking cross-national similarities, however, with respect to *where* respondents place each of the remaining five groups. British, New Zealand, and American respondents all rank the bottom five groups in exactly the same order. Australians 'deviate' from that pattern only because they rate feminists above minorities and Canadians 'deviate' by placing farmers at the very bottom—along with feminists. In every national sample, youth elites consistently place minorities and feminists at the lowest rungs of the influence hierarchy.

It is reasonable to expect that gender will have a significant impact on how respondents rate the influence of feminists. After all, if there is one goal that links the various strands of feminism together, it is the common aim to advance the status of women. In that sense, feminism engages a gender-specific set of interests and if female respondents see themselves as disadvantaged *because* they are women, we would expect them to rate feminists lower than their male counterparts would. Surprisingly, however, when we probe the data further, no consistent gender pattern emerges. Male respondents rate feminists higher than their female counterparts in only two national settings—Canada and Australia—and even in these cases the differences are small. Modest national differences, however, are revealed; British males and females rate feminists lowest on the influence scale, slightly lower than American males and females.

The third broad theme to emerge from these comparisons relates to cross-national similarities in perceptions about the *distribution* of influence. We have noted congruence in the relative placements of the ten groups but there are also similarities in how those groups are spread across the influence scale. As would be expected, there are national differences in how much influence equality, or lack of it, respondents see in their societies. We can provide a rough measure of the perceived 'influence spread', or range, by subtracting the influence scores of the least influential group from the scores of the most influential group. By that calculation we find that Australian respondents (4.03) followed by Britons (3.74) report the greatest inequalities of influence. Americans come next (3.40), while New Zealanders (2.79) and Canadians (2.81) see the least inequality. Far more impressive than these national differences, however, are the cross-national similarities in how the ten groups are clustered. Figure 6.2 plainly indicates two broad clusterings: in every country, respondents see a substantial gap between the five groups clustered at the top of the scale and the five groups clustered at the bottom. That gap is widest in the Canadian case and narrowest for New Zealand; the significant point is that the gap never disappears—the clusters never meet or mingle.

The substantial cross-national consensus in perceptions about the distribution of influence is striking and intriguing. It is also open to a variety of interpretations. Even if we cautiously limit ourselves to the evidence at hand, these data unquestionably underscore broad similarities in the world views of these respondents. Not only do our youth elites organize their political beliefs in similar ways, as the previous chapters show, but there are also significant similarities in how they *see* their worlds, or at least those parts of their political worlds that have to do with the distribution of influence. It might also be argued that the similarities in perspectives are not 'merely ideological' but derive from and reflect the fundamentally similar structural conditions under which these respondents live. The reported distributions of influence, in other words, may indicate genuine similarities in the patterns of conflict that are generic to the dynamics of advanced industrial states (Goldthorpe, 1984). Thus labour and capital are viewed as powerful because they *are* powerful; the media are seen as more influential because they *became* strategically important as a result of the information explosion; and, similarly, minorities and feminists are accorded little influence because they *are* marginalized and have little influence.

That structural explanation, of course, has far-reaching implications. For example, it suggests that with the passage of time and sustained exposure to the similar dynamics of advanced industrialism, such national differences as Australia's radicalism, Canada's Toryism, or Britain's collectivism might well fade. But it is important to emphasize once again that we are reporting beliefs about the distribution of influence. And staying strictly within the bounds of our evidence, we can only speculate about the extent to which common structural conditions contribute to similar perspectives about the distribution of influence. At this juncture, however, it is also useful to recall that respondents were asked two sets of questions about influence, and that each set served quite different purposes.

In asking respondents to make judgements about the actual distribution of influence, the first set of questions invokes a constraint. Respondents are encouraged to describe the world as they see it, to set ideology aside and to report the evidence no matter how fuzzy that evidence might seem to be. The second set of questions relaxes that constraint; respondents are asked to express their preferences about the distribution of influence and to give free play to their ideals. Insofar as ideology entails a mental image, or blueprint, of the ideal distribution of influence, we would expect answers to the second set of questions to be particularly revealing of respondents' ideological world views. After all, respondents were not just presented with an opportunity to express their preferences about the distribution of influence; they were specifically invited to do so. The structural interpretation implies that responses to questions about the actual distribution of influence may be similar because the structural conditions of respondents' societies are similar. While the realities may well be similar, ideals can nonetheless be quite different. Thus we can look at the preferences about influence as a more likely place to find residues of the ideological differences between the five societies—Australia's hostility to privilege (Rosencrance, 1964), Britain's deference, Canada's Loyalist Tory ethos (McRae, 1964), and the egalitarian norms attributed to Americans and New Zealanders (Levine, 1980).

Figure 6.3 reports respondents' *preferences* about the distribution of influence, and a direct comparison of these data with the evidence presented in Figure 6.2 is instructive on a number of counts. First, looking at the spread of influence, we can observe substantial and consistent differences between how much inequality of influence respondents see between groups and how much they would like to see. Regardless of national setting, all would like to narrow the influence spread, and to achieve that they would curb the influence of the most powerful groups and promote the least influential ones. In one sense, to learn that our respondents would like greater equality between groups is not much of a discovery. They would probably like less crime, famine, and pollution as well, and prefer more peace and good will on earth. The findings presented in Figure 6.3 become more interesting, though, when we turn the issue around. These respondents are citizens of democracies that pay considerable lip-service to the idea of equality and they are being asked about what they would *like* to see. We could ask why, in a preferred world, these respondents would not like to see even *more* equality? Or, to take the point to its logical extreme, why would they tolerate any inequality at all?

140 | New Elites in Old States

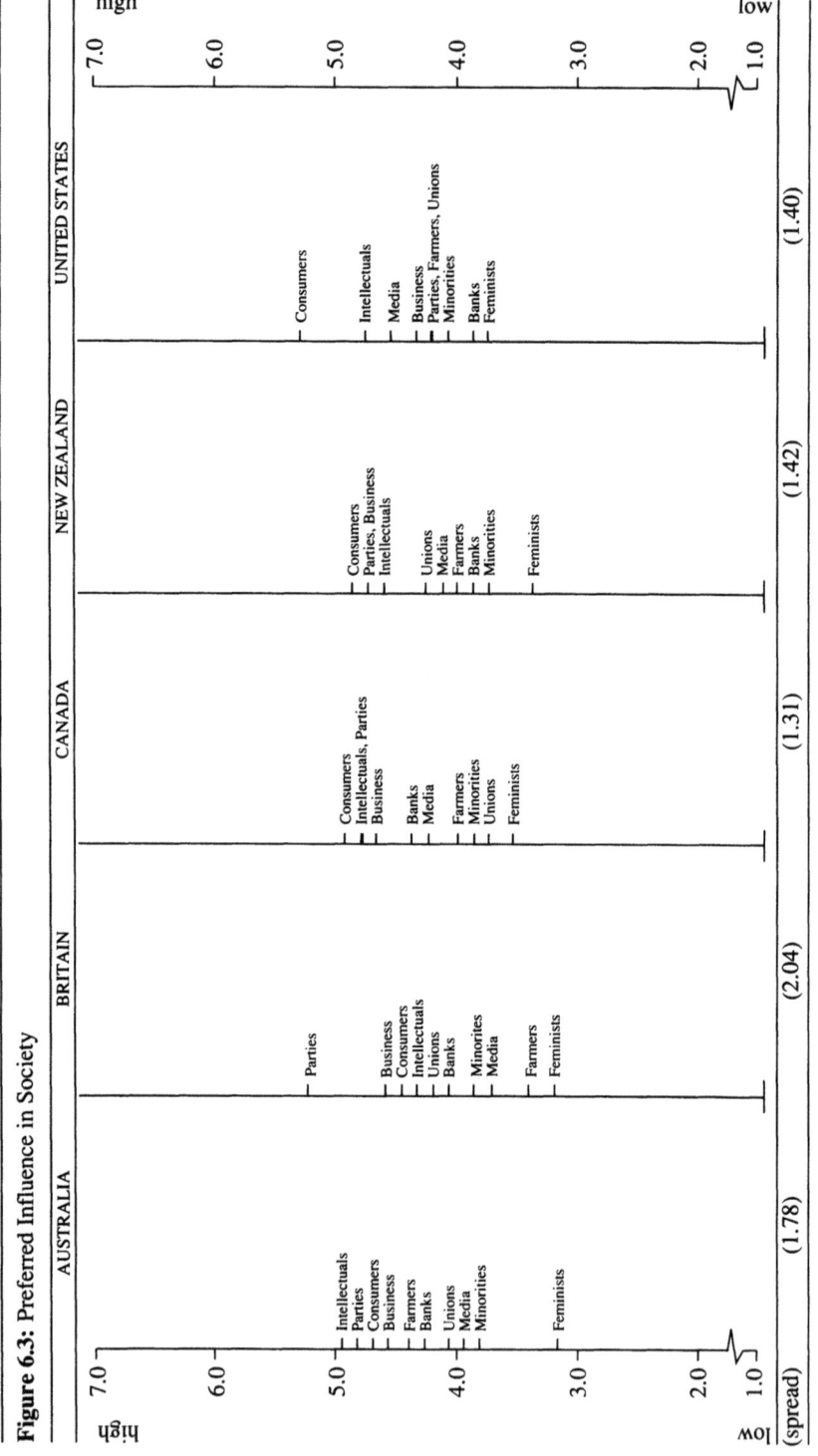

Figure 6.3: Preferred Influence in Society

Clearly, there *are* significant national differences in preferences about group equality. British respondents prefer the most inequality—a spread of 2.04 points across the influence scale (1.63 when parties are excepted) and Australians come next (1.78). By this measure, Canadians are most egalitarian (1.31) and they are followed by Americans (1.40) and New Zealanders (1.42). If these data are indicative of broader attitudes about equality, they provide little indication of Canadian elitism, Australian hostility to privilege,[6] or the collapse of deference in Britain. Indeed, the opposite cases might well be made.

Second, a closer comparison of Figures 6.2 and 6.3 shows that respondents do not just want to flatten the influence hierarchy; they also want a *different* hierarchy. To accomplish that, respondents shuffle the orderings of groups; some groups are demoted and others promoted. The most obvious 'casualties' of that reshuffling are the media; their drop down the influence ladder is the most precipitous, though the extent to which they are demoted varies somewhat according to national setting. Banks are another casualty, but again national variations are evident; their drop down the influence ladder in the Canadian case, for example, is relatively minor. Which groups are promoted? Again we can see cross-national uniformities. Two groups are the principle beneficiaries of the shuffle—consumers and intellectuals emerge from the bottom cluster of the perceived hierarchy (Figure 6.2) to join the top ranks. Indeed, consumers do particularly well; they rise to the very top of the preferred hierarchy in Canada and New Zealand, and even more decisively so in the United States.

In addition to promotions and demotions, there are also patterns of *stability*. Political parties and business hover close to the top of the perceived-influence hierarchy and Figure 6.3 shows that respondents want to keep it that way, though, as we noted before, the top is pegged lower on the preferred-influence scale. A comparison of the placement of feminists and minorities on the perceived- and preferred-influence scales indicates stability at the bottom end of the influence scales as well. In absolute terms, respondents would like to give both groups more influence but, relative to other groups, feminists remain firmly lodged at the bottom of the influence ladder. Minorities fare slightly better. Even so, it is clear that these groups make only modest gains. At best, both still face substantial challenges.

We could go into considerable detail tracking the fortunes of each and every group. We are primarily concerned, however, with the broad cross-national themes and with what those themes might tell us about the similarities and differences between the ideological worlds of our youth elites. Unquestionably, one powerful theme that emerges from these data has to do with the differences between the perceived and preferred influence spreads. Respondents in every national setting want greater parity of influence, and that finding is brought into sharp relief by comparing Figures 6.2 and 6.3. Another theme relates to cross-national similarities in the membership of the top ranks of the preferred-influence hierarchy. Typically, respondents want intellectuals, political parties, consumers, and business to occupy the upper strata; at least they do in all national settings except one—the United States. In that instance political parties rate lower—alongside farmers and unions—and that finding might be explained in institutional terms. Unlike the other four countries, the United States has no tradition of responsible government; it lacks the British-style parliamentary framework that gives greater prominence to parties in the political process. We could speculate that under these circumstances, the media may play a more vital role as political critics. In any event, American respondents certainly have fewer qualms about the role of the media.

A third trend evident in these data concerns the consistently low ratings assigned feminists and minorities on both of the influence scales. That theme is particularly intriguing, and perhaps surprising, in the light of earlier findings. It certainly merits further exploration. We know that these respondents are far from indifferent when it comes to issues that have to do with the status of women and minorities. Chapter 2 clearly demonstrated that attitudes about gender and minorities form two significant cleavages that systematically structure the political belief systems of these respondents. It is reasonable to suppose that preferences about the influence of feminists and minorities would be linked to broader concerns about the status of these two groups. And when we examine our data further, we find that they are. The more sympathetic respondents are to women's issues, the more influence they think feminists should have. The correlations are strong and operate in the predicted direction in *every* national setting (Australia, $r = .56$; Britain, $r = .58$; Canada, $r = .39$; New Zealand, $r = .51$; United States, $r = .52$). The same holds for the correlations between concern for minority issues and preferences about the influence that minority leaders should have (Australia, $r = .58$; Britain, $r = .51$; Canada, $r = .44$; New Zealand, $r = .56$; United States, $r = .56$). Attitudes about how much influence these groups should have, then, are tightly interwoven with those ideological axes that structure the broader political belief systems.

In Chapter 3 we examined the impact of gender on respondents' attitudes toward a broad array of women's issues. We found that in *every* national setting, women and men differed systematically and predictably in perspectives about the status of women. Now, if gender shapes attitudes towards women's issues, and if those orientations in turn are related to respondents' preferences about the influence of feminists, we have good reasons to expect to find gender differences in respondents' preferences about the influence of feminists. Figure 6.4 displays cross-nationally the impact of gender on both the perceived- and preferred-influence ratings of feminists.

Figure 6.4: Gender Differences in the Perceived and Preferred Influence Ratings of Feminists

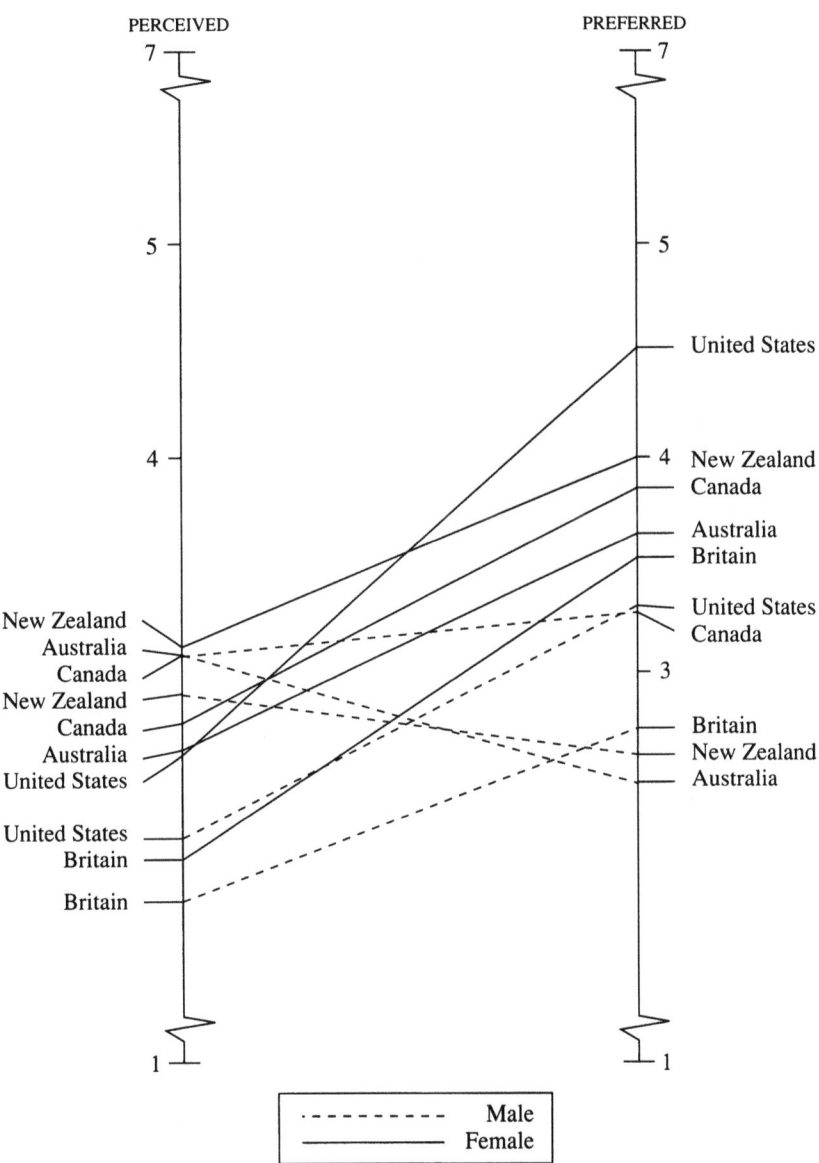

Figure 6.4 indicates no clear gender pattern in respondents' perceptions about the influence of feminists. If anything, traces of national differences can be found. American and British respondents, both male and female,

place feminists at the low end of the scale and New Zealanders put them at the high end. When we turn to consider *preferences*, however, gender differences come into sharp focus. Indeed, the gender differences could hardly be more dramatic. Regardless of national setting, *all* females want feminists to have more influence than male respondents do. All females want to give feminists substantial promotions up the influence hierarchy. Male respondents are far more equivocal on that score. In fact, Australian and New Zealand males would actually demote them. The gap between North American males and their counterparts in Australia, Britain, and New Zealand, moreover, is very wide. Even so, the systematic gender differences are far more remarkable than the national variations. These findings shed additional light on the question of why feminists fare so poorly on the preferred-influence scale (Figure 6.3). In a nutshell, one reason appears to be that male respondents prefer it that way. But what about the case of minorities?

As with the feminist case, we have grounds for speculating that gender may come into play where respondents' preferences about the influence of minorities are concerned. The evidence is more circumstantial and the reasoning more circuitous, but we know that attitudes towards women's issues are linked to concerns about minorities (Chapter 4). In all five Anglo-American democracies, respondents who are sympathetic to women's issues also tend to support minority causes. At a general level, of course, that finding is not very surprising, for historically women have been regarded as a minority, and women and other minorities found common cause on a number of broad policy fronts. Both stood at the margins of society, the economy, and the polity. Both gained protections from an expanding state and both fear, perhaps, that they stand to lose should the enthusiasts for smaller government win the day. A more detailed analysis of our data reveals that in all national settings, respondents' preferences about the influence of feminists *are* positively correlated with their preferences about the influence of minorities, and the correlations are robust.[7]

Figure 6.5 reports perceptions and preferences about minority influence and, as before, the data are broken down by both gender and nationality. The clarity and consistency of the patterns evident in these data are very impressive indeed. With respect to perceptions about minority influence, *national* patterns prevail and they show through much more powerfully than was the case for feminists (Figure 6.4). Male and female co-nationals agree about where minorities stand in the influence hierarchy in all countries except one—Canada. These national patterns, however, must be interpreted cautiously. They may signify national differences in generalized beliefs about minorities; they may reflect genuine national differences in the status of minorities—differences in size, composition, and circumstances; or they may just represent 'noise' resulting from

Ideology and Political Influence | 145

Figure 6.5: Gender Differences in the Perceived and Preferred Influence Ratings of Minorities

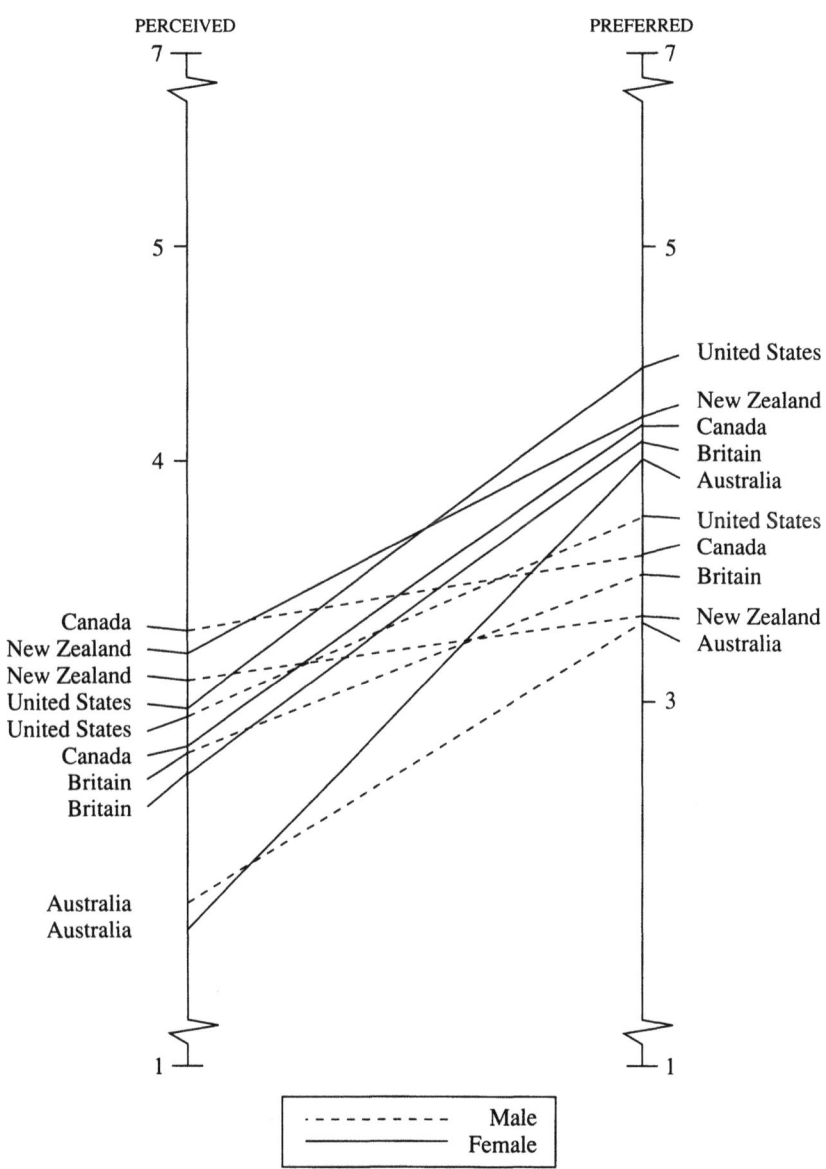

national differences in the survey instrument.[8] Regardless of the reasoning, the national consistencies here are striking.

A very different picture emerges, however, when we turn to consider *preferences* about minority influence. National patterns fade and gender differences take over; the transformation is surprisingly clear. Irrespective of national setting, *all* female respondents place minorities higher on the preferred influence scale than any sample of male respondents. The midpoint on the influence scale (4) operates as a clean gender divide; all female respondents want to place minorities above the mid-point and all males want them below it. These findings are reminiscent of the case of feminists, and when we compare Figures 6.4 and 6.5 we can see that respondent subgroups rate feminists and minorities on the preferred-influence scales in almost precisely the same way. Thus American females want *both* groups highest, and New Zealand females come next. The only exception to this pattern occurs at the middle of the order, where British and Australian switch positions. The rest are exactly the same. The preferred minority ratings, then, essentially amount to a foreshortened version of the preferred feminist rankings. In other words, there is more consensus about where minorities should be on the influence scale; gender produces deeper disagreements on the matter of how much influence feminists should have.

We could delve into these data in even greater detail and point out, for example, that all respondents except American women want to rate minorities above feminists. But the central point is established well enough. National preferences about the preferred influence ratings of *both* feminists and minorities (Figure 6.3) *do* mask systematic gender differences, and the gender divide is both consistent and clear.[9]

Equality of Influence: Left and Right

To this point we have explored beliefs about the influence hierarchy with pooled national samples, and the focus therefore has been upon broad national comparisons. But if competing beliefs about who runs the country and who *should* run the country reflect another face of ideology, then ideological differences should come into view when we decompose the data, when we look at the beliefs about the influence hierarchy from the standpoints of the five national lefts and rights. First and foremost, that analysis will provide us with another vantage point from which we can compare the five national lefts and rights. At the same time, it also presents the opportunity to examine cross-nationally attitudes about social change.

Theories about the origins and dynamics of social change abound. One suggestive explanation places particular emphasis upon the importance of cognitive dissonance, the idea that demands for social change spring from significant discrepancies between how individuals view the world in which they live, and the kind of world in which they want to live. According to this line of reasoning, the larger the gap between the perceived and preferred social, economic, and political realities, the greater the desire for social change. A preference for social change is meaningless in the abstract, and in this instance we shall only be able to explore the potential for change with respect to attitudes about the distributions of influence between the ten groups included in our analysis. But if these ten groups are important gladiators in battles about influence, those comparisons may not be inconsequential. Furthermore, we note that scholars routinely link the ideological categories 'left' and 'right' to preferences about change. For instance, it has been suggested that 'left' usually means advocating social change in the direction of greater equality—political, economic, and social—and 'right' typically means supporting a traditional, more or less hierarchical society, and opposing change toward greater equality (Lipset et al., 1954). By comparing the five national lefts and rights, and by examining the scope and direction of the changes they prefer, we shall also be able to provide a rough test of those speculations.

Figure 6.6 highlights the discrepancies between perceptions and preferences by simultaneously presenting how left identifiers in the five national settings think influence *is* distributed and how they think it *ought* to be distributed. Figure 6.7 reports the same evidence for the five national rights and as before, it is revealing to consider these data together. Before we turn to focus on the five rights or lefts, we note that ideological location does appear to have some bearing upon perceptions of the actual ('is') distribution of influence. Thus, for example, when we consider the 'is' columns for the Australian right and left (Figure 6.4), it is clear that left-identifiers see more inequality of influence between groups than do their right-identifying counterparts. And repeating these comparisons for the British, Canadian, New Zealand, and American samples produces the very same results. In some national settings the differences in the influence spread are substantial, while in others they are more modest.[10] But the differences consistently work in the same direction; all national lefts see a wider influence hierarchy than their co-nationals on the right. Those same comparisons also show that the national lefts and rights broadly agree that there is an influence gap. Moreover, as in Figure 6.2, there is a consensus about which five groups are most influential and which are the least. On the matter of *relative* rankings, the major difference between the left and right perceptions about influence ratings is quite predictable. All national lefts rate business above unions, and all national rights see unions as more powerful than business.

Together, Figures 6.6 and 6.7 present a great deal of data, but when we step back from the details we can highlight a number of common trends. First, when we compare the influence spread of the 'is' and 'ought' columns it is plain that no ideological subgroup is entirely satisfied with what it believes to be the status quo. In all national settings both the lefts and rights want to flatten the influence hierarchy. The two groups consistently differ, however, along two dimensions: over (1) the *extent* to which they would flatten the influence hierarchy and (2) *how*, given their

148 | New Elites in Old States

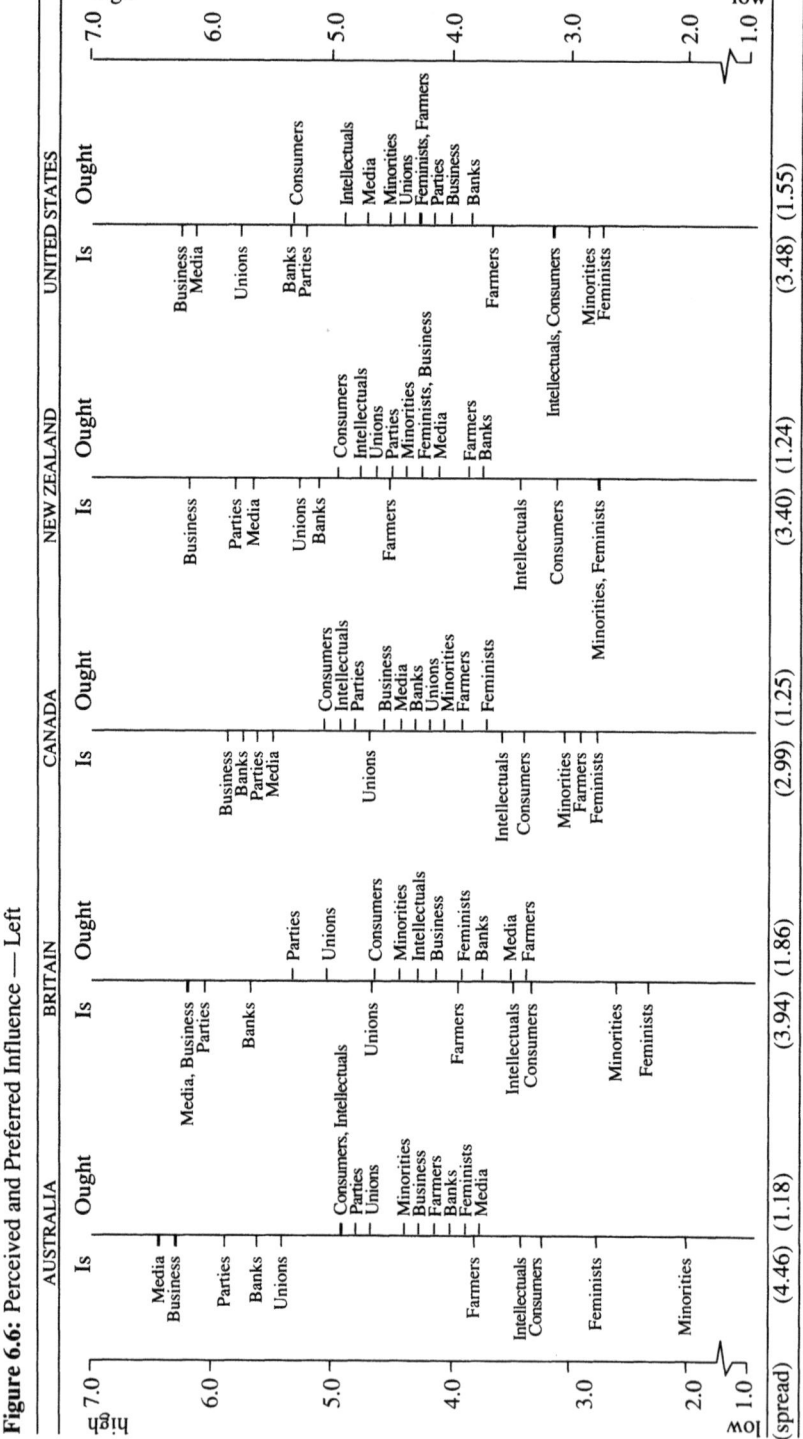

Figure 6.6: Perceived and Preferred Influence — Left

Ideology and Political Influence | 149

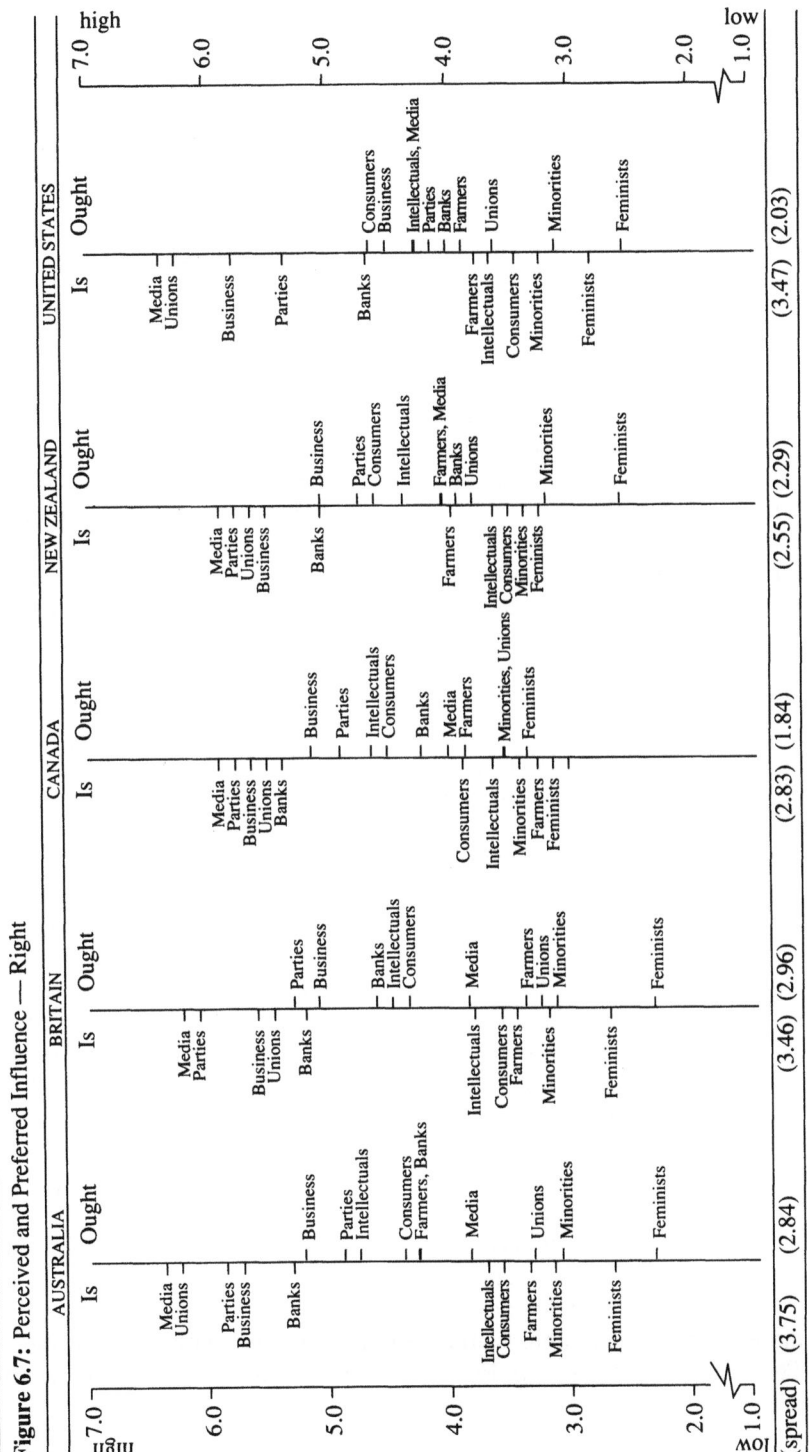

Figure 6.7: Perceived and Preferred Influence — Right

choice, they would go about reordering those hierarchies. The national lefts (Figure 6.6) want less of an influence hierarchy than their counterpart rights (Figure 6.7) and *all* lefts and *all* rights would reduce the influence of those groups perceived to be most powerful. When we turn our attention to the bottom of the influence hierarchy, however, sharp differences between the lefts and rights appear. While all lefts want to promote the least influential groups, the rights do not. With the single exception of Canadian respondents, the rights would like the least powerful groups, minorities and feminists, to have even *less* influence than they appear to have.

Second, these data provide clear support for speculation that the lefts are more egalitarian than the rights. There are, of course, national variations regarding how much equality of influence the ideological subgroups would like to see. As the summary scores at the bottom of the 'is' columns (Figure 6.6) indicate, the Australian left (1.18) is the most egalitarian, followed by the New Zealand (1.24) and Canadian (1.25) lefts. The British left prefers the greatest inequality of influence (1.86) and the American left (1.55) occupies the middle ground. Not surprisingly, there are also national differences between the five rights (Figure 6.5). In rank order, the British right is more inclined towards greater hierarchy (2.96) than are the others (Australia, 2.84; New Zealand, 2.29; United States, 2.03) with the Canadian right (1.84) emerging as the least tolerant of influence inequalities. Both sets of findings suggest that, at least in the British case, national setting is of some importance, for the British left and right are less egalitarian than are their counterpart subgroups in any of the other countries. Indeed, the British left prefers a greater influence hierarchy than the Canadian right!

Left and right, then, clearly are useful indicators of beliefs about the influence spread. But what does left-right self-location tell us about the kind of influence hierarchy respondents would like to see? A comparison of the 'ought' columns in Figures 6.6 and 6.7 provides evidence of some significant differences between the lefts and rights, but then there are similarities as well. All national lefts and rights, for example, prefer to rate consumers, intellectuals, and political parties relatively high on the influence scale. The British left and right both rank parties at the top, and in the American sample, left and right want consumers to have most influence. We can provide a much clearer illustration of the preferences of the five national lefts and rights by isolating four groups for special attention—unions, business, feminists, and minorities.

Unions and business have been the chief gladiators for labour and capital in the epic struggles that have shaped the political landscapes of most Western liberal democracies. Thus we would expect our lefts to be more sympathetic to unions and the rights more sympathetic to business. The evidence presented in Figure 6.8 clearly shows that they are. There are some cross-national inconsistencies in how the lefts and rights perceive the influence of unions, but those inconsistencies evaporate when we look at the preferred influence hierarchy. In every national setting, the lefts consistently place unions higher than their co-national rights on the preferred-influence scale. The rights, in turn, are relatively hostile to unions. We also note that there are significant national variations over the extent to which national lefts and rights are polarized. British respondents are very deeply divided on the matter of how much influence unions should have. The British left, though, is unique; it is the *only national left that wants to promote unions in the influence hierarchy*—a characteristic that is reminiscent of the old left. Conversely, the British right is the most 'anti-union' of all. The Australian lefts and rights hold similar, though less extreme, positions.

Left-right beliefs about business follow a similar predictable pattern; *all* national lefts and rights think business wields more influence than it should and all would demote them. As was the case with unions, what the lefts and rights disagree about is how far business should be pushed down the influence ladder. We could speculate that left-right beliefs about business would present us with the reverse image of left-right attitudes about unions. Significantly, however, the data suggest otherwise. The question of how much influence unions should have is far more contentious than preferences about business; the lefts and rights are spread further apart across the preferred-influence scale in the case of unions.

Figure 6.9 presents the results of a similar analysis for the groups lodged at the bottom of the influence hierarchy—feminists and minorities. In Chapters 3 and 4 we explored how orientations towards women and minorities were connected to broader attitude structures, and we demonstrated that location on the left-right scale worked as a reasonably strong predictor of orientations towards these groups.[11] The evidence presented here amplifies those findings. The cross-national consistencies, again, are striking, particularly so for the lefts. All lefts want to promote feminists and minorities; there is broad agreement about where they would like to place them; and the ordering within the lefts is identical. The New Zealand left is most sympathetic to *both* feminists and minorities, the American left is next for *both* minorities and feminists and so on. By contrast, the rights would leave feminists and minorities at the bottom of the influence hierarchy. All except the Canadian right would demote feminists, and the New Zealand and British rights would demote minorities as well. The differences between the lefts and the rights, then, come into bold relief when we consider the status of feminists and minorities.

Our examination of the perceived- and preferred-influence hierarchies of the five national lefts and rights has moved in several directions. When we gather the threads of our analysis together we can see that our findings both complement and bring into sharper focus the broader structures of political belief systems examined in earlier chapters. More than that, they

152 | New Elites in Old States

Figure 6.8: The Influence Hierarchy of National Lefts and Rights: Unions and Business

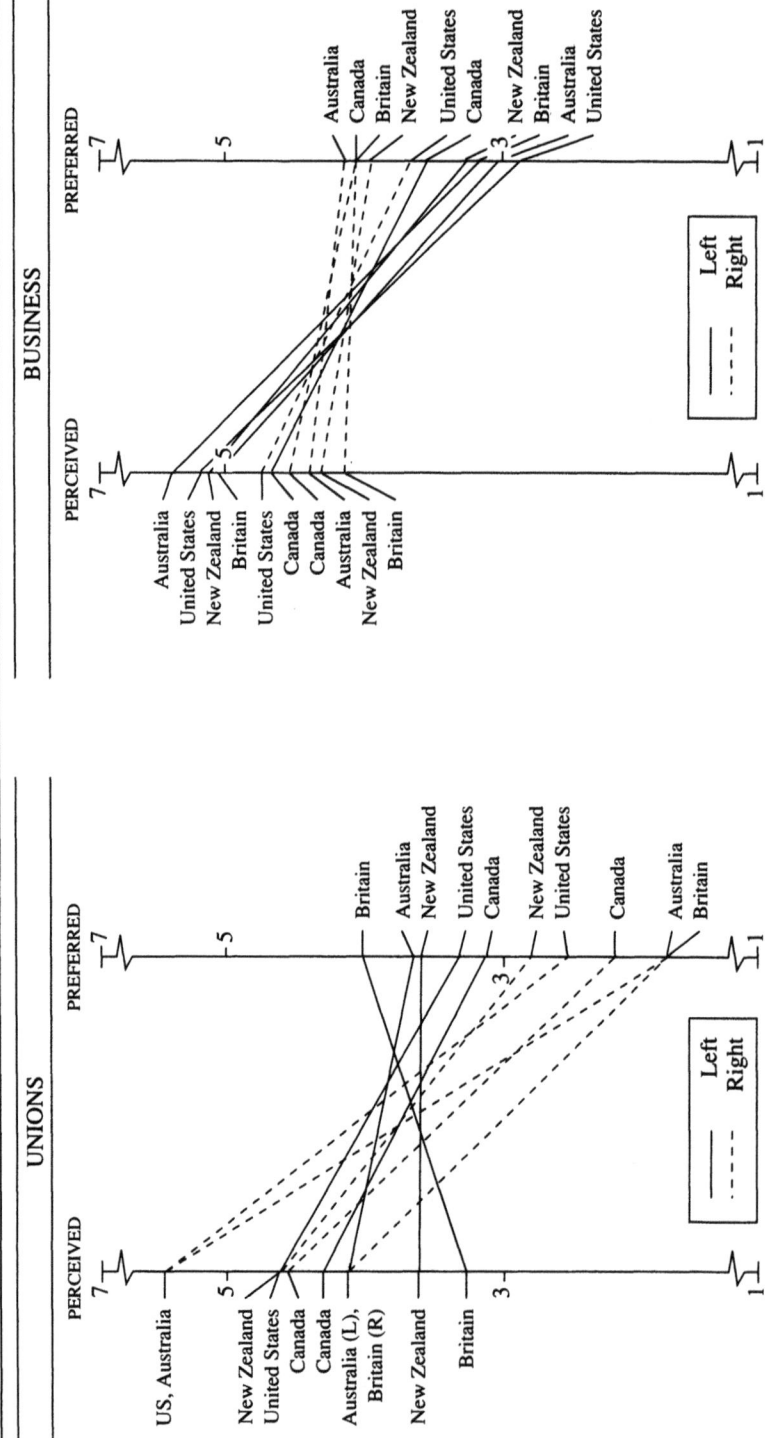

Figure 6.9: The Influence Hierarchy of National Lefts and Rights: Feminists and Minorities

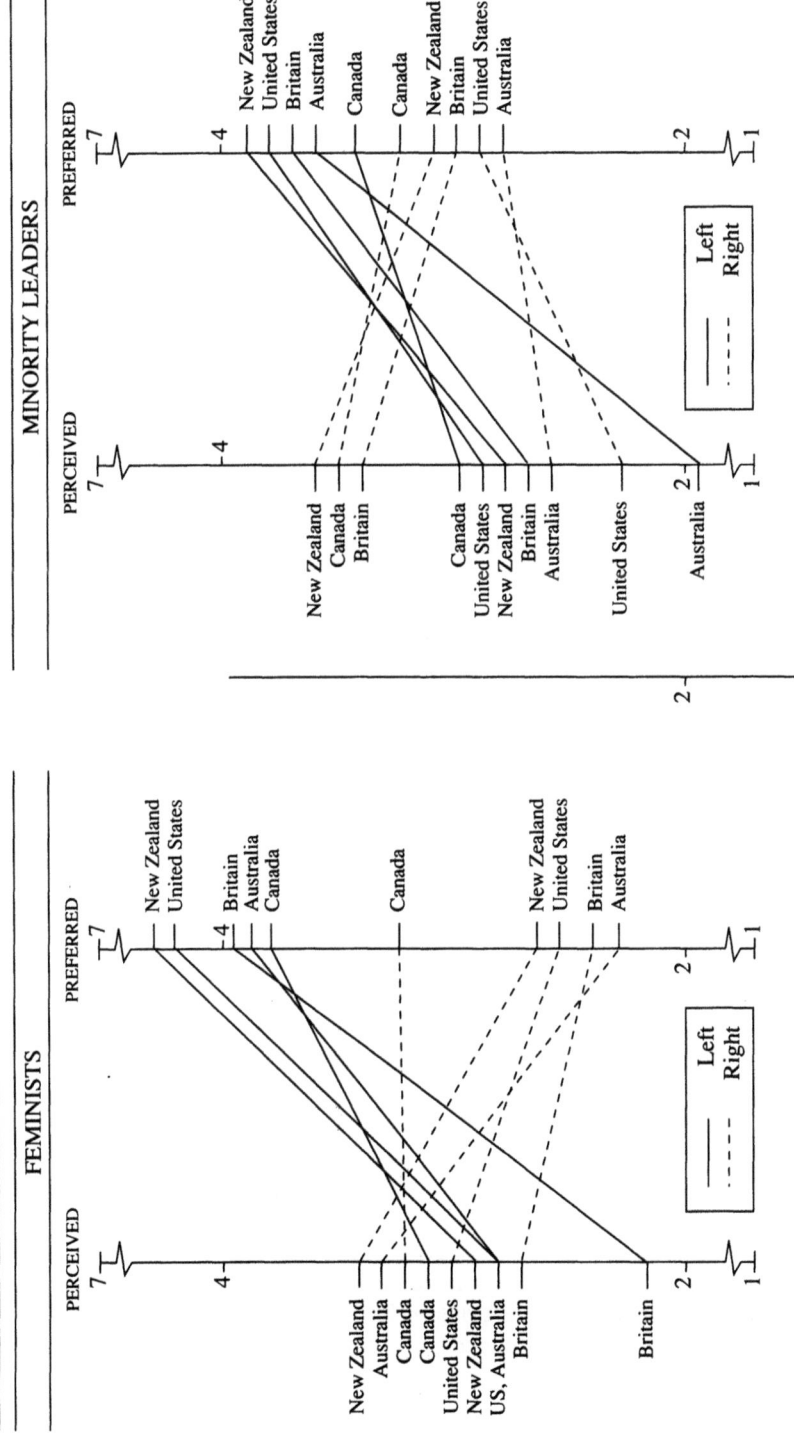

add an evaluative dimension to our understanding of these contemporary lefts and rights. First, the five national lefts and rights clearly *can* be differentiated according to their relative sympathies towards unions and business. But that finding has to be placed in a broader context, for while we can detect echoes indicating that the conflict between labour and capital still resonates within these contemporary lefts and rights, it is also clear that these lefts and rights are not uncritical champions of business, and unions. All rights, irrespective of national setting, plainly want to reduce the influence of business, just as the lefts, with the single exception of Britain, want to reduce the influence of labour.

Second, it is clear that for these respondents the reach of left-right polarity embraces far more than the labour-capital polarity that is traditionally associated with the old left and the old right; it encompasses attitudes towards women and minorities as well. Indeed, the lefts and rights are more deeply divided about the preferred influence of feminists than they are in their preferences about the influence of unions. The lefts and rights are also more deeply divided about the influence minority leaders should have than they are about the influence of business.

These comparisons, however, highlight the contrasts between the lefts and the rights, and they have to be balanced by taking into account the fact that both groups want to narrow the influence spread and both are sympathetic to consumers. As we shall see, all of these themes are reflected in the partisan face of the five national lefts and rights.

Partisanship and Influence

The evidence presented in the previous section clearly implies that ideology does shape views about the distribution of influence. If that were not the case, then we would have found no systematic differences between the lefts and rights in perceptions and preferences regarding the influence hierarchy, its spread and ordering. Moreover, our evidence suggests that left-right self-placement seems to have a more substantial impact upon respondents' *preferences* than their perceptions about the influence hierarchy. Our goal in the final part of this chapter is to bring into focus the ideological similarities and differences between and among the partisan lefts and rights, and to do so we explore partisans' preferences about the distribution of influence.

Our analysis of attitude structures has shown that the belief systems of *partisans* of the left or right do not always match the belief systems of those who locate themselves on the left or right of the left-right scale. Indeed, in some instances, such as the case of the New Zealand left and Labor (Chapter 2), the discrepancies are quite substantial. Consequently, there is little reason to believe that partisans of the left or right will faithfully reflect the positions of left- or right-identifiers when it comes to beliefs about the influence hierarchy. The differences between the lefts and rights might fade or be amplified when partisanship is taken into account. With that caution in mind, we turn to consider the influence preferences of the partisan lefts and rights in Figures 6.10 and 6.11.

First, with respect to the distribution of influence, these data indicate that in *every* national setting left-wing partisans prefer greater equality of influence between groups than do partisans of their counterpart national rights. But there are significant variations as well. In the case of Britain, national setting appears to be particularly important since partisans of both the left and the right want greater inequalities of influence between groups than do their counterpart partisan lefts and rights in the other countries. Indeed, the preferred-influence spread of British Labour supporters is not only larger than that of all other partisan lefts, it is also larger than that of many partisan rights—Progressive Conservatives, Nationals, and Republicans. We note too that the influence spread preferred by British Labour is greater than that of the British left (1.86); the same holds for Australian Labor and the Australian left (1.18).

Second, the rank orderings of groups along the influence scale illustrate a number of common themes, and the consensus across the partisan rights (Figure 6.9) is particularly striking in this respect. The widely held view that parties of the Anglo-American right are 'friendly to business' is shared by our partisan right respondents. Business, parties, intellectuals, and consumers regularly rank at or close to the top of the preferred hierarchy, though again there are some irregularities to that pattern. For example, Australian Liberals rank parties relatively low and farmers high; British Conservatives rate intellectuals and consumers lower; and American Republicans rate the media higher. The point to underscore, however, is that the partisan rights agree not only about which groups they want at the top of the influence hierarchy, but also about which groups they want at the bottom. They are uniformly unsympathetic to feminists, minorities, and unions. Australian Liberals and British Conservatives, in particular, have little time for feminists, and New Zealand Nationals, relative to these other groups, have a benign view of unions.

That right-wing partisans want to place business far above unions comes as no surprise at all; the partisan rights, apparently, are quite clear about where they stand in the classic struggle between capital and labour. What is surprising, however, is where the partisan lefts want to place the same two groups. Figure 6.12 graphically illustrates the sharp differences between the partisan rights and partisan lefts. It also highlights the extent to which Britain's partisan left is unique. British Labour supporters, obviously, are very supportive of unions and hostile to business; the gap between the two is robust—about 1.04 points across the influence scale. For American Democrats the gap is meagre (.28) and for Australian Labor (.08) it has almost disappeared. Partisans of the left in Canada and New Zealand actually place business above unions (NDP $-.14$; Labor, $-.25$).

156 | New Elites in Old States

Figure 6.10: Preferred Influence in Society by National Left Parties

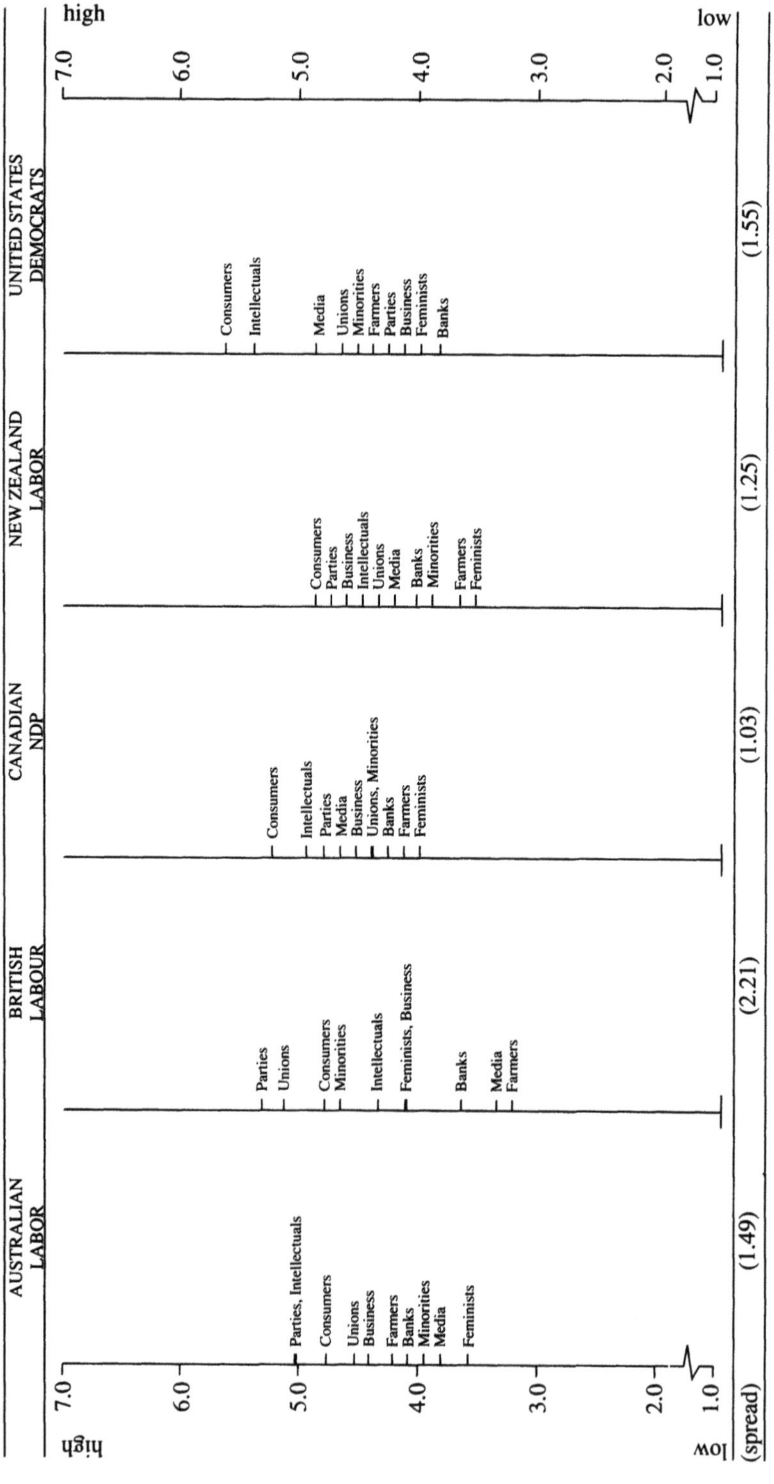

	AUSTRALIAN LABOR	BRITISH LABOUR	CANADIAN NDP	NEW ZEALAND LABOR	UNITED STATES DEMOCRATS
7.0 (high)					
6.0		Parties / Unions			
5.0	Parties, Intellectuals / Consumers / Unions / Business / Farmers / Banks / Minorities / Media / Feminists	Consumers / Minorities / Intellectuals / Feminists, Business / Banks / Media / Farmers	Consumers / Intellectuals / Parties / Media / Business / Unions, Minorities / Banks / Farmers / Feminists		Consumers / Intellectuals
4.0				Consumers / Parties / Business / Intellectuals / Unions / Media / Banks / Minorities / Farmers / Feminists	Media / Unions / Minorities / Farmers / Parties / Business / Feminists / Banks
3.0					
2.0 (low)					
(spread)	(1.49)	(2.21)	(1.03)	(1.25)	(1.55)

Ideology and Political Influence | 157

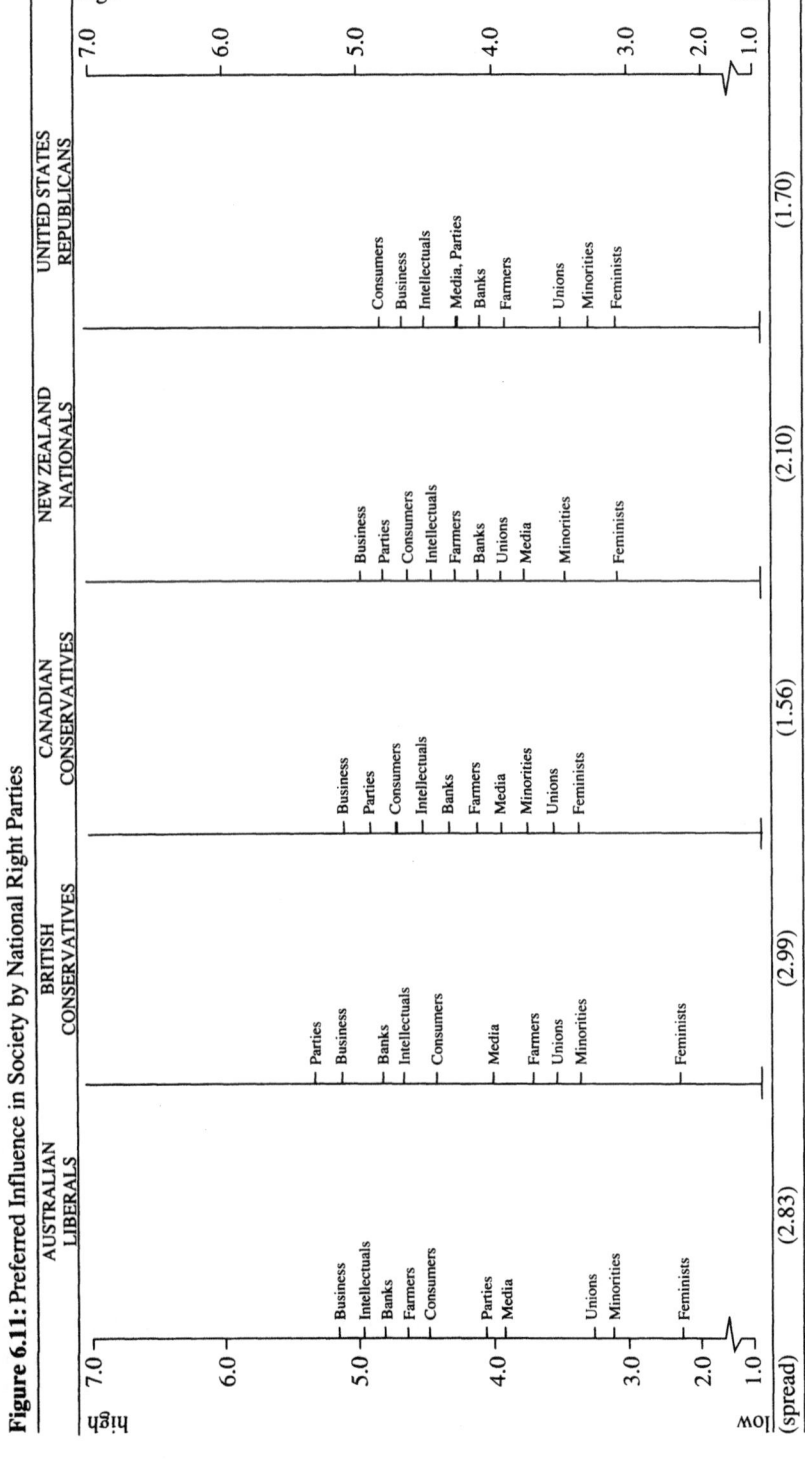

Figure 6.11: Preferred Influence in Society by National Right Parties

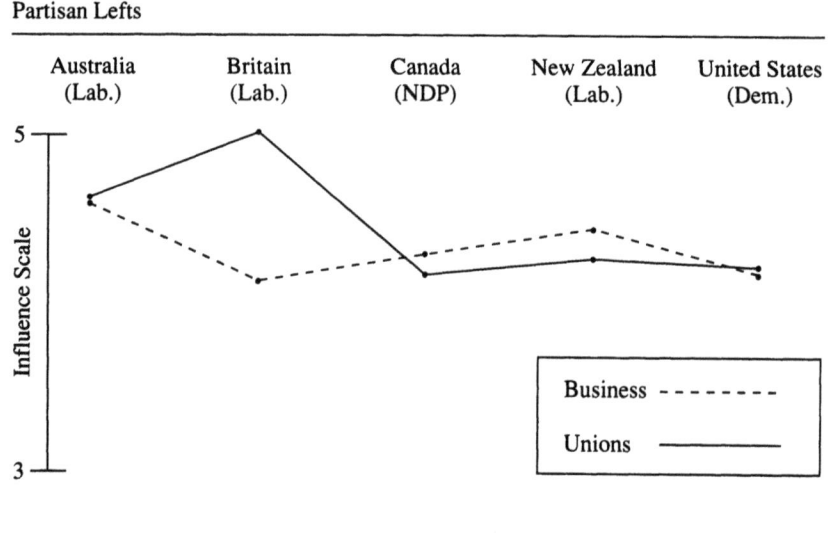

Figure 6.12: Preferred Influence Ratings of Business and Unions by National Partisan Lefts and Rights

A variety of reasons might explain these findings. For example, we could speculate that, perhaps with the exception of Britain, these partisans of the left do not accurately reflect the preferences of all respondents who see themselves as 'on the left'. That reasoning holds for the Australian and New Zealand lefts (Figure 6.4), though even there the case is weak; the gap between unions and business is modest at best. Furthermore, that logic does not travel very well; the Canadian NDP and left-identifiers both place business above unions. We could also argue that these findings reflect disparities in the strength of the organizational ties between unions and parties of the left. Historically, unions have been closely tied to Labour in Britain, but elsewhere—for example, in Canada—the links between labour and parties of the left have been much weaker. But, then again, these data may also foreshadow a genuine shift in the character of the left, a decoupling of parties of the left from organized labour. Regardless of which explanation applies, the evidence points to an intriguing asymmetry: the rights are 'tough' on labour unions, and the lefts, at least this generation of left-identifiers, are relatively 'soft' on capital. The average preferred-influence spread between unions and business for partisans of the right, for example, is a robust 1.5 points on the scale, but for the partisan lefts it is a limp .2 points.

It is much easier to identify common themes uniting the partisan rights than it is to discover commonalities in the preferred rankings of the partisan lefts. Supporters of left-wing parties generally rank consumers, intellectuals, and parties at or close to the top of the preferred hierarchy. At the same time, there is significant national variation, and even less agreement about which groups should occupy the bottom rungs of the hierarchy. But here it is particularly important not to lose sight of why this search for order might be more difficult. The partisan lefts want less of an influence hierarchy than do the rights, and perhaps that is the overriding concern. A flatter hierarchy necessarily means smaller differences between groups.

Table 6.1 summarizes our overall findings regarding the perceived- and preferred-influence spreads. These data enable us to explore a whole variety of within-country and cross-national comparisons. One theme that emerges powerfully from this evidence is that all lefts—left-identifiers and supporters of left-wing parties—see a larger gap between the influence of groups than do the rights. They are less satisfied with the status quo and prefer a narrower influence hierarchy than do the rights and consequently, given their choice, they would support greater social change.

Conclusions

The analysis of influence is a difficult task under the best of circumstances. Certainly no study can claim to provide a comprehensive account of the dynamics of influence in any country without examining such issues as the configuration of elite interactions, how interests are organized, decision-making, opportunity structures, and a host of other contextual factors. We emphasize once again, however, that our focus has been less expansive; we have explored only the world of influence as our respondents *see* it and

Table 6.1 The Influence Gap: Perceptions and Preferences

COUNTRY	PERCEIVED SPREAD	PERCEIVED MEAN	PREFERRED SPREAD	PREFERRED MEAN	DIFFERENCE IN SPREAD
Australia (ave.)	4.03	4.55	1.78	4.24	2.25
Labor	4.22	4.53	1.49	4.35	2.73
Liberal	3.76	4.62	2.83	4.12	0.93
Left	4.46	4.48	1.18	4.36	3.28
Right	3.75	4.56	2.84	4.07	0.91
Britain (ave.)	3.74	4.46	2.04	4.11	1.70
Labour	4.00	4.39	2.21	4.27	1.79
Lib/SDP	3.74	4.48	2.10	4.12	1.64
Conservative	3.54	4.51	2.99	3.96	0.55
Left	3.94	4.41	1.86	4.25	2.08
Right	3.46	4.51	2.96	3.96	0.50
Canada (ave.)	2.81	4.51	1.31	4.32	1.50
NDP	3.08	4.39	1.03	4.48	2.05
Liberal	2.76	4.54	1.66	4.36	1.10
PC	2.89	4.57	1.56	4.24	1.33
Left	2.99	4.46	1.25	4.40	1.74
Right	2.83	4.60	1.84	4.19	0.99
New Zealand (ave.)	2.79	4.58	1.42	4.22	1.37
Labor	3.00	4.54	1.25	4.27	1.75
National	2.72	4.60	2.10	4.12	0.62
Left	3.40	4.47	1.24	4.38	2.16
Right	2.55	4.61	2.29	4.07	0.26
United States (ave.)	3.40	4.45	1.40	4.29	2.00
Democrat	3.70	4.42	1.55	4.45	2.15
Republican	3.42	4.63	1.70	4.00	1.72
Left	3.48	4.43	1.55	4.42	1.93
Right	3.47	4.58	2.03	3.92	1.44

as they would *wish* it to be. If views about influence represent another face of ideology, what do these data show? First, they provide additional evidence about the similarities across the five national rights. As we would expect, these rights are sympathetic to business, unsympathetic to minorities and feminists, and more tolerant of influence hierarchy. Second, they show that the lefts are more likely to see greater inequalities of influence between groups and to prefer greater equality. Consequently, *the lefts are more disposed towards social change*. Third, the data illustrate further and underscore some significant national variations that emerged in our analysis of attitude structures. If it had its way, for example, the Australian left would like to see radical changes to the influence hierarchy. In the case of Britain, the data provide further support for the view that the British left is unique among lefts. It is the most supportive of unions; it is also the most tolerant of inequalities of influence. In the Canadian instance we find more evidence of a weak ideological left-right divide and a benign ideological environment. Compared with those of the other four countries, the Canadian left and right show the narrowest gap of all. For example, they are the closest with respect to the preferred influence assigned to minorities and women (Figure 6.7), dimensions that clearly set other lefts and rights apart. Indeed, the Canadian right is the only right that would promote feminists. The Canadian right places business above unions, but then so does the Canadian left. In the case of New Zealand, Labor supporters are more sympathetic to business than unions, a finding that may help to explain why the Lange government had greater freedom in pursuing policies of privatization.

Perhaps the most intriguing finding to emerge from our analysis of influence relates to the asymmetry between the lefts and rights in the influence they assign to business and unions. Few lefts place the 'agents of capital' at the bottom of the preferred-influence hierarchy. In fact, only the American left does that (Figure 6.4). There are similarities between American Democrats and British Labour in that both rate business and banks relatively low, but that is where the similarities end. British Labour is a party/union left and United States Democrats, like Canadian New Democrats, are a consumer/intellectual left. Our analysis of influence, then, underscores two themes: similarities across the rights and differences within the lefts.

NOTES

[1] The distinctions between power and influence are not central to our analysis and for convenience we use the terms interchangeably.

[2] The Maori Representation Act 1867, for example, divided New Zealand into four Maori electoral districts with the Maori populations in each district entitled to elect one representative to the House. See Allan D. McRobie (1978) 'Ethnic Representation—The New Zealand Experience' in Stephen Levine, ed., *Politics in New Zealand: A Reader* (Sydney: George Allen and Unwin), 270-83.

[3] Whether intellectuals are challengers, mediators, or apologists for the status quo is a matter of conjecture, and thus their precise location is somewhat ambiguous. It

is useful to note, however, that our student respondents might be regarded as 'the constituency' of this leadership group.

[4] In the United States blacks constitute the historically most significant cultural minority. The same holds for aboriginal peoples in Australia and New Zealand, although in both of these instances Aborigines and Maoris represent a much smaller proportion of the total populations. In the cases of Britain and Canada we refer more generally to 'minorities' because in these cases the non-European populations are culturally much more diverse.

[5] Nineteenth-century politicians, of course, complained loudly about the power of the Fourth Estate, a power that emerged under the protection of a free press. It is worth noting that Tocqueville anticipated that a powerful press would emerge under two conditions: (1) when greater social equality prevails, and (2) when associational life was weak (Tocqueville, 1966: Vol II: 119-22).

[6] We are reading these data in terms of absolute differences. As we will later show (Figure 6.10), the size of the gap between perceived and preferred influence equality, or the amount of social change implied by this gap, is greatest within Australian left. In those terms it is most radical.

[7] For Australia, $4 = .62$; Britain, $r = .58$; Canada, $r = .46$; New Zealand, $r = .56$; and the United States, $r = .69$.

[8] The wording for the minority-influence question was different for each country. In Australia, respondents were asked to rate the perceived and preferred influence of Aboriginal leaders; in Britain and Canada, leaders of minorities; in New Zealand, Maori leaders; and, in the United States, black leaders.

[9] We can conduct a rough test of Klein's hypothesis, namely that male support for women's issues derives from broader ideological concerns, by controlling for respondents' location on the minority scale and re-examining the correlations between feminist influence ratings and feminism scale scores. Comparing these partial relationships for males and females shows a weakening of the correlations for males; these data imply that location on the minority scale provides a better predictor of attitudes towards women's issues for men than it does for women.

[10] The spreads are as follows: Australia: left 4.46, right 3.75; New Zealand: left 3.40, right 2.55; United States: left 3.48, right 3.47; Canada: left 2.99, right 2.83.

[11] The correlations for left-identifiers are particularly strong, providing further support for the contention that the lefts, but not the rights, have woven women's and minorities' issues into their agendas.

CHAPTER SEVEN

Common Themes and National Variations

Introduction

We began our investigation with the observation that, in the course of the last twenty-five years, a significant shift has taken place in the way analysts view the Anglo-American democracies. In the 1950s and early 1960s, most observers characterized the Anglo-American democracies as an extended family of nations, different examples of the same type. That characterization was justified on the grounds that the five Anglo-American democracies were remarkably alike with respect to a number of broad-gauge criteria. All were stable, prosperous, advanced industrial states. Each had a large, well-educated and powerful middle class. They had a common heritage, most citizens shared a common language, and the five countries all drew from the same 'core' liberal tradition. Although legal and political institutions in the five countries were not identical, they worked in very similar ways. Furthermore, there was no question that these countries, more than any other comparable cluster, had been knit together by an intricate and powerful web of historical bonds that were both inspired and reinforced by a long tradition of international co-operation. When these characteristics were considered together, and when the five countries were viewed from a global standpoint, the case for the Anglo-American democracies' being 'essentially alike' was powerful indeed, and an idea not easily dislodged.

Nonetheless, a shift in perspective became evident by the mid-1960s, when scholars with an eye on more fine-grained cross-national comparisons became embroiled in a vigorous debate that centred on the question underlying the present research: Are there significant differences between and among the contemporary political cultures of the five Anglo-American democracies? That debate continues to engage scholars from a wide variety of disciplines, and it spans both historical and contemporary perspectives. For example, historians typically emphasize the importance of founding circumstances, focusing on such factors as the social make-up of the founding fragments; the timing of the 'point of departure'; developmental trajectories; and the presence or absence of a revolutionary moment, an aristocracy, a feudal past, exposure to industrialism, and frontier experiences. Others examine contemporary national experiences, and generalize about cultures and values on the basis of such indicators as socio-structural conditions; elite behaviour and recruitment; levels of unionization in the workforce; patterns of social mobility; the structure of political parties; crime rates; and collective decisions about health care, education, and a variety of other social supports.

When we stand back from the details of this lively debate and examine its broader outlines, several intriguing features come into view. First, the debate has produced a burgeoning literature that, by any measure, amounts to an impressive body of high-quality research. It contains insightful hypotheses about value similarities and differences as well as a variety of intriguing speculations about the scope and direction of value change. What is striking is that scholars on both sides of the debate have probed value differences and similarities by imaginatively weaving together qualitative, historical, literary, socio-structural, and other scattered evidence to reach *opposite conclusions*. There are no clear winners or losers; the jury is still out.

If we took a head-count of scholars in both camps, we would likely find that those arguing for 'significant differences' outnumber those who see 'essential similarities'. In that respect, the cumulative effect of the shift in emphasis has perhaps been to undermine confidence in the utility of the Anglo-American democracies as an analytical category. However, it should be noted that scholars making the case for 'significant differences' frequently work from single-country or two-country perspectives. They employ research strategies that are well suited for identifying national differences, and indeed may even impose such differences, but that are less useful for exploring generalizations across all five countries, or for assessing the extent to which values are shared.

Another aspect of the debate worth noting is that, in most instances, conclusions about similarities and differences hinge upon indirect evidence. The difficulty here is that to move from qualitative, contextual, or anecdotal evidence to authoritative statements about national values is problematical and contentious; it entails a leap of faith. Earlier bench-mark studies, most notably Almond and Verba's *Civic Culture* and Alford's *Party and Society*, did rely on direct evidence, but neither study analysed all five Anglo-American democracies. Moreover, the data were collected nearly three decades ago. A substantial body of research (e.g., Barnes, Kaase, et al., 1979; Dalton, 1988; Inglehart, 1990) indicates that important value changes have swept across Western industrialized states in the last twenty years, and have done so for reasons that would suggest ideological convergence among the Anglo-American democracies. Thus the extent to which earlier bench-mark studies can provide a reliable basis from which to draw conclusions about contemporary values in the Anglo-American democracies is increasingly unclear.

When these various aspects of the debate are considered together, it might be argued that the entire research enterprise has been seriously flawed. We have not taken that position, but we have suggested that the debate can move a significant step forward by employing direct evidence from all five Anglo-American democracies. Of course such evidence, presented throughout this study, is too limited to tell the entire story. But when the dust has settled, what kind of story can be told?

The Structure of Political Beliefs

The preceding chapters have presented a great deal of detailed evidence, and a rather complex cumulative analysis. When we look at those findings more broadly, several important themes emerge. The first emerges from the initial factor analysis, which showed that respondents throughout the Anglo-American democracies organize their thinking about the political world in remarkably similar ways. Respondents structure their political ideas around the same four attitudinal areas: (1) government intervention in society and the economy; (2) gender relations; (3) minority-majority relations; and (4) the trade-off between equality of opportunity and equality of result.

A close probing of the factor analysis data shows that while the amount of variance explained by each factor differs slightly from one national setting to the next, each factor captures, with more or less efficiency, the same ideological cleavage in each of the five countries. In itself that finding is not surprising, and indeed it would be remarkable if that were not the case. However, the more impressive findings brought to light by the detailed examination underscore the similarities in the structures that dominate ideological thinking in the five countries. When the factor analysis is replicated in each of the five national samples, the same four factors not only are reproduced, but also appear in the same order. The government factor is *always* the most powerful, the factor dealing with women's issues *always* comes next, and so on. Also impressive is the cross-national stability with respect to the item loadings; when the factor analysis is performed on different national samples, items rarely drop out of a factor (become insignificant) nor do they 'drift' or move from one dimension in one country to a second dimension in another. The results, then, are robust; the same factors emerge in different settings, they have similar power, they contain the same items, and thus they mean the same thing.

More important, perhaps, than the statistical consistency and elegance of these data are their substantive implications. Together, the four dimensions emerging from the factor analysis bring into focus the issues that animate political discourse in the five countries. The government dimension contains a wide variety of items that tap such classic redistributional issues as the gap between the rich and the poor, the role of taxation in reducing disparities of wealth, the fairness of the free-enterprise system, the appropriate size of government, and services to the handicapped and the old. This dimension not only represents the bundle of issues typically associated with the rise of the welfare state; its pre-eminence within the data set also suggests that the ideological battles generally associated with the post-Second World War policy agenda are far from settled.

In the same manner, the second and third factors tap attitudes towards gender equality and the treatment of minorities, issues that are central to new political agendas and that have been brought to the forefront by recently empowered groups. The fourth dimension, the equality of opportunity/result, taps a variety of concerns and attitudes about the use of quotas for particular underclasses in society. In this important sense, the equality dimension is not a part of the traditional cluster of issues surrounding the welfare safety net; it is more focused, it has different reference points, and it envisions the use of novel instruments—quotas— to achieve a measure of equality not just for an economic underclass but for gender and minority underclasses as well.

Here it should be stressed that the dimensions that structure ideological thinking for respondents in all five national settings bear little resemblance to ideological cleavages that can be traced to founding circumstances. Indeed, the pronounced cross-national convergence in ideological patterns argues against any substantive impact from idiosyncratic founding circumstances, or at least against any impact that is still detectable among youth elites in the 1980s. While we cannot and would not contest the reality of idiosyncratic founding circumstances, their impact has been diluted and diluted again by generational change driven by similar structural and economic dynamics. Nor do the ideological dimensions *simply* reflect cleavages that traditionally divided the lefts and rights in the national communities. In addition, they typify a broader cluster of ideological divisions associated with the contemporary agendas of mature industrial states. Within such states, the Anglo-American democracies form a recognizable but by no means aberrant community.

Britain and the United States: The Great Polarities?

To say that respondents' beliefs are structured according to the same general principles, irrespective of national location, is an important finding in its own right. But on the basis of those data alone we cannot conclude that respondents in the five countries therefore agree with each other about *how much* the government should intervene in society and the economy, about *how much* should be done for women and minorities, or about *what kind of balance* should be struck between equality of opportunity and result. When we marshal evidence to pursue this latter line of investigation, the results are intriguing, particularly when they are interpreted in the context of conventional expectations about how values are distributed throughout the Anglo-American democracies.

Britain and America are the 'senior partners' of the Anglo-American democracies, and there are a number of ways in which those two countries stand as the major reference points—often polar reference points—for interpreting the social and political characteristics of the 'junior partners': Australia, Canada, and New Zealand. If the nineteenth century was Britain's, then the twentieth has been America's. Britain symbolizes the past, America the future, and when the United States replaced Britain as the West's great power, the magnet of British influence in the Commonwealth countries weakened and the pull of the United States became more powerful. Although this transformation was most clearly evident in the Canadian case, it was also evident in Australia and New Zealand.

The magnet analogy might well be extended to include ideological dispositions among the Anglo-American Commonwealth countries. Britain, the first industrial nation, experienced deep and institutionalized class differences; it was the home of collectivism of the right and left, Toryism and Fabian-style socialism, and it developed an expansive welfare state. The experience of the United States has been quite different; its liberalism has been individualist and it has a minimal state. So striking are the contrasts that it seems reasonable to suppose that Britain and the United States stand at the two poles of the Anglo-American ideological spectrum. By implication, then, we would expect the Australian, Canadian, and New Zealand centres of ideological gravity to be distributed 'somewhere in between' those two poles. Given the likely impact of proximity, we might further expect the Canadian centre to be closer to the American pole, and the antipodean centres to be closer to Britain. But is there evidence of such a polarity and such a distribution?

The data presented in Figure 7.1 suggest not. These findings bring together evidence presented in various parts of our preceding analysis. They are drawn to scale and report the mean locations of the five national samples on the four additive scales generated from the factor analysis. On the first factor scale we can see that British respondents are true to expected form; they anchor one end of the distribution as the group most likely to support government intervention in society and the economy. But it is Canadian respondents, not Americans, who anchor the other pole on this most powerful dimension. On the second scale, American respondents are most inclined to support women's issues. The intermediate locations of Britain, Canada, and New Zealand are indistinguishable, and in this instance it is Australia that lies at the other end of the distribution. When it comes to minority issues, Americans are most sympathetic and New Zealanders the least. With respect to the trade-off between equality of opportunity and equality of result, all respondents cluster towards the equality of opportunity end of the scale, and it is New Zealand and Canada that anchor the distributions. In *no case* do British and American respondents provide the ideological polarities for the other national samples. In fact, the positions of British and American respondents are either indistinguishable or relatively close to one another on each of the four dimensions. Overall, and quite apart from the polarity of the findings, it should also be noted that national differences are modest at best. Figure 7.1 does not suggest that the five Anglo-American democracies manifest significantly different ideological environments.

Figure 7.1: National Locations on Factor Scales

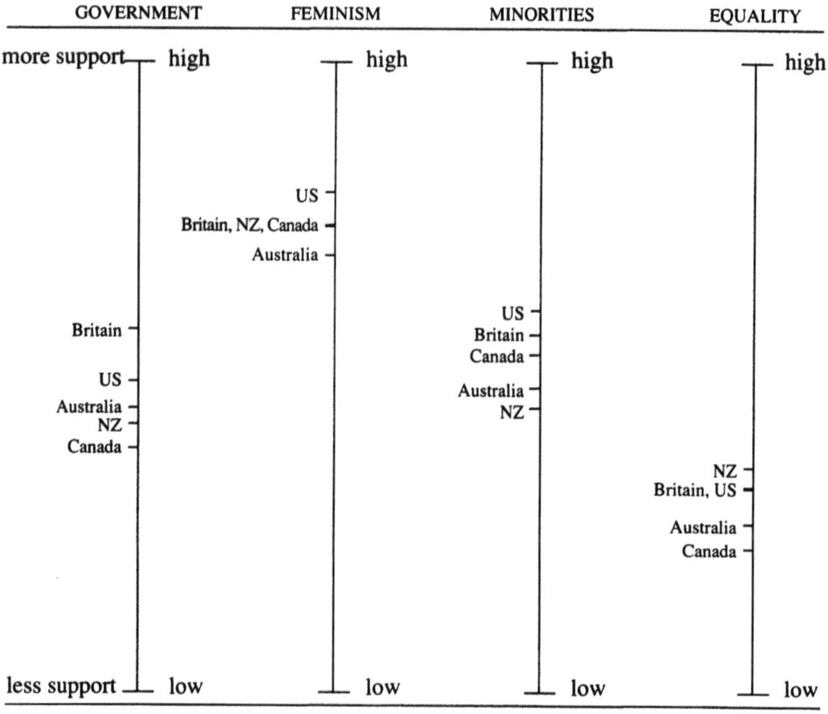

GOVERNMENT	FEMINISM	MINORITIES	EQUALITY
more support — high	— high	— high	— high
	US		
	Britain, NZ, Canada		
	Australia		
		US	
Britain		Britain	
		Canada	
US		Australia	
Australia		NZ	
NZ			
Canada			
			NZ
			Britain, US
			Australia
			Canada
less support — low	— low	— low	— low

It might be argued that presenting national averages for these samples masks important ideological differences *within* national samples, and that if we compared, say, the five national lefts and the five national rights, we would get a very different picture. After all, much of the analysis in previous chapters has clearly demonstrated that 'left' and 'right' are powerful and efficient ideological bench-marks in all five countries, and thus to ignore these distinctions would be to run roughshod over a critical ideological distinction. Figure 7.2, therefore, reports the results of such a breakdown, and again the findings are intriguing. Once more, these data clearly demonstrate that the left-right divide is a meaningful one for all national samples. In no case do the national lefts and rights cross over; the rights cluster together, as do the lefts, and there is a clear, unbridged divide between the two clusters. But when that divide is taken into account, is there any evidence that British and American respondents coalesce into ideological polarities? Again the answer is no. Out of eight different sets of comparisons, British and American respondents appear at the opposite ends of the same scale only once—in the instance of left-identifiers on the equality scale. That frequency is no better than what we would expect from chance alone.

Figure 7.2: Locations of National Lefts and Right on Factor Scales

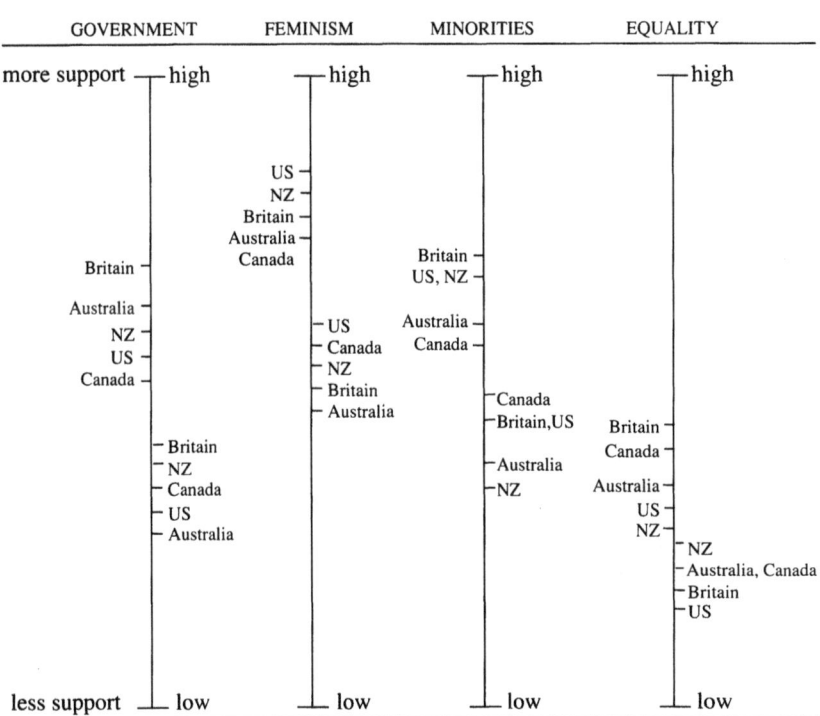

National Lefts and Rights

One of the most striking findings to emerge from this study is the impressive conceptual power of 'left' and 'right' as ideological organizers. Respondents were asked to do a very simple task: to locate themselves on a seven-point scale ranging from far left through centre to far right. Yet despite the simplicity of this measure, the left-right scale proved to be a powerful predictor of respondent attitudes on a wide range of issues and concerns. Put somewhat differently, the left-right scale opens up a panoramic window on the attitudinal and ideological world of respondents. Once we are able to locate a respondent on the left-right scale, we have a very good fix on how he or she feels about government intervention in the economy, about feminism, about minority groups, and about the equality of opportunity and result.

Even more strikingly, once we know where he or she falls on the left-right scale, the national location of the respondent adds virtually no additional information with respect to predicting or explaining political beliefs. Those who locate themselves to the left of centre on the left-right scale share an essentially common outlook on the political world *irrespective of where they happen to live* among the Anglo-American democracies. In a similar fashion, respondents who locate themselves to the right of centre share an essentially similar world view *irrespective of nationality*. Although there are some modest exceptions, such as the outlier positions of the British left on the government scale and the Australian right on the feminism scale, the general conclusion is clear and unequivocal; across a broad policy domain, self-location on the left-right scale overshadows and even eclipses nationality as a predictor of ideological predispositions. If we could ask only one question in trying to predict the attitudinal orientation of respondents towards a host of political issues, we would be much better off asking respondents to locate themselves on the left-right scale than we would be asking where they lived. In this respect, then, the five Anglo-American democracies occupy similar, even strikingly similar, ideological space.

Here it should also be reiterated that, on balance, the five national rights are even more similar to one another than are the five national lefts. This finding is contra-intuitive for several reasons. Historically, the Anglo-American lefts have shared common ideological reference points, a common analytical perspective on industrial society, and in the case of the Labour/Labor parties of Australia, Britain, and New Zealand, common patterns of labelling and partisanship. Conversely, parties of the right have tended to be more closely identified with their idiosyncratic national experience; the right has been conservative in the important sense of defending *national* values, traditions, and mores. Thus there is less reason to expect coalescence on the right than on the left. Yet we find that, if anything, the opposite is true. This finding in turn underscores the cross-national character of neoconservatism; the 'new right' appears to transcend national boundaries in a fashion analogous to that of the 'old left'. At least in our study, right-of-centre respondents did not manifest ideological orientations that were highly reflective of distinctive national circumstances. Rather, they *shared* a wide-ranging ideological perspective common to the five Anglo-American democracies.

Finally, we should stress the absorptive power of left and right. Given that the left-right scale itself is content-free, we must rely on correlational analysis to flesh out the more specific orientations and attitudes that adhere conceptually to left and right. As we might expect, the left-right scale is strongly correlated with the government scale, the scale that incorporates much of the traditional conceptual domain of left and right. At the same time, the correlational linkages between the left-right scale and the remaining dimensions of the factor analysis demonstrate that respondents have little difficulty packing new ideological issues and debates into the conventional terminology of left and right. Thus that terminology readily expands to embrace orientations towards gender relations, towards minority relations, and towards the use of quotas. This versatility suggests in turn why the terminology of left and right has proven to provide such a durable foundation for ideological organization; the basic conceptual polarities are not confined to a narrow or specific policy domain, but rather are elastic enough to absorb new issues and concerns as they arise. While the content of left and right may change with the times, the terms themselves live on and continue to provide a powerful organizing tool for individuals trying to make sense out of a complex political world.

Moreover, our correlational analysis clearly demonstrates that at a given point in time, the terms left and right have virtually identical content across the five Anglo-American democracies. Thus, for example, the American right differs only at the margins from the rights of Britain and New Zealand. This cross-national similarity also extends to perceived and preferred influence rankings; distinctive national patterns can be teased out of the data, but only in a very nuanced form and with considerable effort.

The Organization of Ideological Beliefs

Throughout this analysis, we have been primarily interested in the nature of political belief systems. Given the nature of our samples, we cannot assess whether, for example, Australians at large have different orientations to gender relations than do Canadians or Americans; we can compare student but not national populations. What we *have* been able to explore is whether national differences exist in the way student respondents organize their perceptual and ideological worlds. Thus, for instance, we have examined the manner in which respondents weave orientations to gender relations into larger ideological packages, and the extent to which such packages are similar or different across the Anglo-American democracies.

The findings in these respects are sharp and unambiguous. Respondents display a great deal of constraint in their mental organization of the political world; belief *systems* of considerable breadth and complexity do exist. These systems are anchored in the ideological rubric of left and right, but are expansive enough to encompass a wide range of issues and concerns, and to embrace preferred patterns of political influence. Throughout, the absorptive capacity of left and right has been impressive. Emergent concerns about gender and minority relations have been readily grafted onto pre-existing ideological structures grounded in the post-war political agenda of the welfare state (although it remains to be seen whether new issues such as environmentalism will also be absorbed into the ideological structures observed in this study, or whether they will significantly disrupt, distort, or transform existing patterns of political belief). Moreover, those structures display a remarkable degree of similarity across the five Anglo-American democracies, and particularly across Australia, Britain, and the United States. While the patterns weaken perceptibly in New Zealand, and even more so in the Canadian case, their overall structure remains intact.

The coherence, breadth, and strength of these belief systems suggest that they will persist into the future, that the belief systems of our youth elites in the 1980s will shape their political values and behaviours well into the twenty-first century. However, this expectation of persistence should not suggest that youth elites are captives of their past or present, that they would prefer the status quo to continue. The preceding chapter's discussion of student preferences concerning the distribution of influence makes it quite clear that youth elites would like to see a more equitable distribution of influence, that they would like to curb the perceived influence of the most powerful and enhance the perceived influence of the least powerful. It should also be noted that youth elites would like the greatest enhancement to occur for consumers, among whom they will number, and intellectuals, among whom, as students, they may understandably place themselves. Thus in examining the preferred visions of youth elites, one can detect the unsubtle play of self-interest, something that comes to the fore with even greater force when the preferred futures of men and women are concerned. Nonetheless, a common theme does emerge for virtually all respondents regardless of their nationality, gender, or ideological self-location; the ideal world would be one in which political influence was more equitably distributed than at present.

This discussion of student preferences serves as a useful reminder that our findings on the nature of political belief systems cannot be divorced from the nature of our sample. Students, after all, live in an environment where a premium is placed on constraint and rationality, where individuals are trained to observe patterns within a multitude of social and political facts. Thus a further question remains; do the patterns we observed among student respondents bring into bolder relief patterns that also exist in the broader public, albeit in less coherent and more muted forms, or are such patterns in some important sense unique to the student environment? We have no reason to expect the latter possibility, but it cannot be discounted by our analysis *per se*.

As the curtain falls on any major piece of social science research, it is conventional practice for authors to issue both a number of caveats and a clarion call for further research. In this case, the two come together in the need for more deliberate cross-national analyses employing full *national* samples. As we stated at the outset, it cannot be assumed that our five samples of Anglo-American youth elites are representative of their respective national populations. Indeed, we assume just the opposite, and argue that our samples provide particularly fertile ground for the cross-national examination of political belief systems precisely *because* respondents do *not* constitute a representative slice of their national populations. At the same time, however, it would be fascinating to see to what extent the cross-national picture that has emerged in this analysis finds reflection in representative national samples. Until such data are available, our analysis offers strong evidence for the case that the Anglo-American democracies do share common patterns of political beliefs, and that the similarities across the five countries outweigh, and by a wide margin, national differences. To return to the basic question guiding our research: the Anglo-American democracies appear to share very similar political cultures, and national differences, when found, are seldom significant.

Appendix A

SAMPLE QUESTIONNAIRE

A slightly different questionnaire was used for each national setting. This questionnaire was the one used in Australia.

AUSTRALIAN UNIVERSITIES SURVEY

1. Here is a series of statements. For each please indicate whether you agree strongly with it, agree somewhat, disagree somewhat, or disagree strongly.

   Please use the following numbers in the blank spaces below:

   | Agree Strongly = 1 | Agree Somewhat = 2 | Disagree Somewhat = 3 | Disagree Strongly = 4 | No Opinion = 9 |

   ____ If a company has to lay off part of its labour force, the first workers to be laid off should be women whose husbands have jobs.

   ____ If Aborigines are not getting fair access to jobs, the government should see to it that they do.

   ____ The country would be better off if there was less government control over business.

   ____ White Australians should have a right to refuse to sell their homes to Aborigines or other racial minorities.

   ____ There should be a law limiting the amount of money any individual is allowed to earn in a year.

   ____ It is the right of a woman to decide whether to have an abortion.

   ____ The majority of Australian women do not agree with the leaders of the feminist movement.

   ____ Businessmen have too much power for the good of the country.

   ____ Lesbians and homosexuals should not be allowed to teach in schools.

   ____ Women are usually less reliable workers than men.

   ____ The news media are too critical of Australian institutions.

   ____ There should be more laws which aim at eliminating differences in the treatment of men and women.

   ____ All except the old and the handicapped should have to take care of themselves without social welfare benefits.

___ The government should work to reduce substantially the income gap between rich and poor.

___ Trade unions have too much power for the good of the country.

___ The interests of employers and employees are, by their very nature, basically opposed.

___ The news media pay too much attention to minority groups.

___ The administration of justice in Australia mainly favours the rich.

___ Public funding is a fairer way to pay for political election campaigns than is private funding.

___ The government should pass tougher gun control legislation.

2. Rank the following national goals below in terms of importance to you. Place a '1' next to the most important goal; a '2' next to the second most important; a '3' next to the third most important; and so on down to '10' for the least important goal.

___ Achieving equality for women.

___ Maintaining a strong military defence.

___ Protecting freedom of speech.

___ Curbing inflation.

___ Developing energy sources.

___ Reducing the role of government.

___ Fighting crime.

___ Achieving equality for Aborigines.

___ Reducing unemployment.

___ Giving people more say in government decisions.

3. The following questions cover issues that are in the news these days. In each scale, '1' represents a position held by some people, '7' represents an opposing position, and the other numbers stand for positions between these two. Please circle the number that best represents your opinion on each issue.

The government should see to it that everyone has a job						It is not the role of the government to see to it that everyone has a job
1	2	3	4	5	6	7

If women tried harder they could get jobs equal to their ability						Discrimination makes it almost impossible for most women to get jobs equal to their ability
1	2	3	4	5	6	7

Places should be reserved for Aborigines to ensure their representation in the professions (such as teaching, medicine, law)　　　　　　　　　　　　　Admission to professional training should be based strictly on merit

1　　2　　3　　4　　5　　6　　7

Workers should have more to say in important decisions than they do now　　　　　　　　　　　　　The important decisions should be left to management

1　　2　　3　　4　　5　　6　　7

If Aborigines would try harder they could be just as well off as White Australians　　　　　　　　　　　　　Social conditions make it almost impossible for most Aborigines to overcome poverty even if they try

1　　2　　3　　4　　5　　6　　7

4. Under a fair economic system

All people should earn about the same　　　　　　　　　　　　　People with more ability should earn higher salaries

1　　2　　3　　4　　5　　6　　7

Firms should be made to increase the number of women in good jobs　　　　　　　　　　　　　Job hiring should be based strictly on merit

1　　2　　3　　4　　5　　6　　7

The private enterprise system is generally a fair system for working people　　　　　　　　　　　　　Under private enterprise people do not get a fair share of what they produce

1　　2　　3　　4　　5　　6　　7

Taxing those with high incomes to help the poor is only fair　　　　　　　　　　　　　Taxing those with high incomes to help the poor only punishes the people who have worked the hardest

1　　2　　3　　4　　5　　6　　7

Women would be better off if they stayed at home and raised families						Women would be better off if they had careers and jobs just as men do
1	2	3	4	5	6	7

5. Here are two ways of dealing with inequality; which do you prefer?

Equality of opportunity: giving each person an equal chance for a good education and to develop his or her ability						**Equality of results:** giving each person a relatively equal income regardless of his or her education and ability
1	2	3	4	5	6	7

6. In general, government grows bigger as it provides more services. Do you favour . . .

Smaller government						More government services
1	2	3	4	5	6	7

7. In bringing up children of primary school age, some think that one should teach them that financial security is the most important thing. Do you agree or disagree?

Agree						Disagree
1	2	3	4	5	6	7

8. Below is a list of goals which are frequently thought of as being important to society. For you personally, how would you rank these goals? Place a '1' next to the most important goal; a '2' next to the second most important goal; a '3' next to the third most important goal, and so on down to '12' for the least important goal.

____ Maintain order in society
____ Give people more say in government decisions
____ Fight rising prices
____ Protect freedom of speech
____ Maintain high rate of economic growth
____ Make sure the country has strong defence forces
____ Give people more say in how things are decided at work and in their community
____ Try to make our cities and countryside more beautiful
____ Maintain a stable economy
____ Fight against crime
____ Move to a friendlier, less impersonal society

_____ Move to a society where ideas count more than money

9. Please indicate how strongly you agree or disagree with each of the following statements regarding universities.

| Agree Strongly = 1 | Agree Somewhat = 2 | Disagree Somewhat = 3 | Disagree Strongly = 4 | No Opinion = 9 |

_____ Universities should place less emphasis on the arts and humanities, and put more emphasis on applied technology and business.
_____ Foreign students are taking up too many places at Australian universities.
_____ There should be special funds available for those students in need.
_____ Foreign students should pay higher fees than Australian students.
_____ There should be special university places reserved for students from disadvantaged groups.
_____ The principle of universal access to university education should be folllowed regardless of cost.
_____ University scholarships should be based strictly on merit.

10. Some occupations are listed below. In the first column, please indicate what you think the average annual earnings are for someone in that occupation before taxes. In the second column, please indicate what you think someone in that occupation should earn, again before taxes. (Most people do not have precise information on salaries in other occupations, but we would like your best estimate.)

	Average Annual Salary is	Fair Annual Salary should be
A primary school teacher with 5 years experience	$_____	$_____
Chairman of the Board of one of the top 10 companies	$_____	$_____
A semi-skilled worker in a car assembly plant	$_____	$_____
A top professional athlete (eg Aust. test cricketer, VFL player)	$_____	$_____
A bank teller	$_____	$_____
A cabinet minister	$_____	$_____
An office cleaner	$_____	$_____
A policeman with 5 years experience	$_____	$_____
A civil engineer	$_____	$_____

A university professor	$ _____	$ _____
A doctor in general practice in a large city	$ _____	$ _____
A plumber	$ _____	$ _____

11. What do you anticipate that your salary will be 5 years after you get your degree?

    $ _____

12. In your opinion, should a minimum wage be guaranteed by law, or should all wages be set by the marketplace?

    ____ guaranteed by law
    ____ set by the marketplace
    ____ don't know, no opinion

13. What would you estimate the current annual minimum wage to be in Australia?

    $ _____

14. What do you think this wage should be?

    $ _____

15. Do you think Australia should develop closer or more distant ties with . . . (circle the appropriate number).

	Much Closer	Closer	Same	More Distant	Much More Distant	No Opinion
Britain	1	2	3	4	5	9
Canada	1	2	3	4	5	9
China	1	2	3	4	5	9
France	1	2	3	4	5	9
Indonesia	1	2	3	4	5	9
Israel	1	2	3	4	5	9
Japan	1	2	3	4	5	9
New Zealand	1	2	3	4	5	9
South Africa	1	2	3	4	5	9
Soviet Union	1	2	3	4	5	9
Saudi Arabia	1	2	3	4	5	9
United States	1	2	3	4	5	9

16. How would you describe your interest in international, federal, state and local affairs? (Please write the appropriate number in the space provided.)

One of my major concerns	1		
	2	International Affairs	____
	3	Federal Affairs	____
Moderate concerns	4	State Affairs	____
	5	Local Affairs	____
	6		
I pay little attention	7		

17. Please indicate how strongly you agree or disagree with each of the following statements regarding Australia's role in the world.

Please use the following numbers in the blanks below.

Agree Strongly = 1	Agree Somewhat = 2	Disagree Somewhat = 3	Disagree Strongly = 4	No Opinion = 9

____ Australia should be prepared to use force to prevent the spread of communism.

____ The government should do more to protect Australian businesses from foreign competition.

____ Australia should give economic aid to poorer countries even if it means higher prices at home.

____ We shouldn't think so much in international terms but should concentrate more on our domestic problems.

____ Australia should play a larger role in pushing for a South Pacific Nuclear Free Zone.

____ The main goal of those who make Australian foreign policy is to protect the interests of exporting industries.

____ Australia should play a larger role in the defence of its South Pacific neighbours.

____ We should do more to encourage foreign investment in Australia.

____ As a partner in ANZUS, Australia should allow nuclear-powered American warships into our ports.

18. Some people say that we must concentrate on fighting either inflation or unemployment; the problem is that if we make an equal effort to fight both we probably will solve neither problem. If you had to choose, where would you place the emphasis?

Emphasize fight against unemployment			Emphasize both equally even at risk of solving neither			Emphasize fight against inflation
1	2	3	4	5	6	7

19. Under a fair political system . . .

Appendix A | 181

All States should have an equal say in Australian politics						New South Wales and Victoria, with their larger populations, should have the larger say in Australian politics
1	2	3	4	5	6	7

The rights and freedoms of Australians should be guaranteed by a Bill of Rights						A Bill of Rights is unnecessary. The rights and freedoms of Australians are adequately protected now
1	2	3	4	5	6	7

The Commonwealth government should do more to equalize wealth between have and have not States						It's not Canberra's job to do anything about the distribution of wealth between regions
1	2	3	4	5	6	7

The State Governments, not Canberra, should have the most say in local decisions.						It's up to Canberra to make the important local decisions
1	2	3	4	5	6	7

All Australian citizens born in the country, or not, recently arrived or not, should be treated exactly the same						We should look after Australian citizens born in this country first and others second
1	2	3	4	5	6	7

Government should step in and help remote or rural areas even if it means loss of benefits to the cities						The government should leave well alone differences between rural and urban areas
1	2	3	4	5	6	7

Those citizens who are well informed should count for more in the political system | | | | | | | | All citizens should count the same in the political system

```
1    2    3    4    5    6    7
```

A number of separate Aboriginal seats in Parliament should be established | | | | | | | | There is no need for separate Aboriginal seats

```
1    2    3    4    5    6    7
```

20. We would like to know how much influence you think various groups actually have over Australian life, and how much influence you think they should have. Please rate the groups listed below, using the following scale in which '1' represents 'very influential' and '7' represents 'very little influence'.

Very influential | | | | | | | | Very little influence

```
1    2    3    4    5    6    7
```

	Actual influence	Influence they should have
Trade unions		
Farmers		
Business leaders		
Media		
Academics and intellectuals		
Banks		
Consumer groups		
Feminist groups		
Political parties		
Aboriginal leaders		

21. In general, how would you describe your views on political matters:

___ far left   ___ left   ___ somewhat left
___ centre   ___ somewhat right   ___ right
___ far right   ___ don't know

HERE ARE SOME ITEMS FOR BACKGROUND INFORMATION

22. Gender: _____ male _____ female

23. In what year were you born? _____

24. In what country were you born? _____
If you were not born in Australia, are you presently an
____ Australian citizen
____ other (please specify) _____

25. Where did you go to school? (City and State)

If not in Australia, in which country did you go to school?

26. Was your secondary school:
____ A state school ____ A private school

26a. If PRIVATE, was it:
____ co-educational ____ a single-sex school

26b. If PRIVATE, did it have a religious denomination?
____ YES (please specify) _____
____ NO

27. What part of Australia, if any, do you consider your home?

28. Which university are you currently attending?

29. In which subject will you be getting your degree (please be as specific as possible)?

What are your career goals after you get your degree?

30. What was the highest level of schooling completed by your father and mother?

	Father	Mother
Primary school or less	_____	_____
Some secondary school	_____	_____
Completed secondary school	_____	_____
Some post-secondary education	_____	_____

University degree   _____ _____
Other post-secondary   _____ _____
Some post graduate   _____ _____
Post graduate degree   _____ _____

31. What was your father's occupation at the time you left school? (please describe as fully as possible) _____

32. And your mother's occupation?

33. Compared to other students around you, do you consider yourself to be financially:
____ much better off   ____ somewhat better off
____ average   ____ somewhat worse off
____ much worse off

34. In assessing your academic performance over the last two years, do you consider yourself to be:
____ much better than average   ____ better than average
____ average   ____ worse than average
____ much worse than average

35. In which religion were you raised?

36. What is your present religious preference?

37. How often do you attend religious services?
____ almost every week or more   ____ once or twice a month
____ a few times a year   ____ almost never
____ never

38. Do you think religion is an important part of your culture?
____ very much so   ____ somewhat
____ not at all   ____ it interferes with my culture

39. Generally speaking, do you usually think of yourself as Liberal, Labor, National Party or Australian Democrat?
____ Liberal
____ Labor
____ National

___ Australian Democrat
___ Other (please specify) _____
___ none of the above

40. How strongly do you feel about this party?
___ very strongly   ___ fairly strongly
___ not very strongly   ___ not applicable

41. Which party do you prefer at the **State** level?
___ Liberal
___ Labor
___ National
___ Australian Democrats
___ Other (please specify) _____
___ none of the above

42. To the best of your knowledge, which party has your **father** generally supported?
___ Liberal
___ Labor
___ National
___ Australian Democrats
___ Other (please specify) _____
___ Don't know

43. And to the best of your knowledge, which party has your **mother** generally supported?
___ Liberal
___ Labor
___ National
___ Australian Democrats
___ Other (please specify) _____
___ Don't know

44. Throughout this questionnaire we have explored a number of issues. In closing, is there anything that you would like to add? Here we are particularly interested in knowing the major concerns that you see on your own and on society's horizon. In the years that lie ahead, what do you think will be the major problems that Australia will confront?

Appendix B

UNIVERSITIES SAMPLED

AUSTRALIA

1. Flinders
2. Griffith
3. MacQuarrie
4. Melbourne
5. Monash
6. Murdoch
7. New South Wales
8. Queensland
9. Sydney
10. Tasmania
11. Western Australia

BRITAIN

1. Aberdeen
2. Aberystwyth
3. Bangor
4. Birmingham
5. Bristol
6. Cardiff
7. Dundee
8. East Anglia
9. Glasgow
10. Leeds
11. Manchester
12. Norwich
13. Nottingham
14. Swansea

CANADA

1. British Columbia
2. Calgary
3. Dalhousie
4. Laval
5. Memorial
6. Montreal
7. Queen's
8. Toronto
9. Wilfrid Laurier

NEW ZEALAND

1. Auckland
2. Canterbury-Christchurch
3. Massey-Palmerston
4. Otago-Dunedin
5. Waikato-Hamilton
6. Wellington-Victoria

UNITED STATES

1. California, Berkeley
2. Chicago
3. Duke
4. Harvard
5. Indiana
6. Princeton
7. Rice
8. Stanford
9. Wisconsin
10. Yale

Appendix C

FACTOR ANALYTIC PROCEDURES

The exploratory factor analysis used to discover how our elites structure their political belief systems involves a fairly complex set of statistical procedures. In technical terms, factor analysis is a dimensional statistical technique that reduces potentially limitless relationships between and among co-occurring phenomena—variables—into a manageable number of dimensions (Rummel, 1967). Although this technical definition of factor analysis is somewhat abstract, the logic behind the procedure becomes clearer if we build from a concrete example. Take the case of a single respondent filling out a multi-term questionnaire such as the one used in this study. In a survey questionnaire, a respondent's answer to a single specific question may be given with, or without, reference to answers given to other questions in the survey. That is, responses may be unique, uncorrelated, or they may be systematically connected—that is, correlated. Factor analysis is a procedure that statistically searches *all* respondents' answers to *all* questions, and identifies or 'extracts' stable patterns of intercorrelated responses. These stable patterns are referred to as 'underlying dimensions', or factors.

It is theoretically possible for respondents' answers to items within the questionnaire to be completely uncorrelated, in which case factor analysis would generate a factor that corresponds uniquely to each item entered into the analysis. However, research on political belief systems shows that, generally, people structure, organize, and interpret their political worlds according to what might be called 'economizing principles'. But *how* economically is that world organized? And according to *which* principles? Exploratory factor analysis provides answers to these sorts of questions.

The question of economy is usually answered technically. That is, factor analysis statistically searches for, and extracts, from among all the variables entered into the analysis, clusters of variables that systematically co-vary with each other. Each cluster or factor that is statistically independent of other factors can be set aside.

The question of 'which principles' structure the respondents' political belief systems is answered more intuitively. In practice, researchers scan the items that are clustered within each extracted factor, weigh the relative importance of each item according to its strength of correlation with the factor (factor loading), and 'interpret' the factor by looking for the common conceptual ground that thematically connects the items within the factor.

Our search for common structures in the political belief systems of our youth elites followed entirely conventional exploratory procedures. First, the data from the five national new elite surveys were merged and 44 items common to all the national questionnaires were pooled for an initial screening. Second, the 44 items were entered into a simple factor analysis (unrotated) and the 18 items that failed to load on any of the four extracted factors were dropped from the analysis. The remaining 26 items formed the core items that were retained for the rest of the analysis. Third, we applied strict criteria in the treatment of missing cases. Respondents who failed to answer one or more of the 26 core items were excluded from the next stage of the factor analysis on the grounds that 'common underlying dimensions' generated by factor analysis cannot be common unless each respondent answered all 26 items.

The precise question wording of each of the 26 core items for the five national surveys are as follows:

NOTE: A = Australian Survey; B = British Survey; C = Canadian Survey; N = New Zealand Survey; U = United States Survey

Question Wording of Factor Analysis Items

ITEM 1. In general, government grows bigger as it provides more services. Do you favour . . .
'more government services' v. 'small government' (7 points)

ITEM 2. 'The government should see to it that everyone has a job' v. 'It is not the role of government to see to it that everyone has a job' [ABN]
'The federal government should see to it that everyone has a job' v. 'It is not the role of the government to see to it that everyone has a job' [C]
'The government in Washington should see to it that everyone has a job' v. 'It is not the role of government to see to it that everyone has a job' [U] (7 points)

ITEM 3. The country would be better off if there was less government control over business. [ABN]
The country would be better off if business were less regulated. [CU]
(4 points, Agree/Disagree format, reversed)

ITEM 4. The government should work to reduce substantially the income gap between rich and poor. (4 points, Agree/Disagree format)

ITEM 5. All except the old and the handicapped should have to take care of themselves without social welfare benefits. (4 points, Agree/Disagree format, reversed)

ITEM 6. 'The private enterprise system is generally a fair system for working people' v. 'Under private enterprise people do not get a fair share of what they produce' (7 points, reversed)

ITEM 7. 'Taxing those with high incomes to help the poor is fair' v. 'Taxing those with high incomes to help the poor only punishes the people who have worked the hardest' (7 points)

ITEM 8. 'Businessmen have too much power for the good of the country.' (4 points, Agree/Disagree format)

Appendix C | 189

ITEM 9. 'Trade unions have too much power for the good of the country.' (4 points, Agree/Disagree format, reversed)

ITEM 10. 'Women would be better of if they stayed at home and raised families' v. 'Women would be better off if they had careers and jobs just as men do' [ABCN]
In general, women would be better off if they . . . 'stay home and raise families' v. 'have careers and jobs just as men do' [U] (7 points)

ITEM 11. 'It is the right of a woman to decide whether to have an abortion.' (4 points. Agree/Disagree format, reversed)

ITEM 12. 'If a company has to lay off part of its labour force, the first workers to be laid off should be women whose husbands have jobs.' (4 points, Agree/Disagree format)

ITEM 13. 'Lesbians and homosexuals should not be allowed to teach in schools.' [CU = 'public schools'] (4 points, Agree/Disagree format)

ITEM 14. 'There should be more laws which aim at eliminating differences in the treatment of men and women.' [ABN]
'There should be more laws which aim at eliminating distinctions in the treatment of men and women.' [C]
'The Equal Rights Amendment, which aims at eliminating distinctions in the treatment of men and women, should be ratified.' [U] (4 points, Agree/Disagree format, reversed)

ITEM 15. 'If women tried harder they could get jobs equal to their ability' v. 'Discrimination makes it almost impossible for most women to get jobs equal to their ability' (7 points)

ITEM 16. If 'minorities' are not getting fair access to jobs, the government should see to it that they do. ['minorities': for A = Aborigines; B = ethnic minorities; C = racial minorities; N = Maoris; U = blacks] (4 points, Agree/Disagree format)

ITEM 17. Achieving equality for Aborigines [A]; Minorities [BC]; Maoris [N]; Black [U] (10 points, Most/Least important)

ITEM 18. 'If Aborigines would try harder they could be just as well off as White Australians' v. 'Social conditions make it almost impossible for most Aborigines to overcome poverty even if they try' [A]
'If ethnic minorities would try harder they could be just as well off as whites' v. 'Social conditions make it almost impossible for most ethnic minorities to overcome poverty even if they try' [B]
'If racial minorities would try harder they could be just as well off as whites' v. 'Social conditions make it almost impossible for most racial minorities to overcome povery even if they try' [C]
'If Maoris would try harder they could be just as well off as Pakehas' v. 'Social conditions make it almost impossible for most Maoris to overcome poverty even if they try' [N]
'If blacks would try harder they could be just as well off as whites' v.

'Social conditions make it almost impossible for most blacks to overcome poverty even if they try' [U] (7 points, reversed)

ITEM 19. 'The news media pay too much attention to minority groups.' (4 points, Agree/Disagree format, reversed)

ITEM 20. 'White Australians should have a right to refuse to sell their homes to Aborigines or other racial minorities.' [A]
'White people have a right to refuse to sell their homes to coloured people.' [B]
'White people have a right to refuse to sell their homes to racial minorities.' [C]
'Pakehas should have a right to refuse to sell their homes to Maoris and Pacific Islanders.' [N]
'White people have a right to refuse to sell their homes to blacks.' [U]
(4 points, Agree/ Disagree format, reversed)

ITEM 21. 'Equality of opportunity: giving each person as equal a chance for a good education and to develop his or her ability' v. 'Equality of results: giving each person a relatively equal income regardless of his or her education or ability' (7 points, reversed)

ITEM 22. 'All people should earn about the same' v. 'People with more ability should earn higher salaries' (7 points)

ITEM 23. 'Firms should be made to increase the number of women in good jobs' v. 'Job hiring should be based strictly on merit' [ABN]
'Quotas in job hiring should be used to increase the number of women in good jobs' v. 'Job hiring should be based strictly on merit' [CU] (7 points)

ITEM 24. 'Places should be reserved for "minorities" to ensure their representation in the professions (such as teaching, medicine, law)' v. 'Admission to professional training should be based strictly on merit' [AN] ['minorities' for A = 'Aborigines'; N = 'Maoris']
'Places should be reserved for ethnic minorities to ensure their representation in schools and the work place' v. 'School admissions and job hiring should be based strictly on merit' [B]
'Quotas in school admission and job hiring should be used to ensure the representation of racial minorities' v. 'School admissions and job hiring should be based strictly on merit' [C]
'Quotas in school admissions and job hiring should be used to insure black representation' v. 'School admissions and job hiring should be based strictly on merit' [U] (7 points)

ITEM 25. 'There should be a law limiting the amount of money any individual is allowed to earn in a year.' (4 points, Agree/Disagree format)

ITEM 26. 'Workers should have more to say in important decisions than they do now' v. 'The important decisions should be left to management' (7 points)

Factor Analysis

Three pieces of technical information are critical for evaluating factor analytic solutions: the eigenvalue, the factor loading, communality. The *eigenvalue* of each extracted factor indicates how much of the total variance in the original items is explained by each factor. The *loading* of each item on a factor indicates the extent to which an item can be predicted from extracted factors, and *communality* refers to the proportion of an item's total variance that is accounted for by all of the factors combined.

Following convention, we interpret the simple (unrotated) factor analysis by technical criteria, that is, we identify a factor as having 'emerged' when the amount of variance explained by an extracted factor exceeds the amount of variance that is explained by any single item entered into the analysis: factors with eigenvalues greater than 1.0. Four factors emerged from the initial screening. The first factor had an eigenvalue of 8.9 and explained 34.3 per cent of the variance in the 26 items; the second factor, with an eigenvalue (E) of 1.9 explained 7.3 per cent of the variance (V); the third, E = 1.2 and V = 4.7 and the fourth, E = 1.19 and V = 4.6. Together, then, the four factors explained 50.9 per cent of the total variance of the 26 items.

Unrotated factor analytic solutions are useful for screening purposes precisely because they search for the simplest, most economical solutions. Typically, though, they search for simple structures by (1) limiting the amount of variance between factors and (2) by allowing the first factor to account for as much of the total variance as possible. We relaxed these constraints and clarified the factor structure by repeating the factor analysis specifying an oblique rotation, a rotation that permits factors to become correlated with each other. The rotated factor pattern matrix is shown in Table C-1 (page 192).

Table C-1 Factor Pattern Matrix

ITEM	GOVERNMENT	FEMINISM	MINORITIES	EQUALITY	COMMUNALITY
1. Size of Government	.79499	−.10460	−.03900	−.09948	.59
2. Government and jobs	.70204	.02292	.04503	−.00068	.51
3. Government regulation	.68226	−.04739	−.02445	.05137	.51
4. Rich/poor income gap	.54463	.03320	.12680	.22502	.53
5. Welfare benefits	.52040	.01803	.24597	−.06454	.38
6. Private enterprise	.51184	−.10194	−.01163	.36150	.61
7. Progressive tax system	.49701	.08825	.28664	.17239	.54
8. Power of business	.49255	−.01326	−.02273	.34167	.51
9. Power of unions	.37014	−.11134	.10282	.22567	.37
10. Women's role	−.04327	.72162	−.06107	.01097	.56
11. Right to abortion	−.11247	.71737	.38094	.05560	.52
12. Layoff women first	.13086	.61236	−.11092	−.05099	.41
13. Homosexuals as teachers	−.03013	.48348	−.20130	−.07113	.37
14. Discrimination law	−.15056	.47355	−.23716	.08646	.39
15. Gender discrimination systemic	−.02001	.40238	−.31245	−.21373	.48
16. Minorities and job guarantee	.24201	.07893	.69232	−.15535	.55
17. Equality for minorities	.05560	−.05408	.59135	.25478	.59
18. Minority discrimination systemic	.10122	−.15815	.52966	.21376	.57
19. Media and minorities	.09758	−.17825	.52329	.08437	.47
20. Right to refuse to sell home	.03858	−.11535	.48549	.03335	.31
21. Equality of opportunity or result	.03283	.08943	−.08659	.73745	.51
22. Income similarity	.23317	.03575	.01578	.69489	.68
23. Quotas for women	−.10022	−.23955	.16142	.67146	.63
24. Quotas for minorities	−.08172	−.08273	.33994	.63119	.64
25. Income limit for rich	.33460	.05484	−.09046	.57968	.56
26. Workers and say in jobs	.30142	−.16099	.04344	.34345	.47
Eigenvalue	8.9098	1.9018	1.2093	1.1926	
Variance Explained	34.3%	7.3%	4.6%	4.6%	

Notes: Oblique rotation with listwise deletion of missing cases.

Appendix D

SCALE CONSTRUCTION

To examine relationships among the factors as well as between the factors and other variables in our analysis, scales were built from the items contained within each factor. 'Factor scales' cannot precisely represent the entire underlying dimension of a factor, but they do provide a summary indication, or best approximation, of the underlying general dimension tapped by a factor. Simple additive scales were constructed for each factor by summing respondents' answers to those items that loaded onto each factor. Thus four scales were developed, each of which corresponded to the underlying dimension generated by the terminal factor analytic solution, so that each respondent could be assigned a scale score.

Most of the questions presented to respondents provided answer codes that ranged from 1 to 7. Some questions, however, were Likert-type items that allowed for four responses (range 1 to 4) and others for 10 alternative responses. Responses to items tapped by these questions were weighted by 7/4 and 7/10 respectively in order to avoid losing variance among items with different natural ranges.

Finally, all scales were subjected to a standard scale reliability test (Cronbach's alpha) to determine whether they met the minimum reliability levels required of additive scales. The alpha coefficients reported in Table D-1 indicate that all of the scales are robust.

Table D-1: Standardized Alpha Coefficients for Scales

SAMPLE	GOVERNMENT	FACTORS FEMINISM	MINORITIES	EQUALITY
Pooled	.8592	.6893	.7455	.8041
Australia	.8773	.7087	.7643	.8055
Britain	.8741	.6865	.7928	.8504
Canada	.7937	.6306	.6762	.7415
New Zealand	.8355	.7015	.7379	.7543
United States	.8727	.6415	.7661	.8582

Bibliography

Abramson, Paul R.
1975 *Generational Change in American Politics*. Lexington, MA: Lexington Books.
1983 *Political Attitudes in America*. San Francisco: Freeman.
1989 'Generations and Political Change in the United States'. *Research in Political Sociology*, vol. 4. Greenwich, CT: JAI Press.

Abzug, Bella, and Mary Kelber
1984 *Gender Gap: Bella Abzug's Guide to Political Power for American Women*. Boston, MA: Houghton, Mifflin.

Aitken, Don
1983 'The Changing Australian Electorate'. In Howard R. Penniman (ed.), *Australia at the Polls: The National Elections of 1980 and 1983*. Sydney, London, Boston: Allen and Unwin.

Alford, Robert R.
1963 *Party and Society: The Anglo-American Democracies*. Chicago: Rand McNally.

Almond, Gabriel, and Sidney Verba
1965 *The Civic Culture*. Boston and Toronto: Little, Brown.
1980 *The Civic Culture Revisited*. Boston and Toronto: Little, Brown.

Alt, James
1984 'Dealignment and the Dynamics of Partisanship in Britain'. In Russell J. Dalton, Scott C. Flanagan, and Paul Allen Beck (eds), *Electoral Change in Advanced Industrial Democracies*. Princeton, NJ: Princeton University Press.

Andersen, Kristi
1975 'Working Women and Political Participation'. *American Journal of Political Science* 19, 3: 439-53.

Anwar, Muhammad
1986 *Race and Politics: Ethnic Minorities and the British Political System*. London: Tavistock.

Arian, Asher, and Michael Shamir
1983 'The Primarily Political Functions of the Left-Right Continuum'. *Comparative Politics* 15, 2: 139-58.

Barnes, Samuel H.
1971 'Left, Right, and the Italian Voter'. *Comparative Political Studies* 4, 2 (July 1971): 157-75.

Barnes, Samuel H., Max Kaase, et al.
1979 *Political Action*. Beverly Hills, CA: Sage.

Barry, Brian
1970 *Sociologists, Economists and Democracy*. Chicago: University of Chicago Press.

Bashevkin, Sylvia B.
1982 'Women's Participation in Ontario Political Parties, 1971-1981'. *Journal of Canadian Studies* 17, 2: 44-54.
1985 *Toeing the Lines: Women and Party Politics in English Canada*. Toronto: University of Toronto Press.

Bean, Clive
1980 'Class and Party in the Anglo-American Democracies: The Case of New Zealand in Perspective'. *British Journal of Political Science* 18: 303-21.

Bean, Clive, and Jonathon Kelley
1988 'Partisan Stability and Short-Term Change in the 1987 Federal Election: Evidence from the NSSS Panel Survey'. *Politics* 23: 80-94.

Beaujot, Roderic, and Peter J. Rappak
1988 *Immigration from Canada: Its Importance and Interpretation*. Population Working Paper No. 4. Policy Department. Ottawa: Employment and Immigration Canada.

Beer, Samuel
1982 *Britain Against Itself*. New York: Norton.

Bell, Daniel
1960 *The End of Ideology*. New York: Free Press.
1972 'On Meritocracy and Equality'. *The Public Interest*, Fall 1972: 40.
1973 *The Coming of Post-Industrial Society*. New York: Basic Books.

Bell, Roderick, David Edwards, and Harrison R. Wagner (eds)
1969 *Political Power: A Reader in Theory and Research*. New York: Free Press.

Bishop, George
1976 'The Effect of Education on Ideological Consistency'. *Public Opinion Quarterly* 40: 337-8.

Boston, Jonathan
1987 'Thatcherism and Rogernomics: Changing Rules of the Game: Comparisons and Contrasts'. *Political Science* 39, 2.

Brady, Alexander
1947 *Democracy in the Dominions: A Comparative Study in Institutions*. Toronto: University of Toronto Press.

Braungart, Richard G., and Margaret M. Braungart
1989 'Political Generations'. *Research on Political Sociology* 4: 281, 319.

Brodie, Janine
1985 *Women and Politics in Canada*. Toronto: McGraw-Hill Ryerson.

Buerklin, Wilhelm
1985 'The Greens, Ecology and the New Left'. In H.G. Wallach and G. Romoser (eds), *West German Politics in the Mid-Eighties*. New York: Praeger.

Butler, David, and Donald Stokes
1969 *Political Change in Britain*. London: Macmillan.

Campbell, Angus, et al.
1960 *The American Worker*. New York: Wiley.

Campbell, Donald T., and Julian C. Stanley
1966 *Experimental and Quasi Experimental Designs for Research*. Boston: Houghton Mifflin.

Castles, F.G. (ed.)
1982 *The Impact of Parties: Politics and Policies in Democratic Capitalist States*. Beverly Hills, CA: Sage.

Christy, Carol A.
1985 'American and German Trends in Sex Differences in Political Participation'. *Comparative Political Studies* 18: 81-103.

Converse, Philip E.
1964 'The Nature of Political Belief Systems in Mass Publics'. Pp. 206-61 in David Apter (ed.), *Ideology and Discontent*. New York: Free Press.

Cooper, Barry, Allan Kornberg, and William Mishler (eds)
1988 *The Resurgence of Conservatism in Anglo-American Democracies*. Durham, NC: Duke University Press.

Crewe, Ivor
1980 'Prospects for Party Realignment: An Anglo-American Comparison'. *Comparative Politics* 12: 379-400.

Dahl, Robert (ed.)
1966 *Political Oppositions in Western Democracies*. New Haven, CT: Yale University Press.
1982 *Dilemmas of Pluralist Democracy: Autonomy vs. Control*. New Haven and London: Yale University Press.

Dahrendorf, Ralph
1959 *Class and Class Conflict in Industrial Society*. London: Routledge and Kegan Paul.

Dalton, Russell
1988 *Citizen Politics in Western Democracies*. Chatham, NJ: Chatham House.

Dalton, Russell, Scott Flanagan, and Paul Beck (eds)
1984 *Electoral Change in Advanced Industrial Democracies*. Princeton, NJ: Princeton University Press.

Deane, Phyllis
1978 *The Evolution of Economic Ideas*. Cambridge: Cambridge University Press.

Department of Immigration, Local Government and Ethnic Affairs
1987 *Australia's Population Trends and Prospects, 1987*. Canberra: Australian Government Publishing Service.

Dizard, Wilson P. Jr
1989 *The Coming of the Information Age: An Overview of Technology, Economics, and Politics* (3rd ed.). New York and London: Longman.

Evans, Judith
1980 'Women and Politics: A Re-appraisal'. *Political Studies* 28: 210-11.

Feldman, Stanley
1988 'Structure and Consistency in Public Opinion: The Role of Core Beliefs'. *American Journal of Political Science* 32, 2: 416-40.

Finlay, David J., Douglas W. Simon, and L.A. Wilson
1974 'The Concept of Left and Right in Cross National Research'. *Comparative Political Studies* 7, 2: 209-21.

Flanagan, Scott C.
1982 'Changing Values in Advanced Industrial Societies: Inglehart's Silent Revolution from the Perspective of Japanese Findings'. *Comparative Political Studies* 14: 403-44.

Flora, Peter, and Arnold T. Heidenheimer
1981 *The Development of Welfare States in Europe and America*. New Brunswick, NJ: Transaction Books.

Form, William H., and Joan Rytina
1969 'Ideological Beliefs on the Distribution of Power in the United States'. *American Sociological Review* 34: 19-31.

Fulenwider, Claire Knoche
1981 'Feminist Ideology and the Political Attitudes and Participation of White and Minority Women'. *Western Political Quarterly* 34: 17-30.

Gibbins, Roger
1988 'Conservatism in Canada: The Ideological Impact of the 1984 Election'. Pp. 332-50 in Cooper et al. (1988).

Gibbins, Roger, and Neil Nevitte
1989 'The Ideology of Gender: A Cross-National Analysis'. *Research in Political Science* 4: 89-113.

Glazer, Nathan
1988 *The Limits of Social Policy*. Cambridge, MA: Harvard University Press.

Goldthorpe, John M.
1984 *Order and Conflict in Contemporary Capitalism*. New York: Oxford University Press.

Goodin, Robert, and Julian Le Grand
1987 *Not Only the Poor: The Middle Classes and the Welfare State*. London: Allen and Unwin.

Goodin, Robert, and John Dryzek
1980 'Rational Participation: The Politics of Relative Power'. *British Journal of Political Science* 3: 273-92.

Goot, Murray, and Elizabeth Reid
1975 'Women and Voting Studies'. *Sage Professional Papers in Contemporary*

Political Sociology. Sage Professional Paper No. 06-008. Beverly Hills, CA: Sage.

Graycar, Adam (ed.)
1983 *Retreat From the Welfare State*. Sydney: Allen and Unwin.

Gustafson, Barry
1988 'Regeneration, Rejection or Realignment? The New Zealand Labor and National Parties in 1988'. Paper presented at the Australian Political Studies Association, Armidale, August.

Gutmann, Amy
1980 *Liberal Equality*. Cambridge, London, and New York: Cambridge University Press.

Hansen, Susan B., Linda M. Franz, and Margaret Netemeyer-Mays
1976 'Women's Political Participation and Policy Preferences'. *Social Science Quarterly* 56: 576-90.

Hartz, Louis
1964 *The Founding of New Societies*. New York: Harcourt, Brace and World.

Hay, P.R., and M.G. Haward
1988 'Comparative Green Politics: Beyond the European Context?' *Political Studies* 34: 433-48.

Hayek, F.A.
1960 *The Constitution of Liberty*. London: Routledge and Kegan Paul.

Hewitt, C.
1977 'The Effect of Political Democracy and Social Democracy on Equality in Industrial Nations'. *American Sociological Review* 71.

Hibbs, Douglas A.
1987 *The Political Economy of Industrial Democracies*. Cambridge, MA: Harvard University Press.

Hicks, A., and D.H. Swank
1984 'Governmental Redistribution in Rich Capitalist Democracies'. *Policy Studies Journal* 13.

Hochschild, Jennifer L.
1981 *What's Fair?: American Beliefs about Distributive Justice*. Cambridge, MA, and London: Harvard University Press.

Horowitz, Gad
1966 'Conservatism, Liberalism and Socialism in Canada: An Interpretation'. *Canadian Journal of Economics and Political Science* 32: 143-70.

Hughes, Robert
1988 *The Fatal Shore*. New York: Random House.

Huntington, Samuel P.
1974 'Post-Industrial Politics: How Benign Will It Be?' *Comparative Politics* 6: 147-77.
1975 'The United States'. In Michael Crozier, Samuel P. Huntington, and Joji Watanuki, *The Crisis of Democracy*. New York: New York University Press.

IMF
1986 *World Economic Outlook*. Washington, DC: International Monetary Fund.

Inglehart, Ronald
1977 *The Silent Revolution*. Princeton, NJ: Princeton University Press.
1981 'Postmaterialism in an Environment of Insecurity'. *American Political Science Review* 75: 880-900.
1984 'The Changing Structure of Political Cleavages in Western Society'. Pp. 25-69 in Dalton, Flanagan, and Beck (1984).
1990 *Culture Shift*. Princeton, NJ: Princeton University Press.

Inglehart, Ronald, and Hans D. Klingemann
1979 'Ideological Conceptualization and Value Priorities'. Pp. 203-13 in Barnes, Kaase, et al. (1979).

Jennings, M.K.
1984 'The Intergenerational Transfer of Political Ideologies in Eight Western Nations'. *European Journal of Political Research* 12: 261-76.

Jennings, M.K., and R.G. Niemi
1981 *Generations and Politics*. Princeton, NJ: Princeton University Press.

Kealey, Linda (ed.)
1979 *A Not Unreasonable Claim: Women and Reform in Canada*. Toronto: Women's Press.

Kemp, David
1978 *Society and Electoral Behaviour in Australia: A Study of Three Decades*. St Lucia: Queensland University Press.

Kim, Jae-On, and Charles W. Mueller
1978 *Introduction to Factor Analysis*. Beverly Hills, CA: Sage.

King, Anthony
1975 'Overload: Problems of Governing in the 1970s'. *Political Studies* 23: 284-96.
1985 'Governmental Responses to Budgetary Scarcity: Great Britain'. *Policy Studies Journal* 13, 2: 476-93.

King, Desmond
1987 *The New Right: Politics, Markets and Citizenship*. Chicago: Dorsey Press.

Klein, Ethel
1984 *Gender Politics: From Consciousness to Mass Politics*. Cambridge, MA: Harvard University Press.

Klineberg, Otto, Marisa Zavalloni, Christiane Louis-Guérin, and Jeanne BenBrika
1979 *Students, Values and Politics: A Crosscultural Comparison*. New York: Free Press.

Klingemann, Hans
1979 'Measuring Ideological Conceptualization'. Pp. 215-54 in Barnes, Kaase, et al. (1987).

Lane, Robert E.
1962 *Political Ideology*. New York: Free Press.

Leponce, Jean
1970 'A Note on the Use of the Left-Right Dimension'. *Comparative Political Studies* 2: 481-502.
1981 *Left and Right: The Topography of Political Perceptions*. Toronto, Buffalo, London: University of Toronto Press.

Larrain, Jorge
1979 *The Concept of Ideology*. London: Hutchinson.

LeDuc, Lawrence
1985 'Partisan Change and Dealignment in Canada, Great Britain and the United States'. *Comparative Politics* 17, 4: 379-98.

Le Grand, Julian, and David Winter
1987 'The Middle Classes and the Defence of the British Welfare State'. Pp. 147-68 in Goodin and Le Grand (1987).

Lemons, J. Stanley
1973 *The Woman Citizen: Social Feminism in the 1920's*. Urbana, IL: University of Illinois Press.

Levine, Stephen
1980 'New Zealand's Political System'. Pp. 1-33 in Howard R. Penniman (ed.), *New Zealand at the Polls*. Washington, DC: American Enterprise Institute for Public Policy Research.

Lijphart, Arendt
1971 'Comparative Politics and the Comparative Method'. *American Political Science Review* 65 (September): 682-93.

Lindblom, Charles E.
1977 *Politics and Markets*. New York: Basic Books.

Lipset, Seymour Martin
1968 *Revolution and Counterrevolution*. New York: Basic Books.
1981 *Party Coalition in the 1980s*. San Francisco: Institute for Contemporary Studies.
1988 'Neoconservatism: Myth and Reality'. *Society* (July/August).
1990 *Continental Divide: The Values and Institutions of the United States and Canada*. New York: Routledge.

Lipset, Seymour, Paul F. Lazarsfeld, and Allen Barton
1954 'The Psychology of Voting: An Analysis of Political Behaviour'. In Gardner Lindzey (ed.), *Handbook of Social Psychology* (vol. 2). Reading, MA: Addison Wesley.

Lipson, Leslie
1959 'Party Systems in the United Kingdom and Older Commonwealth Countries'. *Political Studies* 7 (1959): 12-31.

Lowe, P., and J. Goyder
1983 *Environmental Groups in Politics*. London: Allen and Unwin.

Lower, A.R.M.
1953 *Colony to Nation*. Toronto: Longman, Green.
1958 'Theories of Canadian Federalism—Yesterday and Today'. Pp. 3-53 in

A.R.M. Lower, F.R. Scott, et al., *Evolving Canadian Federalism*. Durham, NC: Duke University Press.

Lukes, Steven
1974 *Power: A Radical View*. London: Macmillan.

Luskin, Robert
1987 'Measuring Political Sophistication'. *American Journal of Political Science* 31: 856-99.

McClosky, Herbert, and John Zaller
1984 *The American Ethos*. Cambridge, MA, and London: Harvard University Press.

Macpherson, C.B.
1977 *The Life and Times of Liberal Democracy*. London and New York: Oxford University Press.

McRae, Kenneth
1964 'The Structure of Canadian History'. Pp. 219-74 in Hartz (1964).

Manley, John F.
1983 'New-Pluralism: A Class Analysis of Pluralism I and Pluralism II'. *American Political Science Review* 77, 2: 368-89.

Mannheim, Karl
1954 *Ideology and Utopia*. New York: Harcourt Brace Jovanovich.

Mansbridge, Jane J.
1985 'Myth and Reality: The ERA and the Gender Gap in the 1980 Election'. *Public Opinion Quarterly* 49: 164-78.

Milbrath, Lester W.
1984 *Environmentalists: Vanguard for a New Society*. Albany, NY: State University of New York Press.

Miliband, Ralph
1969 *The State in Capitalist Society*. London: Weidenfeld and Nicholson.

Neuman, W. Russell
1986 *The Paradox of Mass Politics*. Cambridge, MA, and London: Harvard University Press.

Nie, Norman H., Sydney Verba, and John R. Petrocik
1976 *The Changing American Voter*. Cambridge, MA: Harvard University Press.

Norris, Pippa
1985 'The Gender Gap in Britain and America'. *Parliamentary Affairs* 38: 192-201.
1986 'Conservative Attitudes in Recent British Elections: An Emerging Gender Gap?' *Political Studies* 34: 120-8.
1987 *Politics and Sexual Equality*. Boulder, CO: Rienner.

OECD
1988 *Historical Statistics 1960-1986*. Paris.

Offe, Claus
1984 *Contradictions of the Welfare State*. Cambridge, MA: MIT Press.

Pammett, Jon
1987 'Class Voting and Class Consciousness in Canada'. *Canadian Review of Sociology and Anthropology* 24, 2: 269-90.

Pateman, Carole
1970 *Participation and Democratic Theory*. London, New York, Melbourne: Cambridge University Press.

Postgate, Dale, and Kenneth McRoberts
1976 *Quebec: Social Change and Political Crisis*. Toronto: McClelland and Stewart.

Prentice, Alison, et al.
1988 *Canadian Women: A History*. Toronto: Harcourt Brace Jovanovich.

Przeworski, A., and H. Teune
1970 *The Logic of Comparative Social Inquiry*. New York: John Wiley and Sons.

Rae, Douglas
1977 *Equalities*. Cambridge, MA: Harvard University Press.

Rose, Richard, and Guy Peters
1978 *Can Governments Go Bankrupt?* New York: Basic Books.

Rosencrance, Richard N.
1964 'The Radical Culture of Australia'. In Hartz (1964).

Rothman, Stanley
1979 'The Mass Media in Post-Industrial Society'. In S.M. Lipset (ed.), *The Third Century*. Stanford, CA: Hoover Institution Press.

Rummel, R.J.
1967 'Understanding Factor Analysis'. *Conflict Resolution* 11: 444-80.

Sani, Giacomo
1974 'A Test of the Least-Distance Model of Voting Choice: Italy 1972'. *Comparative Political Studies* 7, 2 (July 1974): 193-208.

Sankiaho, Risto
1984 'Political Remobilization in Welfare States'. Pp. 70-92 in Dalton et al. (1984).

Sarlvik, Bo, and Ivor Crewe
1983 *Decade of Dealignment: The Conservative Victory of 1979 and Electoral Trends in the 1970s*. Cambridge: Cambridge University Press.

Sartori, Giovanni
1976 *Parties and Party Systems: A Framework for Analysis*. Cambridge, London, New York, Melbourne: Cambridge University Press.

Schattschneider, E.E.
1960 *The Semi-Sovereign People: A Realist's View of Democracy in America*. New York: Holt, Rinehart and Winston.

Sowell, Thomas
1984 *Civil Rights: Rhetoric or Reality?* New York: William Morrow.

Statistics Canada
1981 *Immigration from Canada: Its Importance and Interpretation*. Population

Working Paper No. 4. Policy and Programme Development. Ottawa: Statistics Canada.

Steinfels, Peter
1979 *The Neoconservatives: The Men Who are Changing American Politics*. New York: Simon and Schuster.

Tabachnick, Barbara G., and Linda S. Fidell
1989 *Using Multivariate Statistics*. New York: Harper and Row.

Taylor, Charles Lewis, and David A. Jodice
1983 *World Handbook of Political and Social Indicators*, 3rd ed. New Haven and London: Yale University Press.

Tocqueville, Alexis de
1966 [1835] *Democracy in America*. New York: Knopf.

United Nations
1984 *The World Population Situation in 1983*. Population Studies, no. 85: New York.

Verba, Sydney
1967 *Participation in Five Western Democracies*. Beverly Hills and London: Sage.

Verba, Sydney, and Garry Orren
1985 *Equality in America*. Cambridge, MA and London: Harvard University Press.
1971 'Cross-National Survey Research: The Problem of Credibility'. Pp. 305-56 in Ivan Vallier (ed.), *Comparative Methods in Sociology*. Berkeley and Los Angeles: University of California Press.
1967 'Some Dilemmas in Comparative Research'. *World Politics* 20: 111-27.

Verba, Sidney, Norman H. Nie, and John R. Petrocik
1979 *The Changing American Voter*. Cambridge, MA: Harvard University Press.

Verba, Sidney, Steven Kelman, Gary Otren, Ichiro Miyake, Joji Watanuki, Ikuo Kabashima, and G. Donald Ferree Jr
1987 *Elites and the Idea of Equality: A Comparison of Japan, Sweden and the United States*. Cambridge, MA, and London: Harvard University Press.

Vowles, Jack
1988 'What About the Workers? Class and the 1987 Election in New Zealand'. Paper presented to the Australian Political Studies Association Conference, Armidale, New South Wales.

Wattenburg, Martin P.
1982 'Party Identification and Party Images: A Comparison of Britain, Canada, Australia and the United States'. *Comparative Politics* 15, 1: 23-40.

Welch, Susan
1977 'Women as Political Animals?' *American Journal of Political Science* 21, 4: 711-30.

Welch, Susan, and Philip Secret
1981 'Sex, Race and Political Participation'. *Western Political Quarterly* 34: 5-16.

Wilensky, Harold L.
1975   *The Welfare State and Equality: Structural and Ideological Roots of Public Expenditures.* Berkeley, Los Angeles, London: University of California Press.

Zipp, John F., and Eric Pulzer
1985   'Gender Differences in Voting for Female Canadians: Evidence From the 1982 Election'. *Public Opinion Quarterly* 49: 179-97.

Index

aboriginal peoples, 87
Aborigines, 33, 87, 44, 17, 162, 93, 90, 88, 91
abortion, 68, 72, 69
age cohorts, 41
Alford, Robert, 4, 6, 11, 164
Almond, Gabriel, 1, 2, 9, 11, 164
American Democratic party, 80
American Democrats, 56, 58, 80, 155
American Republican party, 80, 96
American Republicans, 40, 55, 80, 155
American Revolution, 6
attitude structures, 27, 41, 42
Australian Labor party, 56, 58, 155
Australian Liberals, 40, 80, 155

Bell, Daniel, 12, 19, 113
blacks, 44, 91; American, 86ff
Brady, Alexander, 1
British Conservative party, 96
British Conservatives, 40, 80, 155
British heritage, 7
British Labour party, 57, 58, 96, 155
British Liberal party, 37, 58
brokerage politics, 98
business, 135, 147, 150, 155, 159

Canadian Liberals, 58
challenging groups, 135
Charter of Rights and Freedoms, 65, 88
Civil Culture, 164
cognitive dissonance, 146
cognitive mobility, 15
collectivism, 9, 138, 167
Commonwealth of Nations, 8

constraint, 27, 108, 113, 122, 124, 125
Democracy in the Dominions, 1
democratic ethos, 130
Democrats, 56, 58, 80, 155
distribution of influence, 131, 138, 139, 154

egalitarian norms, 139
employment equity, 75f, 83
environment, 19
Equal Rights Amendment, 70
equality, 25, 44, 109, 121; index, 113; of influence, 130, 150; of opportunity/result, 44, 46, 165; scale, 110, 112, 116, 169
ethnic minorities, 90, 91, 93
European Economic Community (EEC), 26
exceptionalism, 2, 72, 102, 103, 107, 126f

Fabian-style socialism, 38, 167
factor analysis, 42, 44, 45, 46, 165, 171, 187
feminism, 25, 73, 78, 135; scale, 66, 67, 68, 70, 72, 76, 121f
fertility rates, 15
First World War, 73
Flanagan, Scott, 19
founding circumstances, 163
Founding of New Societies, 1
Fourth Estate, 162
franchise, 18
francophones, 18, 33, 86f, 127, 129
Friedan, Betty, 64
frontier experiences, 163

gender equality, 109

gender gap, 74, 75
Gibbins, Roger, 103-4
government intervention, 50, 51, 53, 58, 59, 61, 83, 108
government scale, 49, 100, 103, 121, 170
Great Depression, 10
Great Society programs, 132
Greer, Germaine, 64
group influence, 131

Hartz, Louis, 1, 7, 9
hiring policy, 115
hiring quotas, 110
Hughes, Robert, 6

ideological convergence, 22
immigration, 7, 15, 85, 87
income, individual, 12
income equality, 110
individualism, 9, 46
inequalities, 109, 147
influence, 147, 155ff; equality of, 130, 150; gap, 147; group, 131; hierarchy, 141, 146, 147, 150, 151; individual, 131; of feminists, 142, 143; scale, 137, 141, 155; spread, 138; stratification, 130
Inglehart, Ronald, 19, 29

Keynesianism, 20, 21, 23, 29
Keynes, Maynard, 20
Klein, Ethel, 78

left-right and equality scales, 119
left-right polarity, 30
left-right scale, 34, 35, 36, 38, 40, 41, 81, 82, 84, 93, 95, 96, 98, 99, 100, 101, 105, 106, 113, 119, 120, 123, 125, 126, 129, 130, 169, 170, 171
Liberal party (Australia), 96
Liberal party (Canada), 58, 96
Liberal/SDP (Britain), 37, 58
liberal tradition, 22, 163
linkage, 27
Lipset, Seymour Martin, 1
Lipson, Leslie, 23
Lower, A.R.M., 6

Maori Representation Act 1867, 161

Maoris, 17, 33, 86, 88f, 90f, 93, 162
Marx, Karl, 11
media, 135, 137
mediating groups, 135
merit principle, 115
Mexican immigrants, 87
minority causes, 144; influence, 144; orientations, 100; rights, 25, 121, 122; scale, 92, 94, 95, 99, 103, 105
multiculturalism, 85ff, 103

National Organization for Women, 18, 65
National Women's Coordinating Committee, 65
Native peoples, 17, 33
neoconservatism, 38, 177
Nevitte, Neil, 103-4
New Democratic Party (NDP), 56, 80, 96
New Democrats, 56, 58
new elites, 24
New Right, the, 21ff
New Zealand Labor, 56, 58, 96
New Zealand Nationals, 80, 96, 155
Norris, Pippa, 65

partisanship, 154ff
Party and Society, 164
party identification, 36
political belief systems, 28, 29, 31, 41, 45, 61, 102, 106, 122, 125, 151, 171, 172
political culture, 2, 27
post-industrial societies, 12, 133
preferred-influence hierarchy, 142, 151
Progressive Conservative party, 96
Progressive Conservatives, 40, 55, 80
Progressive movement, the, 74

quality of life, 19
quotas, 110, 166, 171

race relations, 103
racial divisions, 16, 17; minorities, 85, 89ff; relations, 87; tension, 17
radicalism, 138
rainbow coalition, 102
Reconstruction, 86

Republican party, 80, 96
Republicans, 40, 55, 80, 155
Rogernomics, 22
Rothman, Stanley, 137
rugged individualism, 54

Second World War, 25, 75
settler nations, 86
settler societies, 15
settlers, 87
social change, 146, 161
Social Democratic Party (SDP), 56, 58
social mobility, 13, 17, 164
stability, patterns of, 141

stratification of influence, 130

Thatcherism, 21, 24
Tocqueville, Alexis de, 7
Toryism, 9, 138f, 167

unions, 33, 135, 147, 150, 155, 159
United Empire Loyalists, 6

value changes, 164
Verba, Sidney, 1, 2, 9, 11, 164

welfare state, 44, 46, 75, 166, 172
Women's Christian Temperance Union, 64
Women's Electoral Lobby, 18, 65
women's issues, 144

www.ingramcontent.com/pod-product-compliance
Ingram Content Group UK Ltd.
Pitfield, Milton Keynes, MK11 3LW, UK
UKHW022228230426
12048UKWH00016BA/1121